Letter from the editor

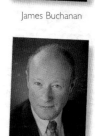

Dear Honeymooner,

Welcome to the second edition of *Special Honeymoon Hotels*. Our launch last year of this specialist book was a great success. So we are back, bolder and better than before, to bring you the 1999 edition, with a stylish new look packed with even more of the world's most tempting destinations and resorts.

Over the following pages you will find more than 170 quality hotels and resorts specially selected by our experts. On each, we provide you with well-researched details about the atmosphere, setting and facilities, as well as colour photographs to give you the best overall picture of potential honeymoon spots. Our editorial team is equipped with great knowledge of the resorts featured, and the regional travel articles that kick-off each chapter will give you more insight into these most alluring and romantic destinations.

I wish you happy honeymoon hunting on behalf of me and our senior board directors, Bill Colegrave, of the world famous *Everyman Travel Guides*, and James Buchanan, managing director of Britain's No.1 wedding and honeymoon magazine, *You & Your Wedding*. From Bermuda to Bora Bora we, and our globetrotting researchers, journalists and marketing team, have spared no effort to uncover the most romantic hotels on the planet. Now it's up to you to choose which one to visit.

Best wishes,

Melanie Garrett
Editor

James Buchanan
Publisher

Bill Colegrave
Publisher

James Buchanan

Bill Colegrave

Special Honeymoon Hotels

Editor
Melanie Garrett

Publishers
James Buchanan, Bill Colegrave

Administrator
Rebecca Kendall

Contributors
Jennifer Alcazar, Liz Booth, Sandy Cadiz-Smith, Susan Cameron, Jo Canning, Helen Foster, Linda Freeman, Matthew Inman, Marc Harris, Marguerite Hartley, Robert Johnson, Nigel O'Brien, Catherine Small, Matthew Tanner

Production Director
Andrew Wilson

Sales & Marketing
Ed Purnell, Linda Johnston, Jasim Adili, Andrea Eisenhart, Philip Eisenhart, Clare Smith

Most images provided by
The Image Bank,
17 Conway Street, London W1P 6EE
Additional images supplied by respective tourist organisations.

Reproduction
Colourpath, London

Printed and bound by
Hunters Armley Ltd, England

A catalogue record for this book is available from the British Library
ISBN 0-95347-050-4

Published by **World Destinations Publishing Ltd**
Silver House
31-35 Beak Street
London W1R 3LD

Distributed in North America by
The Globe Pequot Press
6 Business Park Road
PO Box 833
Old Saybrook, CT 06475-0833

Copyright ©1999
World Destinations Publishing Ltd

contents

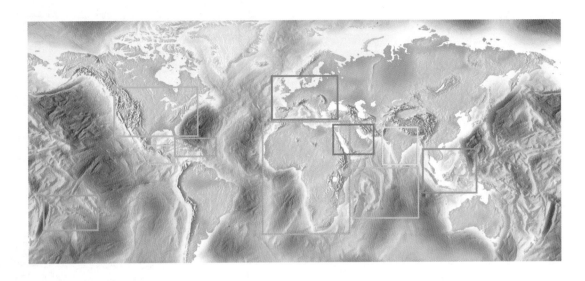

Index by regions

Information & Internet Indexes

hotel listings

hotel listings

hotel listings

you & your
wedding

Britain's Biggest and

We have over 12 years experience in recommending perfect honeymoon hotels for our readers. We visit the countries, stay in the hotels and sample the service. Then we recommend. We are unrivalled in the quality and depth of our honeymoon coverage, helping you, the bride-to-be, to choose from a brilliant selection of wonderful honeymoon destinations.
We apply the same research and understanding of your needs to the rest of the magazine.
Our aim is to provide you with inspiration and advice, including fashion and flowers, gift lists, planning and shoppers' guides. If you havn't bought You & Your Wedding yet, treat yourself. You deserve it!

Best Bridal Magazine

Honeymoons have a lot to live up to, and are viewed by most love-struck couples as the trip of a lifetime with long, lazy days filled with champagne and romance. It is important that you approach this special holiday with your eyes wide open and your feet firmly on the ground. Great honeymoons do not just happen.

Decisions

First, decide where you want to go. Choose a destination neither of you has visited before. Do not even consider going somewhere you have stayed with a previous lover. Your married life should be a fresh place to start.

Work out how much time you can both take off work and how much you can afford to spend. Do not use up all your annual leave with pre-wedding plans, and remember that if you are going to a long-haul destination you will lose about two days of holiday travelling.

Think ahead

Consider carefully about what you both want. That isolated island in the brochure may look like true paradise, but will there be enough to do? A good compromise is to book a two-centre

honeymoon. Unwind first at a beach resort and then visit a city for some sightseeing and nightlife.

One way to start the honeymoon ball rolling is to ask your friends and family to recommend destinations they have experience of, and use your travel agent. More and more agents have wedding co-ordinators who will have plenty of ideas and will be able to tell you the best time of year to visit.

If you prefer a more high-tech approach, the Internet is a growing information source. After a few hours' surfing the net, you should have quite a few ideas for your ideal hideaway spot.

There are plenty of opportunities for sporty honeymooners too. Many resorts offer all the usual watersports, and some include Scuba diving. Diving holidays offer the best of both worlds – exotic locations and stunning sport – and places like the Red Sea and the Seychelles are hot-spots for divers and honeymooners alike.

Once the decision is made, book as soon as possible so that hotels can reserve the honeymoon suite for you. And remember, don't travel too far on your actual wedding day. Spend a night locally and arrive relaxed and refreshed.

Off on the right foot

- Set your honeymoon budget as early as possible, along with the rest of the wedding budget.
- Pay attention to what is included in any package price. If only breakfast is mentioned, this may be why the hotel sounds like such a bargain. Remember that additional meals at luxury hotels can be extremely expensive.
- Allow extra money for drinks, tips, service charges and airport tax. An all-inclusive resort or hotel may seem expensive at first glance, but the price you pay includes everything.

- Talk to your doctor well in advance about health requirements and what, if any, injections are recommended.
- Some vaccinations need to be given at least a month before you travel, and it may be that you need a course of anti-malarial tablets.
- Make sure everyone involved in your holiday arrangements knows you are on honeymoon. You will be amazed how many gifts and special offers suddenly come your way. Many hotels will offer flowers and a free bottle of champagne on arrival. Most will give upgrades if a better room is available, especially in the low season. Don't forget to take along your marriage certificate as proof of your new status.
- Do take out comprehensive travel insurance. Keep your passports in your hand luggage along with any plane and rail tickets, hotel confirmations and your marriage certificate.
- Think ahead if you are changing your name. Make sure the registrar has signed the relevant form to apply for a new passport in advance. Inform the airline so that the name on your ticket matches the name on your passport.
- Fewer and fewer countries now require British passport-holders to have a visa, but your travel agent will be able to advise you.

Travel checklist
Don't leave home without...

Paperwork
Passports
Airline tickets
Car documents, if driving
Hotel booking confirmations
Tour confirmations
Travel insurance
Foreign currency
Traveller's cheques
Credit cards
Vaccination certificates
Marriage certificate

Health and beauty
Vaccinations
Malaria tablets
Mosquito night-burning oil/mosquito net
Insect repellent
Sting cream
Headache tablets
Sun cream
After-sun lotion
Lip protection

Beauty/skincare products
Haircare products
Make-up

Clothing (hot)
Swimsuit
Shorts
Tops
Sundresses
Sunhat
Sunglasses
Casual eveningwear
Smart eveningwear
Beach shoes
Sports gear

Clothing (cold)
Woolly jumpers
Hats
Gloves
Warm boots
Coats
Sports gear
Casual eveningwear
Smart eveningwear

9

10

The thought of a wedding without little arguments over the guest list and the seating plan is more than enough to justify escaping to an exotic clime. Add the spice of a romantic, tropical wedding, exchanging vows on a deserted sandy beach with palm trees rustling in the breeze, and the idea becomes tantalising.

Wherever you get married, the more effort you put in at an early stage, the happier and more relaxed you will be on the day itself. Some tour operators have a weddings department and a dedicated brochure with staff to guide you to the right destination and give you plenty of practical advice. Most like at least four months' notice to deal with all the formalities.

Countries that are already popular honeymoon destinations have realised they can take advantage of the growing trend to marry overseas and are now changing their local regulations. Even in the Far East, where one might have thought strong local culture may have made overseas marriages difficult, has become a relatively easy option.

Bali, Thailand, Fiji and Australia are becoming increasingly popular, along with Kenya and a whole host of Caribbean islands such as Barbados, Jamaica, Grenada and St Kitts & Nevis. In most places most arrangements can be tailored to your wishes.

If you're looking to have a wedding with a difference, your first thoughts should be about the USA. Las Vegas reigns supreme in the world of the weird and wonderful wedding stakes. There are drive-through wedding chapels and kiosks, you can have an Elvis lookalike to serenade you or take to the skies in a hot-air balloon. In Florida, you can tie the knot underwater or join Mickey Mouse & Co. at Disney World.

The easiest and most efficient way to arrange your wedding is to purchase a package through a tour operator. Typical deals include the services of a minister, all the necessary paperwork, a cake, flowers, accommodation, and often a basic set of photographs. If the two of you want to travel on your own, most hotels will arrange witnesses for you.

Weddings overseas are usually feasible for those with strict religious beliefs, and most ministers are non-denominational if that is a concern. Catholics may face particular difficulties in marrying abroad, and the authorities in some countries such as Bali require that both bride and groom are of the same religion.

Abroad

The only other major hurdle couples will face is their age. For example, the groom must be 23 in Bali, while in Sri Lanka both parties must be over 21. Most places, however, set the limit at 18.

Most larger hotels have an on-site wedding co-ordinator who will make sure the day runs perfectly. Normally they will travel with you if you need to visit the local authorities and will arrange the wedding breakfast and any 'extras', such as photographer, videographer, music and flowers, on your behalf.

Brides should think carefully about what style of dress they want to wear. A huge billowing silk dress may not be practical in the heat while high heels could prove a nightmare on a sandy beach. And remember, as soon as you arrive, hang the dress up to allow any creases to fall out – the natural humidity in the tropical heat will help.

Remember
- Pack all originals of your required documents.
- Ask the airline in advance if you can carry your dress as hand baggage, and maybe even hang it up during the flight.
- Make friends with the hotel wedding co-ordinator – you are much more likely to have unusual demands met.
- Go easy on the sunbathing – you don't want to be lobster-red in your photos.
- Video the ceremony to appease any relatives and friends who couldn't make the journey with you.
- Do not expect too much of the ceremony. It will be quick and informal although most registrars will be happy to include a favourite reading or poem. Remember, you just have to ask.

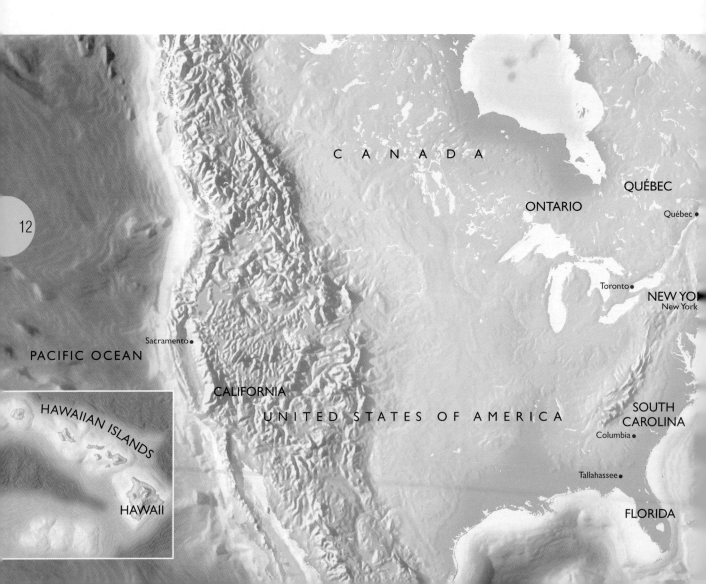

12

CANADA

QUÉBEC

ONTARIO

Québec •

Toronto •

NEW YO[
New York

Sacramento •

PACIFIC OCEAN

CALIFORNIA

UNITED STATES OF AMERICA

SOUTH
CAROLINA

Columbia •

HAWAIIAN ISLANDS

Tallahassee •

HAWAII

FLORIDA

An American journey embraces not only dramatic and widely varied scenery, but a melting pot of cultures, thanks to generations of immigrants, and absorbed into the American way of life as we know and love it today.

Not least into the American kitchen with its Italian pizzas, German hot dogs, Chinese noodles, spicy French Creole gumbo...and it goes on and on.

With some of the most spectacular scenery in the world, including the awesome Grand Canyon, Niagara Falls, the vast expanses of the Great Parks and Lakes and unbeatable mountains and beaches, there is no better place to take up the challenge of nature. Activities like whitewater rafting, ballooning, hiking and riding with cowboys on a dude ranch are all on offer. In California, Colorado, Canada and New England you can combine snowboarding, a bit of skiing and even sunbathing with sightseeing.

There isn't a leisurely option that someone in America hasn't thought of. Take a balloon ride over the plains, cruise the Mississippi on a steamer, laze around the Lowcountry, or partake of a gourmet wine-tasting tour. It is true that America has it all.

ATLANTIC OCEAN

13

California

Perhaps the most varied and inspiring of all the American states, with snow-capped mountains, incredible forests of giant redwood trees, national parks, sun-burned deserts, Pacific beaches, theme parks and all action cities, California is also the most perfect touring destination.

flying time
To: LA/San Francisco
London: 11 hrs
NY: 5-6 hrs

climate
California weather
varies from hot
desert to distinct
seasons in the
cooler north.

when to go
Theme parks and
beauty spots like
Yosemite National
Park get crowded in
the summer holidays.
You can catch the
San Francisco 49ers
in football action
Aug-Dec.

getting around
Consider flying in to
one Californian city
and out of another,
driving the distance
between.

Start off in San Francisco – so picturesque and impossibly hilly that, even if it does not steal your heart, it will take your breath away. Let a clanging cable car carry you up to lofty heights for splendid views over San Francisco Bay, then hold on tight as it hurtles downhill towards the irresistible seafood restaurants of Fisherman's Wharf.

Drive north and soon you are in the Napa Valley, touring the vineyards, and tasting vintages from California's leading winemakers. Head inland and you come to the blue waters of Lake Tahoe, surrounded by pine forests, mountains and ski resorts with snow from December right through until May.

One of America's most scenic drives follows famous Highway 1 south of San Francisco, passing seals playing on the wave-lashed grey rocks. It twists around the craggy Pacific coast between Monterey (where you should be sure to see the vast aquarium), and pretty Carmel, with its quaint but stylish shopping streets and old Spanish mission.

The further south you go in California, the stronger the Hispanic connection. Characterful, hacienda-style

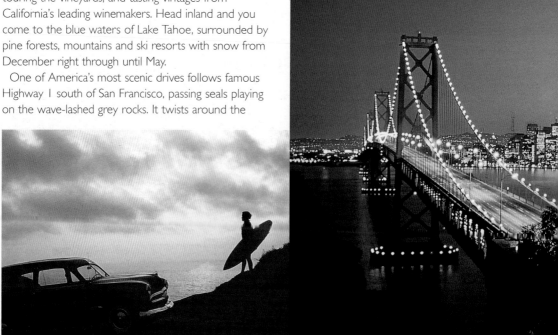

buildings, mission churches and place names are all Spanish legacies; and from beautiful San Diego you can board a trolley bus heading for the Mexican border and browse Tijuana for a day.

Los Angeles rewards those who brave its smog and sprawl and make time to get to know it. For LA is not only Hollywood, but also the wacky seaside strips of Venice Beach and Santa Monica; the shopping street of the stars, Rodeo Drive; the hip restaurants serving up *nouveau* Californian cuisine; and the wealth of theatres, galleries, museums, and hot-spots for music and dance.

Shutters On The Beach

One Pico Boulevard
Santa Monica
California 90405
USA

✈ Los Angeles Int. 16km
tel +310 458 0030
fax +310 458 4589

Toll Free:
US/Canada 800 223 6800
UK 0800 181 123

shutters@specialhotels.com
www.specialhotels.com

16

Member of:
Leading Hotels of the World

Shutters On The Beach is the only luxury hotel nestled right on the warm sands of Santa Monica Bay in Los Angeles. Recalling the architecture of historic southern Californian beach resorts of the early 1900s, the hotel has the look and feel of a sumptuous ocean-front home. The structure comprises three separate buildings, linked by elaborate slate-grey shingled siding, flower-covered trellises, balconies and striped awnings.

Each of the rooms and suites has warm walnut desks, lounge chairs and sliding shuttered doors opening onto the balmy ocean breeze and panoramic coastal views. All rooms have large marble bathrooms and whirlpool bathtubs with huge glass windows; while the suites feature wooden flooring and tiled fireplaces.

One Pico, the hotel's formal restaurant, offers a front row seat to the Pacific Ocean and the stirring sunsets. With the emphasis on local and regionally grown produce, celebrated chef Desi Szonntagh creates entrées with a discreet and unobtrusive quality. Pedals, a casual restaurant at the edge of the beach promenade, has an Italian *trattoria* feel.

Shutters is situated near the historic pier in this seaside resort and is minutes from fashionable shopping districts, fine restaurants and art galleries.

🛏 from US$385 (186)

🛏 US$750-2,000 (12)

🍽 US$40

☕ US$14

Honeymoon specials

Two or four night packages include champagne and chocolates, dinner for two, daily breakfast, mountain bike hire, his and her massages and facials, limousine to and from the new Getty Centre and keepsake.

Sightseeing and leisure

Museums (including the new world class Getty Centre), art galleries, Rodeo Drive boutiques and speciality bookshops are just minutes away.
Pool, Jacuzzi, spa, health club, aromatherapy, massage, reflexology are available at the hotel.

Information & Reservations
UK 0870 606 1296
INT. +44 870 606 1296

150 E. Carmel Valley Road
Carmel Valley 93924
California

✈ Monterey 10 miles

tel +831 659 2245
fax +831 659 5160

stonepine@specialhotels.com
www.specialhotels.com
director@stonepine.com
stonepinecalifornia.com

Member of:
Relais & Chateaux

For the ultimate in perfect American-style luxury, Stonepine offers an incredible once-in-a-lifetime experience. Guests are met at Monterey airport by a cream Phantom V Rolls-Royce and whisked away to the heart of the Carmel Valley to what was once the home of a millionaire horse breeder.

There are just 14 suites set in 300 acres of magnificent, secluded Californian countryside and meandering trails among the oaks and redwoods where deer and horses roam. Each suite is unique and the epitome of elegance.

The heated pool is surrounded by fragrant lemon, olive, orange and fig trees as well as the Italian stone pines planted 65 years ago which gave the estate its name.

There are plenty of other activities, including tennis, archery and horse-drawn carriage rides and for wine lovers there is even a private winery.

Evenings can be spent with champagne and *hors d'oeuvres* in the lounge with its Lalique crystal and wood-burning fires. Stonepine manages to combine exquisite decor and style with a relaxed atmosphere, providing the best of both worlds.

Weddings are a Stonepine speciality – this is the place where (among others) Brooke Shields and Andre Aggassi tied the knot.

17

US$295-550 (10)

US$400-750 (4)

US$65

included

Honeymoon specials
Flowers and champagne on arrival. Romantic carriage ride. The property can be booked as an exclusive, please enquire.

Sightseeing and leisure
Situated close to the famous 17-mile Drive, the delights of Carmel, Monterey and Fisherman's Wharf. Big Sur is nearby as are some of the most famous golf courses in the world, such as Carmel Valley Ranch and Pebble Beach.

Florida

flying time
To: Fort Lauderdale,
Miami, Orlando.
London: 9-10 hrs
LA: 4-5 hrs
NY: 3 hrs

climate
Winters are mild, at
15-20°C with mainly
sunny days. Summer
is hot and humid,
especially in central
Florida, and you will
be thankful for an air-
conditioned car.

when to go
Avoid the busy US
public and school
holidays when visiting
the theme parks.
May, June and Nov
are generally good
months to visit.

They call it the Sunshine State, but it could easily be known as the Happy State. Florida is a fun place.

Every evening is party time in Key West, as street entertainers and visitors from all over the world gather to cheer and celebrate the glorious sunset at Mallory Point. Two hundred miles away at Miami's hip South Beach, the stylish set preen and pose outside the pastel lemon and lilac Art Deco facades.

In the world's theme park capital, Orlando, just as many adults as kids get delightedly dizzy on Disney World's amazing selection of rides.

If sports are your idea of fun, Florida is your dream destination. It has more than a thousand golf courses and excellent tennis centres. All sorts of watersports are on offer, with Scuba diving off the Keys and exciting deep-sea fishing trips from Miami and Fort Lauderdale. The island paradise of Longboat Key, near Sarasota, offers the chance to sample the combination of all of these. And of course there are the legendary beaches – more than 1,800 miles of sugary coastline with something to suit everyone.

There is also the chance to sample delights like the splendid art collection at Ringling Museum, in Sarasota, historic plantation mansion houses and Florida's natural wonders. These include the famous Everglades, miles of lakelands and state parks where you can say hello to pelicans, meet manatee, and swim with dolphins.

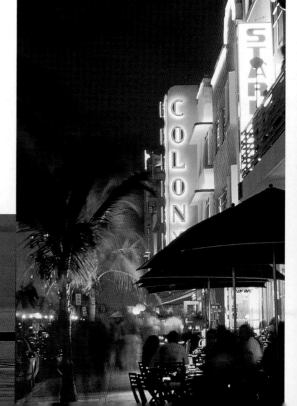

The Colony Beach &
Tennis Resort

1620 Gulf of Mexico Drive
Longboat Key
Florida 34288
USA

✈ Sarasota 18mins
✈ Tampa 65mins

tel +941 383 6464
fax +941 383 7549

colonybeach@specialhotels.com
www.specialhotels.com
www.colonybeachresort.com

For those who love their beaches and their tennis, the Colony on Longboat Key in Florida is the place to be. With 21 tennis courts, and miles and miles of white sand beach, all under a warm tropical sun and flanked by the azure waters of the Gulf of Mexico, the resort promises to pamper its guests in a friendly and relaxed environment.

Tennis court time at the Colony is complimentary. Whether it's just a knock-about or something a little more serious, tennis programmes for all abilities can be arranged. There is also a range of watersports on offer – from Hobie-cat sailing to windsurfing – as well as a state-of-the-art fitness and aerobics centre and health spa, complete with steamroom, sauna and massage.

The casually elegant suites and rooms are decorated with fresh flowers and warm furnishings and fabrics to make new arrivals feel at ease. And after a hard day in the sun, the award-winning Colony Dining Room, which overlooks the Gulf, offers an original and lavish menu, plus a stupendous selection of fine wines. For a more casual evening, The Bistro and outdoors at The Patio and Bar, both offer traditional American favourites.

Weddings can also be arranged on the Colony's private 800-foot sugar sand beach.

 US$195-1,025

 US$40-65

US$10-15

Honeymoon specials

Discerning Choices packages cost from US$250-450 per night and include a $100 daily credit to be used anywhere on the property (except towards rooms), such as the spa, restaurants, tennis lessons and clinics, fitness centre, gourmet market, watersports centre, the designer boutique and sports shop for logo merchandise.

Sightseeing and leisure

Tennis, extensive fitness centre, aerobics and massage, sauna and steamroom at the health spa. Watersports, golf and deep-sea fishing are also available. Not far away is Sarasota, great for museums, galleries and concert halls. Disney World and Sea World are also nearby, as are the famous film studios Universal and MGM.

Hawaii

flying time
To: Honolulu, Oahu
London: 18 hrs
LA: 6 hrs
NY: 12 hrs

climate
Sunshine and mild temperatures all year. Aug-Sept are humid and hottest (25-30°C). Winter (Oct-Apr) is cooler and wetter, rain being most likely Feb-Mar.

when to go
Avoid Christmas and New Year and school holidays, when rates are high and hotels, golf courses and beaches busy. Try to catch the islanders celebrating during the Aloha Festival (mid Sept-Oct).

getting around
Internal flights link the six main islands. Helicopter trips show off the dramatic scenery.

Hawaii is an excellent choice for a honeymoon destination, a place where American efficiency overlays romantic and charming South Seas traditions.

You will be guaranteed a warm welcome – greeted by friendly locals with a garland of flowers, invited to dance the *hula* and to taste the Polynesian barbecue, otherwise popularly known as a *luau*.

Try to visit at least two of the islands during your stay. Of the six main islands – Oahu, Hawaii, Maui, Kauai, Molokai and Lanai – many people vote Kauai the most beautiful. Nicknamed the Garden Isle because of its lush, colourful scenery, it has featured in movies including *South Pacific* and *Jurassic Park*.

And be sure to surf the swells – body-surfing on a board is the easy option; and make the most of a rare opportunity to go whale-watching. Should one of the islands' volcanoes decide to perform while you are there, count yourself lucky and prepare for a spectacle more grand and thrilling than anything America's theme parks can offer.

Mauna Lani Bay Hotel & Bungalows

68-1400 Mauna Lani Drive
Kohala Coast
Hawaii 96743
USA

✈ Kona 37km

tel +808 885 6622
fax +808 885 1483

mauna@specialhotels.com
www.specialhotels.com
www.maunalani.com

Tour operators:
US Pan Pacific Worldwide

Member of:
Preferred Hotels

There's not one but two silver sand beaches on the doorstep of the Mauni Lani Bay Hotel & Bungalows. The resort sprawls out beautifully over 3,200 acres and maintains a secluded atmosphere amid lush gardens and a stretch of shoreline that is home to myriad marine life. Here there is luxury in spoonfuls: two championship golf courses (carved from a 16th-century lava flow), a Tennis Garden, Racquet Club and fitness centre.

If guests opt for one of the luxury bungalows they will probably believe they've died and gone to heaven. Four thousand square feet of luxury await. Fax through your preferences before arrival and find your favourite CDs in the player, your choice of magazines on the coffee table and your favourite snacks in the fridge (there's even a telescope for star-gazing). To ensure an easy time, discrete staff are on hand to arrange everything: from massages to helicopter rides.

The big island of Hawaii offers a diverse tropical paradise to explore, as do the resort's restaurants which, like everything else here, are larger than life and twice as wonderful. Whether it's a hamburger and fruit smoothie on the beach, or Hawaiian Tempura at the award-winning Canoe House, no one leaves disappointed.

21

US$335-4,550 (350)

US$925-5,180 (10)

🍽 US$19-50

US$14-22

Honeymoon specials

1999 Romantic Interlude Package includes fresh flower lei on arrival, special check-in with fresh squeezed fruit juice, rose petals with champagne and candles at turndown, romantic dinner at the resort, breakfast in bed each morning, picnic basket with camera and mat, plus special gift from the hotel. Prices on application.

Sightseeing and leisure

Two championship golf courses, tennis and swimming pool. Beauty salon, health spa, massage and Jacuzzi. The Big Island has the most active volcano in the world, 'Kilauea', which can be viewed brilliantly by helicopter. There are also Monarch Festivals, pro golf tournaments, Cuisines of the Sun in summer months, and historic sites along the Kohala Coast.

New York

flying time
To: JFK/Newark
London: 6-7 hrs
LA: 5-6 hrs
Miami: 3 hrs

climate
Summers can be very hot, winters can be bitterly cold with thick snow. Spring and autumn are more pleasant.

when to go
The street parades are quite a sight; St Patrick's Day in March and Thanksgiving Day in Nov offer the biggest and best. Most travel agents offer special, low weekend fares.

getting around
The grid layout of the streets make travelling on foot a good option. Yellow taxis and buses abound. The tubes are confusing, but comparatively cheap.

Yellow taxis, flashing neon lights, the classic curves of the Chrysler Building – images of New York are familiar to us all. The city is one of the world's most popular tourist destinations, yet it remains surprisingly untouristy.

There are sights in abundance: the Statue of Liberty, Radio City Music Hall, the Metropolitan Museum of Art, even the hectic, hustling street life itself. But for most people, the main attraction is in the doing rather than the seeing: shopping like mad in the countless stores and boutiques along Madison and Fifth Avenues, enjoying a scintillating evening on Broadway before a night to remember in one of the Big Apple's innumerable swanky bars and restaurants.

New York can justly lay claim to be Entertainment Capital of the World. Life here is a distillation of the remainder of the planet's most exuberant entertainment played double-time – with jazz, *samba*, cinema, dance, and over 500 galleries and nightclubs to while away the hours.

Nevertheless, there are still more than enough opportunities to wind down. Pick the right spots and this can be an extremely relaxing place. Take a romantic carriage ride from The Plaza or stroll round the lake in Central Park and finish up in one of the quiet, homely diners that dot the city; or take a privileged view down First Avenue from the vantage point offered by the overhead cable cars. New York – it's a world unto itself.

Hôtel Plaza Athénée

37 East 64th Street
New York 10021
USA

✈ JFK Int. 16 miles

tel +212 734 9100
fax +212 772 0958

athenee@specialhotels.com
www.specialhotels.com
www.plaza-athenee.com

Tour operators:
UK Elegant Resorts

Member of:
Leading Hotels of the World

Between the quiet elegance of Park Avenue and the boutiques and art galleries of fashionable Madison Avenue, the Hôtel Plaza Athénée is just one block from Central Park. This prime location provides the perfect base to explore the vibrant city of New York, being within walking from most of the city's main attractions.

The stylish lobby is the last word in elegance with Italian marble floors, French antique furnishing and hand-painted murals. The newly renovated rooms combine European style with meticulous attention to detail. Most feature pantries with refrigerator and two-burner stove.

To underline that feeling of luxury, the sumptous bathrooms in Rose Aurora marble come complete with fresh flowers and bathrobes. Meanwhile, the award-winning Le Régence restaurant, described by critics as 'a fairytale setting where dinner is an event', offers exquisite dinners, including a grand seven-course chef's tasting menu. The Sunday brunch has also been rated 'best in the city'. The state-of-the-art Health Lounge gives guests the chance to work off all that good food.

With so much to offer, it's no surprise that *Condé Nast Traveler* (US) voted the hotel best service in NY City in its January '99 Gold List.

23

 US$410-620 (117)

 US$890-3,500 (36)

 from $36

 from $25

Honeymoon specials
Honeymoon weekend rates from US$285, traditional room; $355 deluxe and $495 for a one-bedroom suite, subject to availability. Bottle of champagne included.

Leisure facilities
The Health Lounge offers top-class facilities, including stairmasters, treadmills, lifecycles and free weights.

Sightseeing
Located on the fashionable Upper East Side of Manhattan, the hotel is within walking distance to Central Park, Fifth Avenue, art galleries, boutiques and New York's finest department stores.

South Carolina

flying time
To: Charleston
From: London 11hrs
via Washington

climate
Pleasant climate all year; sea breezes keep temperatures down in summer (20°-25°C) and up in winter (14°C). Most rainfall occurs in Mar and Nov.

24

when to go
With such a mild climate, there are fun outdoor activities throughout the year. Except in hurricane season, in Aug and Oct, the beaches are pretty and golden all year long.

getting around
Coach, train and bus services all operate around the state, but car hire is the best way to explore. Also, in Charleston take a horse-drawn carriage around to get a real feel for the quaint city. Ferries operate to the barrier islands.

Magnolia blossoms, rustic wooden porches and cool mint juleps are all part of life in charming South Carolina where the pace is just that bit slower and gentler – the perfect place for total relaxation and long, lazy days.

This state in the Deep South retains the grandeur and elegance of times gone by, combined with a modern outlook and up-to-date amenities that make it a perfect, enviable mix of both old and new.

Whether you visit the grand old city of Charleston or the tiny towns of the Lowcountry where laid-back fishermen line the waterways, you will discover the calm and peace of the region. Be sure to tour the many beautifully preserved antebellum homes, pretty clapboard churches and town museums.

The south is known for its outdoor lifestyle and the national and state parks are a great place to see it all in action. Find out more about its founders and rich history at one of the many Civil War sites throughout the state, or search for Indian artefacts along the banks of the charming, aptly named Salkehatchie, Combahee or Coosawhatchie rivers.

For golfers and those in search of limitless activities, Myrtle Beach awaits, while Hilton Head Island offers quiet, upmarket fun and, again, a lot of fine golf.

And don't forget the stunning coastline with its many tiny islands dotted offshore providing the perfect haven for honeymooners wanting a world all of their own.

Litchfield Plantation

PO Box 290
Kings River Road
Pawleys Island
South Carolina 29585
USA

✈ Myrtle Beach Int. 25 miles

tel +843 237 9121
fax +843 237 1041

litchfield@specialhotels.com
www.specialhotels.com
www.litchfieldplantation.com

Tour operator:
UK Whole World Golf Travel

Member of:
Small Luxury Hotels

Built in 1740 to be home to colonial rice planters in South Carolina, Litchfield Plantation, with its live oak-lined drive, wrought iron gates and white columned entrance would not be out of place on the set of Gone with the Wind. Secluded and steeped in history (the house even has its own ghost), the hotel is set in 600 acres of serene glades. Close by is a charming coastline with great beaches, marshes and lush groves.

The guest rooms and cypress-clad cottages, with their fireplaces, artworks and antique furniture, have a colonial charm and discrete sense of ease. The house was built at a time when the days passed slowly and whether guests are relaxing in a fire-side armchair in the lounge, dining in the elegant Carriage House restaurant, or living it up at the ocean-front clubhouse, the warm Carolina graciousness is every bit as present now as it was 250 years ago.

A good range of amenities from deep-sea fishing, championship golf courses and wildlife preserves to theatres, restaurants and nightclubs, is within easy reach. Many guests, however, never stray far from the grounds. For them, the plantation becomes a place in which to relax and settle, summed up by a simple word – home.

25

 US$132-202 (30)

 US$194-242 (8)

US$8-27

US$8-27

Honeymoon specials
Complimentary champagne and flowers on arrival (minimum stay of three nights).

Leisure facilities
Tennis, swimming pool, Beach Clubhouse, championship golf. Watersports nearby.

Sightseeing
Historic tours to typical Southern plantations, plus daytrips and sightseeing in nearby Georgetown and Charleston, both charming old Southern towns. The award-winning Brookgreen Gardens are just up the road. Also, river tours and exhibitions and museums devoted to blues music.

Canada

flying time
To: Toronto
London: 8 hrs
NY: 2 hrs
Plus 4 hrs to
Vancouver

climate
Summer averages
24°C. Winter can be
icy, but Canada is
geared for the cold.

when to go
Winter Carnival in
Quebec City in Feb
provides 11 days of
revelry. In Calgary,
for 10 days in July,
there is a showcase
for cowboy skills
and showmanship
called Stampede.

currency
Canadian dollar.

language
English is generally
spoken; French
predominates in
French territories.

getting around
Travel within the
country by air, but
trains are a good
alternative, especially
on scenic routes.

Canada is the second largest country in the world, with a stunning variety of locales, from the Rocky Mountains to Niagara Falls; from the glittering skyscrapers of Toronto to the lonely, glass-like lakes and forests of the vast Algonquin Provincial Park.

There is a rainbow of nationalities and cultures too, producing a tantalising variety of cuisine and some unique shopping opportunities: Inuit and Native Indian crafts, textiles and furs, traditional patchwork quilting, woodcarving, cowboy outfits and pottery aplenty. Coastal waters provide oysters, scallops, lobster and salmon, as well as clams for the famous chowder. The prairies offer grain-fed beef and delicious breads, and in the French territories you find classic *haute cuisine* as well as hearty, herby French colonial nosh.

Nightlife in Toronto lives up to anything the USA has to offer. The lakes are great for sailing, and there is Alpine and cross-country skiing all winter. On the west coast, Vancouver is a vibrant city and a good starting point for jaunts into the wilds of British Columbia – like a trip on the Rocky Mountaineer, a splendid train that hugs mountainsides and edges along lakes, past breathtaking scenery. Niagara Falls, one of the most popular honeymoon destinations, is a short hop away. The Algonquin Provincial Park, just three hours' drive from Toronto, offers 3,000 square miles of wilderness complete with wolves, vast lakes and primordial forests.

Quebec has a largely rugged terrain, and a truly French air. Experience the *joie de vivre* of the Winter Carnival, pop into a croissanterie for breakfast, or while away the afternoon with the chic clientele at a Montreal pavement cafe.

La Pinsonnière

Cap-à-l'Aigle
Charlevoix
Quebec
Canada

✈ Quebec City 150km

tel +418 665 4431
fax +418 665 7156

pinsonniere@specialhotels.com
www.specialhotels.com
pinsonniere@relaischateaux.fr

Closed 31 Oct–17 Dec

Member of:
Relais & Chateaux

This exclusive family-run inn perches high above the broad St Lawrence River in the heart of Quebec's stunningly beautiful Charlevoix region.

Set on a rambling property in the picturesque village of Cap-à-l'Aigle, many of the inn's luxuriously appointed rooms feature a double whirlpool bath and private sauna. Canopy beds and fireplaces provide a welcoming, comfortable atmosphere. Elegant bay windows open out onto spacious private balconies looking out over the river. The refined interior is heightened by a stunning collection of artwork.

Award-winning cuisine is served in a sophisticated softly lit dining room decorated with the owner's impressive art collection, and is complemented by one of the country's most highly rated wine cellars.

A nature trail leads through a cedar wood to a secluded beach that is ideal for sunbathing and picnicking. In summer, guests can try out activities as diverse as whale-watching cruises, outdoor concerts with Sunday brunch and carriage rides.

And during the winter months, there is skiing, romantic sleigh rides, or try dog-sledding and snowmobiling. Daredevils can experience the thrills of white-water rafting or sea kayaking, or try their luck at the glamourous casino.

27

 CAD$140–450 (26)

 CAD$450 (1)

 from CAD$45

 from CAD$13

Honeymoon specials

Honeymoon package includes welcome cocktail, a celebratory seven-course dinner, breakfast, champagne and souvenir gift. The package is available for three and five nights, cost: CAD$945-1,875 and CAD$1,425-2,975 per couple respectively.

Sightseeing and leisure

Outdoor concerts, boat cruises, wine tastings, art galleries and casino nearby. Whale-watching, skiing, sleigh rides, dog-sledding, snowmobiling, golf, horseriding, white-water rafting and sea-kayaking can be arranged. Swimming and tennis. Sauna and massage by appointment.

The Inn at Manitou

McKellar Centre Road
McKellar
Ontario POGICO
Canada

✈ Toronto 250km

tel +416 245 5606
fax +416 245 2460
Toll free: +800 571 8818

manitou@specialhotels.com
www.specialhotels.com
www.manitou-online.com

28 Open May-October

Member of:
Relais & Chateaux

Two hundred and fifty kilometres north of Toronto, the Inn at Manitou nestles in 550 acres of woodland. Located on the shores of one of Ontario's unspoilt lakes, it offers five star luxury deep in the Canadian wilderness.

Just 33 luxurious guest accommodations are available. All are built chalet-style on the hillside overlooking the lake and are furnished with soothing colours. Many contain log fires.

Meals are included in the room rate. Breakfast is served in the sun-filled dining room with views over the grounds. Lunch ranges from light bistro fare to hearty American barbecues. Dinner is normally three courses and features strongly the modern French Cuisine the hotel is known for. There are formal evenings four nights a week.

The Inn is world famous for its tennis facilities and it has a brand new spa opening in May 1999. Many other activities are also offered. Exact timings appear in the daily INNOVATION newsletter. If you'd prefer more independent activities, mountain biking, horseriding and many watersports can be arranged. Finally, despite its wilderness location the hotel offers the opportunity for sightseers to explore many delights of Canada – including a helicopter trip over stunning Niagara Falls.

 CAD$218-308*

 CAD$305-370*

 CAD$35

 CAD$20

Honeymoon specials

Flowers in room on arrival, pre-breakfast wake-up with champagne, juice and strawberries in room, candlelit dinner. Plus, for her a manicure, pedicure and Swedish massage (or tennis lesson); for him a facial or massage plus tennis lesson. Three-day package costs from CAD$565-1,217*.
* Prices are per person per day, plus all meals. Exclusive of taxes and 16% service charge.

Sightseeing and leisure

Recreation is the name of the game at Inn at Manitou. Choose from golf, tennis, spa facilities and watersports such as skiing, sailing and canoeing. Also, you can take boat fishing excursions (from CAD$90), pontoon trips (from CAD$80), float plane trips (from CAD$60) and sunset champagne flights (from CAD$110 per person).

All of the best bars, restaurants, cafes, shops, festivals and things to see and do, in more than 40 destinations around the world.

The best of the world in the palm of your hand

"practically the only thing they can't do is call you a cab!"
ELLE

SEVILLE AND ANDALUSIA

BALI

CRETE

AMSTERDAM

PRAGUE

PROVENCE

RAJASTHAN

ITALY

EVERYMAN GUIDES

Paris
Everyman City Guides

New York
Everyman City Guides

Madrid
Everyman City Guides

EVERYMAN TRAVEL GUIDES

at all good bookshops from £9.99.
or order from © +44 171 539 7600
email guides@everyman.uk.com

Amsterdam
Athens & the Peloponnese
Bali
Barcelona
Berlin
Brittany
Brussels & Southern Belgium
Crete
Egypt
Florence
The Holy Land
Ireland
Istanbul
Italy
Lisbon
The Loire Valley
London
Madrid
Milan
Morocco
Naples and Pompeii
New York
Paris
Prague
Provence & Côte d'Azur
Rajasthan
Restaurants of Paris
Rio de Janeiro
Rome
The Route of the Mayas
Saint Petersburg
San Francisco
Seville & Andalusia
Singapore & Malaysia
Thailand
Venice
Vienna

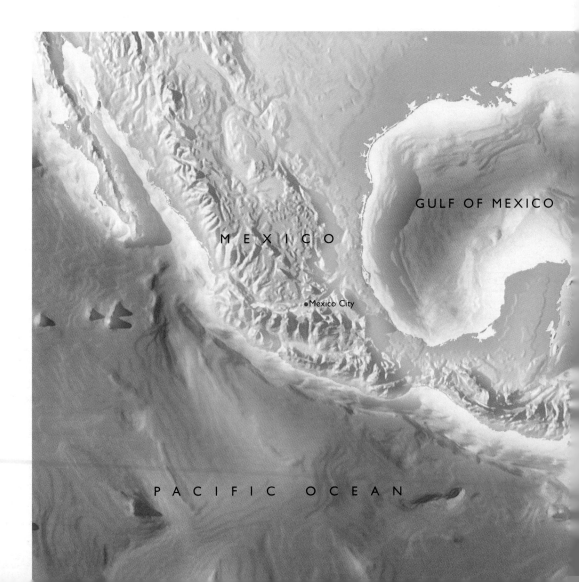

GULF OF MEXICO

M E X I C O

•Mexico City

P A C I F I C   O C E A N

Here, at 'the sweet waist of America', a fantastic range of political, ethnic and environmental forces have collided, creating a magical hybrid.

In the big cities, a version of Coca-Cola culture moves to the rhythm of Colombian *salsa*. Deep in the forests, species of birds, beasts and plants from north and south live beside local species that are found nowhere else in the world.

There are places where it is not wise to travel, but the beautiful bays and rainforests of Costa Rica, and the soaring, creeper-clad ruins of the ancient Mayan Indian civilisation in Guatemala, are truly unforgettable honeymoon locations.

Neighbouring Mexico, a more cosmopolitan country, with long, gorgeous beaches, pulsating resorts and magnificent monuments, is already a mainstream holiday destination.

The whole region is incredibly romantic: for its scenery of smouldering volcanoes rising above green and gold highland valleys; for its still, dark lakes and mysterious cloud forests shrouded in swirling mists; for its tropical jungles hiding ancient pyramids; for its crumbling, elegant colonial architecture; for its thrilling music and certainly for its kind, passionate people.

The great driving forces here are land, family and religion, and throughout the whole length of Central America a fiery and unforgettable Latin heart beats just below the surface of all things.

COSTA RICA
• San José

Costa Rica

flying time
To: San José via
Bogotá
London: 12 hrs
Miami: 3 hrs
NY: 7 hrs

climate
Tropical country with
two seasons: wet and
dry. Dry between
late Dec-Apr, wet
rest of the
year. Temperatures
vary little between
seasons. In San José
the climate is eternal
spring (15°-25°C),
coastal areas are
hotter (30°C+).

when to go
Late Dec-Apr is drier
but prices are higher.
Note that hotels
book up early.

currency
Costa Rican colón.
But be sure to take
US dollars with you.

getting around
By air to almost all
the main towns. The
bus service is the
best on the isthmus
but services are
scarce off main
routes. Car hire
can be expensive.

The second smallest of the Central American nations, Costa Rica is an increasingly popular destination with travellers.

Nature-lovers and sports enthusiasts in particular are finding this country of such diversity a terrific place to explore. But it is still relatively undiscovered – and cleaner, greener and more relaxed than its neighbours.

No less than 20% of the country has been set aside for nature conservation in a superb network of national parks, all alive with the overwhelming fertility of the tropics, and offering a unique and intriguing opportunity to see wildlife in the raw. The country is home to more than 750 species of bird – more than in the entire United States – and protected areas include steaming volcanic peaks, undisturbed tropical forests, vast lakes, islands, dry grassland, superb beaches, mountains and rambling pre-Colombian ruins.

In this country of natural wonders and astonishing beauty, highlights include Corcovado National Park, diving off the Cocos Islands, carnival in Puerto Limón, the Gold Museum in San José, Arenal Volcano, and a whole raft of sports. Pacific rollers pound the coast, attracting surfing enthusiasts. River rafting is a developing sport that requires no training. River and deep-sea fishing are superb. The gruelling ascent of a volcanic peak and wading through jungle mud. Wildlife viewing, too, is in a league of its own.

Lapa Rios

Pto. Jiménez
Costa Rica

✈ Pto Jimenez 12 miles

Contact:
PO Box 025216
SJO-706
Miami, Florida 33102-5216

tel +506 735 5130
fax +506 735 5179

rios@specialhotels.com
www.specialhotels.com
info@laparios.com
www.laparios.com

Set in a thousand acres of private, lush rainforest, high up on the Osa Peninsula, overlooking the vast Pacific Ocean, owner-operated Lapa Rios is one of the most deluxe jungle and beach hideaways in all of Costa Rica.

Fourteen luxury thatched bungalows are dotted throughout the jungle. Each has a private deck and patio garden with magnificent views over the ocean, showers with solar-heated water, and two queen-sized beds. The bungalows are furnished in wood and bamboo with tropical printed fabrics. Constant breezes pass through the screened window walls. Although isolated (no phones), service at Lapa Rios is sophisticated. Staff are outgoing and experienced. Electricity is provided 24 hours a day. The main lodge, soaring 50 feet into the air, has a full service bar and restaurant serving quality cuisine, with the accent on fresh fruits, vegetables and meat, and local seafood.

While here, you can relax on safe, unspoiled sandy beaches, watch the continuous parade of colourful birds, butterflies and animals native to Costa Rica, and take part in adventurous organised activities – from jungle hikes to sea kayaking.

 US$330-450 (14)

 US$25

 US$10

Honeymoon specials
Flower arrangement on bed on arrival. Welcome cocktail.

Leisure facilities
A romantic swimming pool set in tropical rainforest and a private tropical plant and orchid garden. Massage.

Sightseeing
Resident naturalists give guided tours around the private reserve and the famous Corovado National Park. Orchid Garden and Mangrove River tours. Guided hiking, horseriding, kayaking, fishing, surfing.

Mexico

flying time
To: Mexico City
London: 10-12 hrs
LA/Miami: 3 hrs
NY: 5 hrs

climate
Generally the north
west coast, northern
Baja California and
central plateau are
coolest. Overall, the
weather is temperate
and dry Nov-May,
with temperatures
rising and rainfall
heavier June-Oct.

when to go
High season, with
crowds and action, is
Dec, Feb, July-Aug.
The quiet months
are Apr-May.

currency
Mexican peso.

getting around
Frequent flights
between major cities,
together with a vast
bus network and a
rather slow rail
system.

Mexico's famous shimmering coastline along the Pacific, the Caribbean and the Gulf of Mexico is just one element of this vast country's extraordinary range of attractions.

The captivating landscape varies from snow-capped mountains to arid deserts, and lush, tropical forests to temperate valleys, while numerous archaeological sites and historic cities inspire visitors with their mysticism and almost unbelievable beauty.

Mexico City is rambling, cosmopolitan and modern, and a tribute to earlier civilisations with magnificent Aztec temples and the floating gardens of Xochimilco, where people still live on the canals, as the Aztecs did 500 years ago. The city is also an ideal base from which to visit the pyramids of Teotihuacan, one of the world's most impressive archaeological sites, the temple of Tlahizcalpantecuhtli in Tula, with its gigantic

Atlantes statues, and the colonial cities of Taxco, Toluca and Tepotzotlan.

The southern area of Mexico was home to the Maya, one of the greatest of the country's civilisations dating from 3,000 years ago. Chichen-Itza is the most renowned of all Mayan cities, with some of the greatest monuments, including the great pyramid known as El Castillo.

Heading north, Guadalajara is hailed as the essence of Mexico, upholding traditions like the *charreadas* (rodeos) and *jaraba tapatlo* (hat dance), while the famous *mariachis* create amazing amounts of atmosphere in Plaza Tapatio.

Acapulco offers glittering nightlife and beaches surrounded by tall mountain ranges, with the famous divers of la Quebrada soaring from a cliff 45m high.

Spectacular scenery, including pine forests, can be seen from the Chihuahua-Pacifico train which joins the altiplano of Mexico with the Sea of Cortez. The train travels through historic towns like Bahuichivo, a good base from which to explore the staggering Copper Canyon. And try travelling down to the southern tip of the Baja Peninsula where you'll be mesmerised by cactus-laden desert spectacularly meeting the Sea of Cortez, and perhaps as importantly, by the rich and famous who zoom down from LA for long, lazy weekends.

Rich flavours of the native cuisine are also a trademark, with three indispensable elements: *tortillas*, beans and chillies. And no meal is complete without Mexico's other homegrown staple: tequila.

Information & Reservations
UK 0870 606 1296
INT. +44 870 606 1296

Baja Catita S/N
Carrerera Escencia Km
14 Acapulco
Guerrero 39867
Mexico

✈ Acapulco 15 mins

tel +52 74 66 1010
fax +52 74 66 1111

diamonte@specialhotels.com
www.specialhotels.com
www.caminoreal.com/acapulco/

36

Tucked into the side of a mountain along the shore of the beautiful Puerto Marques Bay in the exclusive Pichilingue Diamante area, the Camino Real is surrounded by hills and lush tropical vegetation with a sandy beach and warm waters on its doorstep.

The 150 or so rooms and suites are tastefully decorated in sun-rich colours, with soft lighting, marble floors and warm, blonde furniture. All have their own verandahs and enjoy marvellous views. Some of the suites include a Jacuzzi, solarium and spacious terrace to flop out on.

Swimming, waterskiing, sailing and snorkelling await on the beach or, if guests prefer, a luxurious dip in one of the hotel's three pools is also a distinct possibility. Allow time for a rousing game of tennis or a challenging round of golf on the nearby golf course.

All this exercise tends to create a healthy appetite and Camino Real delights in satisfying hunger pangs. At La Vela, seafood is on the menu, the speciality being the famous red snapper while at Cabo Diamante an international menu is served in elegant yet informal surroundings. For those who can still move after the feast, Acapulco, with its scintillating nightlife, is just a wish away.

🛏 from US$500 (11)

🛏 from US$170 (156)

🍽 US$25

☕ US$25

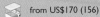

Honeymoon specials
Champagne and flowers in room on arrival.

*There is also the Camino Real Club offering guests exclusivity in services and amenities in its 11 luxurious and spacious rooms with ocean views which include private registration area, breakfast daily, cocktails and *hors d'oeuvres* every evening, bathrobes and concierge services.

Sightseeing and leisure
The Beach Club has three swimming pools and a beach with watersports available: jet-skiing, waterskiing, deep-sea fishing, snorkelling, Scuba diving and sailing. There is also one lighted tennis court available.

Camino Real Cancun

Punta Cancun S/N
Zona Hotelera
Cancun Q. Roo 7750
Mexico

✈ Cancun 20 mins

tel +52 98 83 0100
fax +52 98 83 1730

cancun@specialhotels.com
www.specialhotels.com
www.caminoreal.com/cancun/

The ultra-luxurious five-star Camino Real Cancun sits at Punta Cancun, the utmost tip of the island of Cancun, surrounded on three sides by the sparkling Caribbean and smooth, white stunning Mexican beaches. The architecture of the hotel is inspired by ancient Mayan pyramids and designed by world-renowned Mexican architect, Richard Legorreta. Balconies overlook the miles of stunning sea and give guests the chance to sample the awe-inspiring sunrises and sunsets.

Two secluded beaches and a private inlet offer that taste of paradise as well as a huge array of watersports, including snorkelling, windsurfing, Scuba diving, jet skiing, fishing and sailing. For those guests who prefer to be on solid ground, there are three lighted tennis courts, a fully-equipped fitness centre and spa and an 18-hole golf course nearby.

At night there are a wide selection of local restaurants and bars to choose from. Fresh fish and seafood abound at the Mezquite Grill La Brisa where you can enjoy your meal to the sound of sultry Latin jazz.

Or if dancing the night away is your idea of the perfect evening, the Azucar Caribbean Bar gives you the chance to salsa, merengue or learn a host of other Latin dances.

37

 US$195-230

 US$275-380

 from US$25

 from US$10

Honeymoon specials
Champagne on arrival, room upgrade subject to availability. Special honeymoon package "Affairs of the Heart" includes special gift, welcome cocktail, daily breakfast, one dinner for two, champagne on arrival. Cost from US$953-2,102, including taxes.

Sightseeing and leisure
Watersports abound, including diving, snorkelling, sailing, kayaking. At the hotel there are tennis courts, beauty salon and full gym. Trips to local archaeological sites can be arranged.

Information & Reservations
UK   0870 606 1296
INT. +44 870 606 1296

Camino Real
Las Hadas Manzanillo

Peninsula de Santiago
PO Box 158 Manzanillo
Colima 28200
Mexico

✈ Playa de Oro 28km

tel +52 333 40 000
fax +52 333 41 950

hadas@specialhotels.com
www.specialhotels.com

38

Las Hadas is the Spanish word for fairies and it's a fitting name for this magical, self-contained resort magnificently located on the edge of the beautiful Manzanillo Bay.

Between narrow streets and cool shady plazas lie 233 rooms and suites offering high standards of comfort combined with perfect peace and quiet. White spires and ornate domes characterise the complex's architecture, while fountains and palm trees line the grounds.

At night two restaurants offer fine dining using local produce like succulent seafood. Mexican dishes are a speciality of the house and will enliven even the most jaded palate with their rich mix of spices and textures.

The resort also houses La Mantarraya golf course, considered one of the finest courses in Mexico. If you'd prefer to tee-off your tan visit the hotel's golden sand beach featured famously in the movie *10* starring Bo Derek and Dudley Moore.

For the explorer the surrounding area has much to offer. Take out a boat from the hotel's private marina to try your hand at deep-sea fishing or, on land, explore the nearby fishing towns and sleepy villages of the Mexican countryside. At the 'hotel of the fairies' your every wish can be granted.

 US$250-970 (192)

 US$200-920 (41)

¶◎¶ US$6-35

☕ US$6-9

Honeymoon specials
Deluxe ocean view room, welcome cocktail, daily American breakfast, one round of golf per room, one hour of daytime tennis, flowers on bed, special gift, one romantic dinner with one bottle of domestic wine. Price on application.

Sightseeing and leisure
Professional tennis courts, La Mantarraya golf course, lagoon-shaped pool, windsurfing, waterskiing, snorkelling and Scuba diving. Locally, there are magical plazas with fountains, tropical tours, sunset cruises and gastronomical festivals throughout the year.

Camino Real
Puerto Vallarta

Playa de Las Estacas
S/N 48300
Puerto Vallarta, Jal
Mexico

✈ Puerto Vallarta 20 mins

tel +52 322 150 00
fax +52 322 160 00

vallarta@specialhotels.com
www.specialhotels.com
www.caminoreal.com

Sandwiched between the palm-covered Sierra Madre mountain range and the sparkling waters of Banderas Bay, the Camino Real is a relaxing haven of modern comforts within a rustic setting. Once a quaint seaside village, Puerto Vallarta is now a world-famous resort. Yet it is still one of Mexico's most picturesque coastal cities, with charming cobblestone streets, lined with old-fashioned white adobe buildings.

The Camino Real overlooks a secluded cove and boasts a kilometre of private beach. The 300-plus comfortable rooms and suites are decorated in Mexican style with richly coloured fabrics and

artworks. Each overlooks Banderas Bay, which is the seventh largest bay in the world and home to numerous dolphins, whales and giant manta rays. But don't worry, no sharks.

Besides the resort's five restaurants serving authentic Mexican and international cuisine, Camino Real also features shimmering swimming pools, tennis courts and a health club. Fishing trips, safaris and a golf club are all nearby as well as every facility to enjoy watersports.

Just five minutes away lies the village of Puerto Vallarta, which is great for shopping, sightseeing, and has an abundance of cafes, bars and restaurants.

39

US$160-220 (326)

US$400-600 (11)

US$4-35

US$9

Honeymoon specials
The hotel offers an 'Affairs of the Heart' package for US$600. It includes a three-night stay in a Club suite with private Jacuzzi, flowers and champagne on arrival, welcome cocktail, breakfast daily, dinner including a bottle of house wine, plus all taxes. Room upgrade subject to availability. Prices on application.

Sightseeing and leisure
Tennis courts, all watersports at Camino Real. There are also sea tours, deep-sea fishing excursions and golf nearby. Puerto Vallarta is a bustling town full of markets and bazaars, largely catering to those on 'leave' from the many cruise lines that stop off here. Don't miss the sunsets over Banderas Bay and Pacific Ocean beyond.

Fiesta Americana
Cancun

CP 77500
Cancun
Quintana Roo
Mexico

✈ Cancun 20mins

tel +529 8 831400
fax +529 8 832502

fiesta@specialhotels.com
www.specialhotels.com

Tour operators:
UK Kuoni, British Airways
US Travel Impressions

40

Set on one of the finest beaches on the Cancun peninsula, the Fiesta Americana Cancun overlooks the smooth blue expanse of Mexico's Caribbean.

The Mediterranean inspiration of the hotel's design is reflected in the red-tiled roofs and stone balustrades of the private balconies. All rooms are sea-facing, decorated with Mexican elegance, and furnished with oak. Large picture windows lead out to private balconies which overlook the ocean.

A dining experience to suit all tastes is assured by the range of restaurants and bars in the hotel. Friendly staff serve traditional Mexican dishes at Chulavista Cafe, and local seafood specialities are prepared by the pool at La Palapa.

There are a wide range of watersports here, including snorkelling, Scuba diving, sailing and waterskiing. Jungle and catamaran tours can also be organised. You can venture further afield as well, to archeological sites at Tulum and Chichen-Itza, take a boat to some of the surrounding islands, or explore the natural aquariums.

The hotel can organise receptions for weddings. Ceremonies may take place on the beach, at the poolside, or an a special deck by the ocean.

 US$97-250

 US$303-504

 US$25

 US$10

Honeymoon specials

Complimentary champagne and flowers on arrival, special romantic dinner and room service or breakfast buffet each day. Ocean-view room guaranteed and complimentary bathrobes. (Minimum of three-night stay.)

Leisure facilities

Spa in the hotel as well as fitness centre, beauty salon and swimming pool.

Sightseeing

Flea and craft markets nearby. Numerous discos, restaurants and nightlife. A plethora of golf and other sports nearby.

Las Mananitas

Ricardo Linares 107
Apartado Postal 1202
62000 Cuernavaca
Morelos
Mexico

✈ Mexico City 80km

tel +52 73 14 14 66
fax +52 73 18 36 72

mananitas@specialhotels.com
www.specialhotels.com
mananita@intersur.com

Member of:
Relais & Chateaux

Las Mananitas is a small and friendly, privately run hotel in Cuernavaca, located 40 miles south of Mexico City. The hotel is small because its owner likes it that way and over the 40 or so years since it was founded, Las Mananitas has built up a reputation which could be the envy of many larger establishments.

The 22 suites are charmingly old-fashioned with wood beams, stone floors and antique furniture. Bright Mexican fabrics add a splash of colour and art works by some of Mexico's better known artists grace the walls. In the gardens serenity is the key as exotic birds wander freely among the sculptures and manicured lawns. Guests can enjoy a cocktail and dine *al fresco* in one of the covered terraces overlooking the garden or sit beneath the shade of a poolside palm.

The hotel's restaurant has many admirers and the *à la carte* menu featuring Mexican and international dishes offers a selection of culinary delights. Once visitors have exhausted the sites of Cuernavaca, there are countless other excursions nearby. Among them are the silver town of Taxco, famous for its colonial architecture, the beaches of Acapulco and, of course, Mexico City with its museums, galleries and intriguing architecture.

41

 US$137-374* (21)

 US$91-118* (1)

US$12-25

US$10-20

Honeymoon specials
Complimentary champagne, fruit and flowers in room on arrival.

* Prices do not include 15% tax or 5% service charge.

Sightseeing and leisure
Cuernavaca, called 'The City of Eternal Spring' by the Aztecs, plus other sites within walking distance. City tours and shopping, local craftsmanship, flower festival during Easter, day trips to Mexico City, Anthropology and History museum. Golf and tennis also nearby, massage by appointment.

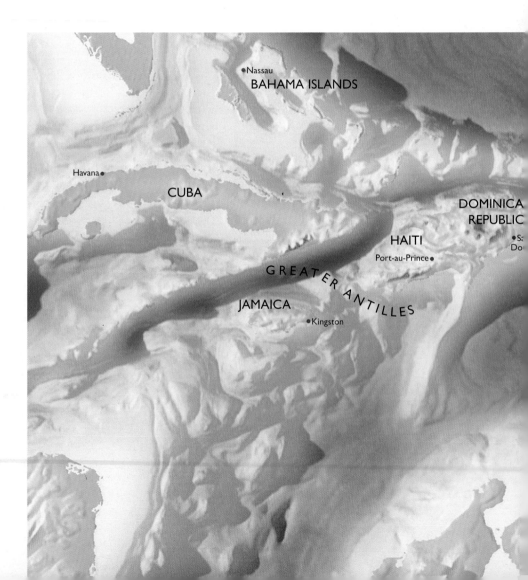

BAHAMA ISLANDS

Nassau

Havana

CUBA

DOMINICA
REPUBLIC

HAITI

Port-au-Prince

GREATER ANTILLES

JAMAICA

Kingston

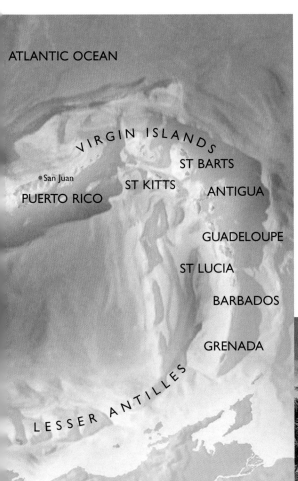

ATLANTIC OCEAN

VIRGIN ISLANDS

ST BARTS

• San Juan

ST KITTS   ANTIGUA

PUERTO RICO

GUADELOUPE

ST LUCIA

BARBADOS

GRENADA

LESSER ANTILLES

The alluring Caribbean is the world's most popular honeymoon destination by far – and so it should be.

Here you are bombarded by intense sensations – the sweet flavours of ripened fruits, the fragrance of jasmine in the night air, the impossibly bright plumage of a scarlet ibis and music played loudly, everywhere.

You can dive in crystal seas to a glittering extravaganza of colourful corals and tropical fish, take an unforgettable trip on a catamaran, feel the surge of a windsurfer beneath you as you race off on the trade winds, or simply lie back and absorb the sun's warmth.

The region is an extraordinary melting pot of cultures including Parisian chic, English country churches, American-style cable television and large cruising cars, Hindu prayer flags, Moslem minarets and the spirit of Africa.

In places it can be difficult to find an isolated beach and would-be island-hoppers should plan their route with care. Elsewhere there are sugary, quiet beaches from paradise, and certainly some of the most romantic and exclusive resorts to stay in the world.

43

Antigua

flying time
London: 8 hrs
Miami: 3 hrs
NY: 4 hrs

climate
Warm year-round with temperatures from 20°-25°C.

when to go
Apr for regattas, July for carnival, Oct for the jazz festival.

currency
Eastern Caribbean dollar, fixed to the US dollar. Life can be expensive; the government raises taxes through sales of food and goods.

language
English.

getting around
Daily flights to the other islands. No scheduled boat services and few local buses, but an abundance of taxis, bicycles, hire cars. Roads are poor. Hire a 4-wheel-drive to venture off main routes.

The largest of the Leeward Islands, Antigua is famous for cricket matches, yachting parties, soft manners and gentle shores, and of course rum parties and soaring frigate birds.

And it is one of the prettiest. Within the sweeping curves of bays on the protected shores of the Caribbean Sea, gentle wave action on the reefs has pushed up miles of blinding white sand. Between the main beaches there are any number of small coves, and reefs on all sides with plenty of wrecks to dive.

In Antigua's capital, St John's, many of the old wood and stone buildings with overhanging balconies remain, and traditional West Indian life can be still be seen – in the chaos of the market, and by the glistening water where fishermen mend their nets. And at English Harbour, a pretty enclave in the southeast, Nelson's Dockyard is a centre for tourism and yachting that is touristy but nevertheless charming.

In the 18th century the island bristled with forts and fortlets, and today many visitors enjoy rooting around the ruins, now 15 feet deep in scrub, and taking in the glorious views for which the forts were originally built.

Yachting is a big activity, with a major regatta at the end of the winter season that attracts sailors from everywhere, and is a good excuse for a 'jump-up'.

There are a few fine hotels tucked away in their own coves. Some sit in splendour in the historical setting of English Harbour and offer fine international cuisine as well as fiery West Indian fare.

Siboney Beach Club

PO Box 222
St John's
Antigua

✈ VC Bird Int. 10km

tel +268 462 0806
fax +268 462 3356

siboney@specialhotels.com
www.specialhotels.com
siboney@candw.ag
www.turq.com/siboney

Tour operators:
UK Thomas Cook
US Silkcut Travel

'How pleasant it would be,' wrote the naturalist Charles Darwin, 'to pass one's life in such quiet abodes.' In Antigua, it is not only the fittest which have survived but the most beautiful as well. Brightly-coloured papaya, mangoes and guava abound, growing under flamboyant trees and palms and amidst this miniature jungle beside a sheltered mile of white sand and emerald waters is the intimate Siboney Beach Club.

The suites are individually decorated in rich, earthy colours and furnished with tropical prints, comfortable sofas and king-size beds. Twin double doors open onto balconies affording glimpses of the Caribbean through a profusion of palm fronds and bougainvillea.

The food is a riot of colour and taste and attests to the Antiguan proverb 'Better man belly bus' than good food waste'. Delicious concoctions of fresh lobster and seafood, spicy curries, thick steaks, bright salads, barbecues, baby back ribs and even Conch Fritters are all available nearby.

Weddings are easily arranged. Couples can exchange vows barefoot in the sand or, for a more formal ceremony, at the Siboney Beach Club itself. Wedding extras can include anything from cake and champagne to steel pan soloist.

45

 US$155-310* (12)

 US$15-35

 US$5.50-8.95

Honeymoon specials

Welcome cocktail, wine, flowers, use of snorkels, masks, beach lounges and towels, plus full day of sailing. Packages cost from US$695* per couple for a four-night stay.

Prices subject to 18.5% gratuity and government tax.

Sightseeing and leisure

Sailing, Scuba diving, snorkelling, golf, tennis, windsurfing, fitness club, cycling. Also, Trips to Nelson's Dockyard, wind-powered sugar mill, historic naval buildings, Redcliffe Quay, Museum of Antigua and Barbuda, St. John's Cathedral, Jolly Harbour, Indian Town and Devil's Bridge. There are festivals and events, like Antigua sailing week in April, Carnival in July.

Barbados

flying time
London: 3¹/₂ hrs by
Concorde, or 8 hrs
by jet
LA: 9¹/₂ hrs
Miami: 3¹/₂ hrs·
NY: 4¹/₂ hrs

**climate/
when to go**
You can visit the
island any time, but
May-June and Oct-
Nov are wet seasons
with fewer festivals
and regattas.

currency
Barbados dollar,
fixed to US dollar.

language
English.

getting around
There are relatively
frequent air and sea
services to the other
islands. On Barbados
use the friendly local
buses or plentiful
unmetered taxis. Car
hire is expensive.

Barbados stands alone, out in the Atlantic, about a hundred miles beyond the rest of the Eastern Caribbean. It's a small coral island with some of the finest golden sandy beaches anywhere and a most agreeable climate. The island is long established as a winter getaway, and its famous west coast, second home to a crowd of international celebrities and sophisticates, has given it the nickname 'millionaires' playground'.

At just 21 miles by 14 miles, the island can get fairly crowded, but it is easy to have an idyllic holiday here. As well as some of the smartest, and certainly most expensive, hotels in the Caribbean, Barbados has a growing tradition of fine food. The Bajans know a thing or two about service; the result being a string of great restaurants, wine bars and lively beach bars where you can eat well in charming locations. Bajan fare includes plenty of seafood, especially flying fish, and sea egg, the roe of the white sea urchin, which is supposedly an aphrodisiac. As well as the ubiquitous cocktails, fruit punches are particularly good.

The island's British heritage has left a delightful and

often old-fashioned charm in its manners, buildings and even its language. (You can hear distinct traces of a West Country accent in Bajan speech.) Gorgeous and well-preserved plantation houses stand in swathes of sugar-cane, cricketers in whites play beneath palm trees. In the thriving capital of Bridgetown, grand old colonial structures with filigree metal balconies jostle with glass-fronted shops and offices.

Spectator sports include horseracing and polo, but cricket is the national sport, with weekend matches all over the island and less formal games being played by children in the backstreets.

Top-class hotels provide most sports you can think of, including horseriding, deep-sea fishing and golf. Watersports operators on the main beaches on the west and south coasts can fix you up with a kayak, small sailing boat, windsurfer or jet-ski; arrange a ride in a glass-bottom boat or on a bouncy banana. Windsurfing is excellent on the south coast. The east coast boasts big surfing waves, and an excellent hiking district known as Scotland.

The highlight of the festival year is Cropover, which culminates in early August (the crop referred to is the sugar-cane harvest). This is a major blow-out along Carnival lines, with calypso-singing competitions, steel band music and carnival bands made up of hundreds of costumed players who strut to *soca* music.

There is a jazz festival in early January, and in the middle of the month there is an international regatta. In February, the Holetown Festival celebrates the first settlement of the island in 1627 with a week of grand exhibitions and a general jamboree.

Colony Club Hotel

Porters St James
Barbados

✈ Grantley Adams 35km

tel +246 438 4690
fax +246 438 4696

Contact:
tel +44 (0) 171 495 5588
fax +44 (0) 171 495 1444

colonyclub@specialhotels.com
www.specialhotels.com

Tour operators:
UK British Airways Holidays, Kuoni
US Liberty GoGo, Travel Impressions

Member of:
Elegant Hotels Group

One of the Caribbean's premier hotels, Colony Club, is set in seven acres of resplendent gardens on the famous platinum coast of Barbados, shaded by coconut palms and cooled by the waters of four twisting freshwater lagoons.

Once a gentleman's club, today the hotel is the epitome of sophisticated elegance. With breathtaking views of the turquoise seas, Colony Club's facilities are unrivalled. Here you have state-of-the-art sports equipment and complimentary activities from waterskiing to catamaran sailing, windsurfing to tennis. Horseriding along the beach and even a submarine tour can be arranged.

Impeccable service complements award winning cuisine. Dine in the Laguna restaurant, which stretches two stories high, and sample both international and Caribbean fare. Or choose Colony's *á la carte* restaurant, the Orchid Room, and two cocktail bars which provide refreshments Caribbean-style. Or you may choose to take the complimentary water taxi to make use of one of Colony's sister hotels on the island.

Colony Club is a popular choice for weddings and honeymoons alike. The hotel's own wedding co-ordinator is more than happy to deliver and meet your every expectation.

US$136-308* (64)

US$161-349* (34)

US$20-40

US$15

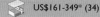

Honeymoon specials

Tropical flowers and bottle of sparkling wine on arrival. Champagne breakfast served on balcony, romantic dinner with photos of the evening. Special gift from hotel. Luxury and Ultimate Wedding Packages available, please enquire for further information.
* Prices quoted are per person per night. Half board or room only available.

Sightseeing and leisure

Waterskiing, sailing, snorkelling, windsurfing, tennis, fitness centre, golf, biking, horseriding, deep-sea fishing, shopping tours, helicopter tours, submarine tours, and trips to neighbouring Caribbean islands.

Information & Reservations
UK 0870 606 1296
INT. +44 870 606 1296

Paynes Bay
St James
Barbados

✈ Grantley Adams Int. 15km

tel +246 432 1346
fax +246 432 1094

treasure@specialhotels.com
www.specialhotels.com
barbados.org/hotels/h64.htm
treasure@caribsurf.com

Tour operators:
UK Elegant Resorts
Caribbean Connection

Well positioned on the stunning coral island of Barbados is Treasure Beach. An attractive hotel with an outstanding restaurant, Treasure Beach is an intimate hideaway and with just 29 secluded suites, each of which enjoys pleasant views of the garden, pool or Caribbean Sea, it is more like a club than a hotel. Days spent here stretch out, just like the sandy beach on its doorstep, full of simple pleasures and warm hospitality.

The spacious suites are elegant and unfussy. Each has a private balcony or patio – the Hemingway suite has a four-poster bed – and private terraces. After a dip in the freshwater pool or the invigorating surf, hearty appetites can be appeased in the award-winning restaurant, which boasts a very well-selected wine list to match the cuisine.

Barbados, at only 22km by 34km, has everything for the perfect honeymoon. A clear ocean, pink and white beaches, lots of sunshine and a culture that combines modern-day Caribbean living with the resonance of its charming colonial past.

The delights of the Caribbean – Calypso music, limbo dancing, restful beaches and stunning tropical scenery – are served in generous portions on the island. It is a winning recipe and one that the Treasure Beach hotel knows well.

49

 US$188-1,704 (29)

 US$27-100

 US$11.50-34.50

Honeymoon specials
Treasure Beach's wedding package includes room upgrade if available, wedding co-ordinator, marriage license, bridal posy and groom's buttonhole, Minister's fees, transfers, two witnesses at ceremony, one-tiered fruit cake, one bottle of champagne and dinner on the wedding night. Cost: US$540. Other options are available, such as photographer and music, to be paid locally.

Sightseeing and leisure
Festivals are a big part of Bajan culture; the highlight of the year is Cropover, held in August, with Calypso-singing competitions and steel bands at every corner. Also, watersports and fresh water pool are available at the hotel. Golf and tennis nearby.

Bermuda

flying time
London: 7 hrs
Miami: 3-4 hrs
NY: 2 hrs

climate
Summers (May-Oct) can be hot and humid. Winters are quite mild.

when to go
For watersports the summer months are best. Golf and riding are best enjoyed in spring and autumn. In June of alternate (even-numbered) years go for the great Newport to Bermuda Ocean Yacht Race.

currency
Bermuda dollar, on a par with the US dollar.

getting around
Distances are small, and buses and taxis abound. Visitors hire bicycles and mopeds rather than cars. For a romantic jaunt, there is no better way to see Hamilton than from a horse-drawn surrey with a fringe on top.

A subtropical paradise set in the warm Atlantic some 600 miles off America's east coast, Bermuda actually comprises a 21-mile curve of linked islands.

Blessed with a balmy climate, lush green countryside, a profusion of colourful flowering shrubs and beautiful beaches of fine coral-pink sand, Bermuda is a special place indeed. With a wide range of top-notch hotels, from US-style high-rise to quaint country cottages, and plenty to see and do, it is the perfect destination.

Discovered by Spanish mariner Juan de Bermudez in 1503, the islands were claimed in England's name in 1609 and they remain English speaking and loyal to Britain to this day. Their proximity to North America has given them a New World feel and made them a popular cruise ship destination, while the mild climate, clean, safe environment and excellent sports facilities continue to attract many repeat visitors.

Bermuda offers all types of holiday. History buffs will love St George's Town, the island's first capital, founded in 1612. A stroll through the narrow streets is a walk back in time – see the Town Hall, Old Rectory, St Peter's church, several museums and the Deliverance, a full-size replica of a 17th-century sailing ship.

At the other end of the islands you can visit Gibbs Hill Lighthouse, which affords wonderful, sweeping views over Great Sound and the whole archipelago. Then in Sandys parish you cross the charming Somerset Bridge, the world's smallest drawbridge.

Be sure not to miss Scaur Hill Fort Park with its 19th century fortress and the old Royal Navy Dockyard, beautifully restored and now one of Bermuda's main attractions, with its Maritime Museum, Arts Centre, Craft Market and Pottery.

In today's capital, Hamilton, you find high-class shops and stores facing the cruise ships which tie up right alongside Front Street, and a number of quaint and interesting buildings including Sessions House and the famous Perot Post Office.

Other attractions include the Bermuda Aquarium, Crystal Cave, Botanical Gardens, and the dozens of beaches, bays and coves which dot the coastline. Watersports enthusiasts will be in their element. Plus, there is tennis, fishing and riding, while golfers will have a tough time choosing which of the eight top-rated championship courses they should tackle first.

Cambridge Beaches

30 Kings Point
Sandys MA 02
Bermuda

✈ Bermuda Int. 35km

tel +441 234 0331
fax +441 234 3352

cambridge@specialhotels.com
www.specialhotels.com
www.cambridgebeaches.com

Tour operators:
UK Elegant Resorts
Caribbean Connection

52

This elegant cottage colony, situated at the western end of Bermuda on a stunning 25-acre peninsula and surrounded by five private, soft pink, sandy beaches, is the perfect romantic getaway.

Individually decorated rooms and suites offer privacy and comfort and include balcony or terrace. Many have spectacular ocean views.

Award-winning gourmet cuisine can be enjoyed in a variety of settings, both indoor and outdoor. Afternoon tea is served daily at four o'clock in the Clubhouse. For a truly magical evening, guests can dine *al fresco* beneath the stars on the beautiful Mangrove Bay Terrace.

The resort offers a wealth of activities and all watersports imagineable. Guests can choose to take a private shuttle to Hamilton, Bermuda's charming capital, for a day's shopping, or simply escape to one of the many beaches and coves which provide romantic, secluded locations for swimming, sunbathing and snorkelling. Don't miss the European Health Spa.

This is also an absolutely ideal setting for both weddings and receptions for up to 50 guests. These can be arranged by the hotel and take place on the grass terraces or in the lounge overlooking picturesque Mangrove Bay.

 US$255-560 (62)

 US$385-650 (17)

🍽 included

🍷 included

🍾 🥂 ▣

Honeymoon specials

Heart and Soul Honeymoon package includes six nights deluxe accommodation, all taxes and gratuities, breakfast, afternoon tea and dinner, fruit basket and champagne on arrival, airport transfers, sunset sailing trip, personalised photo, massages, plus use of all facilities. Prices cost from US$3,310-4,660 per couple. Wedding packages are also available ranging from US$4,400-5,660.

Sightseeing and leisure

Ferry excursions to Hamilton. Visits to historic dockyard, maritime museum, arts and crafts centre and galleries. Private beaches, pool, croquet, tennis, marina, reef snorkelling. Moped and bicycle hire is also available. European solarium and spa with a range of treatments, sauna, steamroom. Access to nearby golf courses, deep-sea fishing and Scuba diving.

Horizons & Cottages

South Shore
Paget, PGBX
Bermuda

✈ Bermuda Int. 15km

tel +441 236 0048
fax +441 236 1876

horizons@specialhotels.com
www.specialhotels.com
www.bermudasbest.com

Member of:
Relais & Chateaux

As its name suggests, Horizons & Cottages is famed for its views, sitting on a hilltop with panoramic vistas of the countryside and ocean beyond. One of the oldest plantation estates in Bermuda, the hotel was originally owned by the Middleton family, made famous by Captain Lewis Middleton who saved the Turks islands from the French and Spaniards back in 1710.

The Horizons' house itself is typical Bermudian architecture with whitewashed keystone corners, knee-high cedar fireplaces and tray ceilings. Outside guests can enjoy 25 acres of rolling lawns and beautiful, stylish gardens. Horizons has its own

nine-hole golf course, three tennis courts and a swimming pool.

All the rooms and cottages are air conditioned and some bathrooms are equipped with private Jacuzzi. And of course all the rooms have their own individual stunning views.

With the emphasis on personal service, guests can dine on the terrace during the summer months enjoying uninterrupted sea views and step inside to the warmth of open log fires in the stonewashed dining room in the winter. And those staying in one of the cottages even get their cooked breakfast prepared fresh right in their own kitchen.

🛏 US$310-720 (40)

🛋 US$540 (3)

🍽 from US$55

☕ US$25

Honeymoon specials
Breakfast and dinner, complimentary champagne, tax, service, use of all sports facilities. The package costs from US$2,100-5,000 per couple.

Leisure facilities
Tennis, Mashie golf course, putting, pool and full leisure facilities two minute walk away at Coral Beach Club. Other golf courses include Mid Ocean and Port Royal.

Sightseeing
The beautiful pink sands of the South Shore beaches, St George's, Gibbs Hill Lighthouse, Dockyard, Aquarium and Hamilton, the capital of Bermuda is close by.

Pink Beach Club

116 South Road
Tuckers Town
Bermuda

✈ Bermuda Int. 7km

tel +441 293 1666
fax +441 293 8935
For reservations contact:
UK 0800 964 470
US +800 355 6161

pink@specialhotels.com
www.specialhotels.com
info@pinkbeach.com
www.pinkbeach.com

54

Closed: 14 Dec '98-1 Mar '99

Tour operators:
UK Prestige Holidays

Poised among acres of rolling hills and lush gardens, overlooking two magnificent, pink coral beaches, is the deluxe cottage colony known as the Pink Beach Club. Soft pink-painted cottages dotted throughout the grounds house large suites, also decorated beautifully in light pastel shades, with wooden furniture and teeming with local species of plants. Each room has two double beds, some king-size, and views of the ocean. Breakfast is served in the main Clubhouse, or brought to your suite or private balcony by a personal maid.

Dinner is served by candlelight in the ocean-front restaurant, or under the stars poolside, where a range of dishes are prepared by top European chefs.

Guests can discover the sights of Bermuda by moped, scooter, taxi or horse-drawn carriage; try Scuba diving and experience the wonders of marine life; or simply sip cocktails by the pool.

For a nice, relaxed evening in the bar or on the pool terrace, a pianist, jazz musicians and steel drum bands provide a range of live music from Calypso to Swing.

For those wishing to marry here, couples can exchange their vows, in true Bermudian tradition, under the 'moongate' – a coral ring said by locals to bring happiness and good fortune.

 US$425-495* (91)

 included

 included

Honeymoon specials
Wine, cheese and fruit in room on arrival. Also, one day's complimentary snorkel gear and moped rental.

* Prices subject to 17.25% gratuity and government tax.

Sightseeing and leisure
Moped rental, tennis and gym on site. In-room massage by appointment. All watersports, reef and deep-sea fishing, parasailing, sailing and golf nearby. Only 15 minutes from the historic centre of Hamilton, and five minutes from Crystal caves, nature reserve and aquarium.

Waterloo House

Pitts Bay Road
33 Hamilton
Bermuda

✈ Bermuda Int. 15km

tel: +441 295 4480
fax: +441 295 2585

waterloo@specialhotels.com
www.specialhotels.com
www.bermudasbest.com

Member of:
Relais & Chateaux

55

Colonial elegance is the hallmark of this historic hotel which sits in four acres of terraced gardens right on Hamilton Harbour.

One of only two Relais & Chateaux properties in Bermuda, the hotel dates back to 1815 when it was built as a sumptuous manor house. Today it retains the elegance of days gone by and is filled with fine antiques and elaborate soft furnishings while providing the very latest in 1990s amenities to ensure every visit is truly luxurious.

Known around the world for its fine cuisine, the hotel offers the choice between the relaxing waterside Poinciana Terrace, where diners can enjoy stunning views of the bustling harbour, or the more formal, but magnificent, Wellington Room.

As a waterfront hotel, the choice of sports is excellent, varying from charter deep-sea fishing boats to windsurfing or swimming in the hotel's freshwater pool.

But for romantic beach picnics, take advantage of the hotel's private launch which will ferry you to uninhabited and unspoilt islands that surround Bermuda, or spend the evening aboard for a cocktail cruise with beautiful sunset views.

🛏 US$260-400 (22)

🛋 US$450-650 (8)

🍽 US$50-65

☕ US$10-18

Honeymoon specials
A six-night stay in either a garden view room, harbour or suite, including membership to Coral Beach Club for sports, plus gift for the bride and photograph, costs between US$2,110-2,890 per person. The price includes all taxes, gratuities and hotel transfers.

Leisure facilities
Coral Beach Club. One day's picnic on board hotel launch, with breakfast and tea, US$562.80 per person.

Sightseeing
Hamilton is two minute's walk away. Other sites include Napoleonic forts, Dockyard, St George's, Gibbs Hill Lighthouse, South Shore beaches.

Grenada

56

flying time
Direct to Port
Salines or via St
Lucia, Trinidad or the
Bahamas
London: 8-9 hrs
Miami: 3-4 hrs
NY: 4-5 hrs

**climate/
when to go**
Warm, constant
temperatures all year.
Travel in Aug for
Carnival and the
island's most lively
sailing regatta.

currency
Eastern Caribbean
dollar, fixed to the
US dollar.

language
English.

getting around
Local buses, taxis,
ferries and island-
hopping planes all
offer services. Hiring
a car is a good way
to see the island if
you are prepared to
brave the somewhat
erratic roads.

Grenada, in the far south of the Windward Islands, is typical of this chain of islands in its tropical beauty.

It has excellent beaches and the capital, St George's, is the prettiest harbour town in the whole Caribbean. Set in a massive volcanic bowl, its slopes lined with red-tiled roofs that descend to the edge of the way, where yachts and old-fashioned schooners have long lined the waterfront. In the valleys of the interior there are large fruit and spice plantations.

Grenada sees a steady stream of tourists to its broad range of hotels. The nightlife is generally pretty quiet, but most hotels and restaurants have bars and there are clubs that attract a young crowd. The island is also well positioned for exploring the Grenadines, by yacht, ferry and island-hopping plane.

Secret Harbour Resort

Lance aux Epines
St George's
Grenada

✈ Point Salines 10km

tel +473 444 4439
fax +473 444 4819

secret@specialhotels.com
secret@caribsurf.com
www.secretharbour.com

Tour operators:
UK Hayes & Jarvis
US Go Go Tours

The hideaway resort of Secret Harbour is tucked into a tropical hillside overlooking Mount Hartman Bay on the island of Grenada. This is an island of outstanding natural beauty with stunning mountain vistas, cascading waterfalls that invite bathers, palm-fringed beaches and picturesque harbours.

The rooms retain the Mediterranean influence of the early explorers and feature four-poster beds, sunken sitting rooms, vaulted brick ceilings, and sumptuous   bathrooms with Italian-tiled tubs. French windows lead out onto private balconies with views encompassing the ocean, dotted with sailing boats, and the busy little harbour.

Guests can dine *al fresco* at the restaurant, with Moorish arches framing the ocean views, or relax casually at the poolside terrace restaurant.

There are a wealth of activities on offer from windsurfing along the shores of the private beach to the new PADI five-star dive operation on site. The resort also offers excursions to local islands on skippered or self-skippered yachts, and can arrange 'Sail and Stay' packages combining four days on a yacht with three days at the resort.

Wedding ceremonies are also staged under a rustically-tiled archway with a canopy of local flowers, or at one of the village churches.

57

US$130-250 (20)

 from US$17

 from US$15

Honeymoon specials
Flowers and champagne in room on arrival. Room upgrade subject to availability.

Sightseeing and leisure
Waterfalls, mountains and beaches. Annual carnival and sailing festivals. Trips to daily farmer's market. Tennis and watersports including sailing, kayaking and windsurfing. Fitness centre and beauty salon, plus 9-hole golf course nearby. Also, private beach and swimming area. 'Sail and Stay' packages can also be arranged.

Guadeloupe

flying time
London: 9 hrs
NY: 3 hrs

**climate/
when to go**
Tropical tempered by
trade winds; very
similar year-round.
It can get busy in
summer months.

currency
French franc, though
US dollars are usually
accepted.

language
French but English is
widely spoken.

getting around
A variety of links via
sea plane and ferries.
Local bus services
are good.

Legend has it that when Christopher Columbus first glimpsed Guadeloupe, he placed the island in a casket to be presented to the king and queen of Spain.

The island's romantic history continued when it was used as a base for 16th-century pirates to store their cargoes of rum and sea-booty. Since that time, this jewel of the French Caribbean has developed into a thoroughly modern, chic and, above all, thoroughly French tropical playground. Sun, sea, surf and of course champagne combine deliciously in these extravagant fantasy islands to produce an exciting and unique mix of cultures and nationalities.

The Gallic influence is overt: shops are filled with Lacroix and Givenchy, *boules* is played in dusty town squares, and bakeries provide a daily supply of *baguettes* and *croissants*. And under-pinning all this is a Caribbean sensibility. Leisure and pleasure are assiduously pursued: sunbathing, snorkelling and windsurfing throughout the day, dining and dancing all night.

Guadeloupe also abounds in natural beauty. Lush vegetation strikingly frames the waterfalls and rivers, rich with crayfish. Norfolk pines and great ferns surround the sleepy towns where fresh sea breezes gently rock the sun-blistered boats moored by the wharf. Numerous little restaurants serve up fantastic local produce — breadfruit, plaintains, congo peas and salted pork — to create the rich and wonderful Creole cuisine for which the region is justly famous.

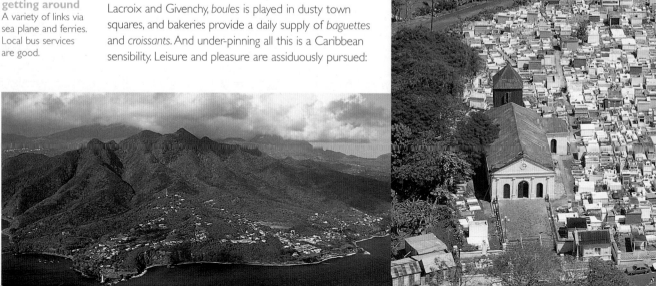

La Cocoteraie

Avenue de L'Europe
97118 St Francois
Guadeloupe

✈ Pôle Caraïbes 30km

tel +590 887 981
fax +590 887 833

cocoteraie@specialhotels.com
www.specialhotels.com
cocoteraie@wanadoo.fr
www.antilles-info-tourisme.com/
guadeloupe/coco.htm

Nestled between one of the most beautiful lagoons on Guadeloupe and the impressive golf course designed by Robert Trent Jones, La Cocoteraie combines the charm of a colonial habitation with the luxury of a first-class hotel.

Each of the 52 personalised suites is exquisitely decorated in typical Creole style. The bathrooms are spacious with hexagonal-shaped, raised baths providing magnificent views of the sun setting over the lagoon. Each has a colourful and comfortable living room and flowered terraces overlooking the swimming pool and sea beyond.

At La Varangue restaurant chefs prepare refined and imaginative local specialities based on local produce, such as fish and shellfish freshly landed at the port of Saint François.

Guests can sail away in a catamaran, play a round of golf on one of the neighbouring islands or just relax in the magnificent swimming pool decorated with Chinese vases while enjoying a few traditional rum-based cocktails at the Indigo Bar.

The hotel is happy to organise anything from a Corsair party with a steel band or a full-blown carnival party to the rhythm of a *zouk* band, which comes complete with limbo dancers.

A one-day sailing excursion, discovering the small neighbouring island of Petite Terre, will add the finishing touch to a truly unforgettable honeymoon.

59

FF1,500–3,400 (52)

à la carte

FF95

Honeymoon specials
Welcome gift, champagne and flowers in room on arrival.

Sightseeing and leisure
Championship golf course designed by Robert Trent Jones, parachuting, windsurfing, swimming and tennis. The hotel has its own private beach.

Jamaica

60

Jamaica is one of the liveliest islands, its allure the strongest of all the former British territories.

Physically the island is spectacular. Greenery bursts into life everywhere. You might almost expect a pencil to take root. And the scenery is fantastic; within a few hundred yards of the sea you can be at an altitude of 1,000 feet with stunning mountains all around you.

For the visitor, Jamaica has the most romantic allure of all the Caribbean islands. Neglected stone gateposts and decaying walls of abandoned plantation houses witness times when the island was the focus of British dreams, and source of fortunes for the planters. Noel Coward, Winston Churchill, Ian Fleming and Errol Flynn all fell in love with the place.

There is something for everyone here: humming resorts that specialise in sun, sea, sand and golf, elegant hotels and huge plantation hideaways that preserve a glorious air of old Jamaica.

The tourist areas are on the north coast, between Negril and Ocho Rios. This is where the beaches and main facilities are, and the liveliest crowds. Be sure to climb Dunns River Falls while here. In the west, Negril has all the trappings of a resort, but without the frantic atmosphere. Ocho Rios is more developed, with some outstanding hotels. Close by, there are exotic botanical gardens, and a genuine Jamaican countryside of steep valleys watered by numerous rivers and falls.

Montego Bay, the tourist capital, is large and busy, with beaches and watersports, and a lively nightlife. The most famous great houses are here; and historic Falmouth, which is site of some of the finest Georgian architecture on the island.

Port Antonio is a charming, dozy town in the far east, the loveliest and most strikingly fertile part of the island. From here you can venture up into the Blue Mountains, a region of spectacular natural beauty.

The capital of Kingston is well worth a visit. Check out the wonderful mayhem of the markets downtown, where limers loiter, chatting, amidst the constant calls of 'Bag-juice!' and the pulse of Bob Marley's ever-present reggae sounds. This is definitely the Jamaicans' Jamaica – energetic, lively, noisy and sometimes tricky.

Grand Lido Negril

PO Box 88
Negril
Jamaica

✈ Montego Bay 88km

tel +876 957 5010
fax +876 957 5517

lido@specialhotels.com
www.specialhotels.com

Tour operators:
UK SuperClubs,
British Airways Holidays
US International Lifestyles,
Apple Vacations

This luxury super-inclusive resort hotel is tucked into a protected cove at Negril, along Jamaica's popular west coast.

Stunning marble and glass architecture and cool, elegant interiors blend beautifully into the natural contours of the landscape. Luxurious suites have king-size beds, large private bathrooms and room service provided round the clock.

There are a number of award-winning restaurants, all serving an array of dishes from around the world, including traditional Jamaican fare such as the famous jerk chicken.

Secluded hammocks and Jacuzzis are scattered throughout acres of tropical gardens where you can while away lazy afternoons in peace and total privacy. For the more active, sports facilities are unusually comprehensive.

Evenings can be spent enjoying live entertainment featuring Jamaican artists, or perhaps dancing the night away in the disco, and ending with a romantic stroll along the moonlit beach, feeling the warmth of the Caribbean beneath your toes.

Wedding ceremonies are free to guests and can be arranged in a romantic gazebo by the water or aboard the yacht where Prince Rainier and Princess Grace spent their honeymoon.

 US$260–360 (210)
 US$380–440 (24)
🍽 included
☕ included

Honeymoon specials
Rose for the bride and champagne in room on arrival. Dinner in Piacere on wedding night. Manicure and pedicure for the bride. Weddings, including marriage officer, licence, cake, champagne, flowers and decorated location in hotel's grounds or aboard the M/Y Zein yacht.

Sightseeing and leisure
Glass-bottom boat rides, waterskiing, diving, tennis, golf, volleyball, fully equipped fitness centre, cycling and croquet are some of the activities available at no extra cost. Trips to Dunn's River Falls, shopping excursions, river rafting, plantation tours, horseriding and other excursions can also be arranged.

Hotel Mocking Bird Hill

PO Box 254
Port Antonio
Jamaica

✈ Kingston 112km

tel +876 993 7267
fax +876 993 7133

Contacts:
Island Inns +860 364 1100
Euro-Marketing-Connections
+49 211 940273/4

mocking@specialhotels.com
www.specialhotels.com
mockbrd@cwjamaica.com
www.hotelmockingbirdhill.com

The unspoilt region of Port Antonio, with its lush valleys, sleepy fishing villages and quiet coves, provides the perfect backdrop for an intimate getaway. Hotel Mocking Bird Hill, overlooking the coast and Blue Mountains, is ideal for those wishing to enjoy peace and tranquillity off the beaten track.

Large and airy rooms with cool white tiles, handcrafted bamboo furniture and original artwork offer splendid ocean views from their balconies and provide a restful, fresh atmosphere. Tropical plants, attractive floral fabrics and hammocks add a touch of Caribbean comfort.

The Mille Fleurs restaurant is as romantic as they come with terrace dining overlooking the harbour of Port Antonio with its spectacular sunsets. Fresh produce and homemade pasta, ice creams and breads, and an inspirational chef produce some of the best food in Jamaica.

The hotel has its own art gallery with works of local artists and by the co-owner Barbara Walker.

Enjoy lounging on the beach – Frenchman's Cove is just minutes away. Also, a gentle rafting trip down the Rio Grande River is the ideal way to enjoy romantic seclusion after an intimate wedding. In this privately owned resort, the managers take care of all your wedding arrangements personally.

63

 US$150-230* (10)

 US$36

US$12.50

Honeymoon specials
Five nights' accommodation, welcome cocktail, fruit basket, bottle of sparkling wine, breakfast each morning, one afternoon tea, two picnic lunches, one massage each, three dinners, transport from Port Antonio, surprise gift. Cost: from US$1,330-1,550 per couple depending on season. Wedding packages also available. * Prices are inclusive of all taxes.

Sightseeing and leisure
Snorkelling, Scuba, fishing and yacht charter available. Free shuttle to the beach. Also, horseriding, bicycle tours, golf, tennis and hiking. Massages and beauty treatments. Nearby is Frenchman's Cove, rain forests and highland valleys, home to the largest specie of butterfly in the Northern hemisphere. Tours available with trail guides. Bustling local markets.

St Barts

flying time
London: 13-14 hrs
via Antigua
Miami: 3½ hrs
NY: 4½ hrs

**climate/
when to go**
There is hardly any
rain here but July and
Aug still have the
best weather.
Temperatures range
from 20°-25°C.
There is a great
music festival in Jan.

currency
French franc,
although US dollars
are usually accepted.

language
French but Engligh is
widely spoken.

getting around
Linked to other
islands by a variety
of plane and sea
services.

The exclusive and very French St Barts provides an idyllic environment for transient millionaires and glamour-seekers, with glorious sandy beaches and luxury Riviera-style hotels.

At only 10 square miles, St Barts (St Barthelemy) is little more than a pebble in the midst of French Antilles. For all its Lilliputian proportions it manages to cram a lot in and attests to the maxim that less is more. Steep-sided mountains laden with cactus and fragrant frangipani, a coastline full of rugged cliffs and exceptional beaches and kaleidoscopic panoramas combine to create a feeling of endless variation.

The island's capital and only town, Gustavia, is graced with a harbour as calm as a pool but is also lively and welcoming with a good but stylish mix of restaurants and nightlife. With a population of mainly French and Swedish origins, St Barts has less of the hot pepper sauce and steel bands about it, but the welcome and vibrancy is entirely Caribbean.

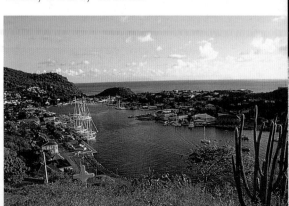

Le Toiny

Saint Barthélémy

✈ Saint Jean 6km

tel +590 278 888
fax +590 278 930

toiny@specialhotels.com
www.specialhotels.com
www.letoiny.com

Closed 1 Sept-20 Oct

Tour operators:
UK Elegant Resorts,
Caribbean Connection

Member of:
Relais & Chateaux

Tucked into the hillside of St Barts, a tiny but charming outpost in the Caribbean, is the stylish hotel hideaway of Le Toiny.

The hotel's architecture is influenced by the old plantation houses of Guadeloupe and Martinique. There are 12 cottages here, each decorated in typically Caribbean pastel shades and featuring handmade terracotta and mahogany furnishings and four-poster beds. Each has a private swimming pool and terrace with teak *chaises longues* where guests can contemplate the romantic views of a lagoon fringed with coconut palms, and the vast blue sea beyond.

The renowned French chef Maximé Déschamps prepares a harmonious blend of traditional French and innovative Caribbean cuisine in the Le Gaiac restaurant. Meanwhile, nightlife here is centred around the many restaurants with their lively atmosphere and well-stocked wine cellars. After a gourmet meal, guests can enjoy a nightcap on the rambling terrace of the main pool with chirping tree frogs and songs of cicadas for entertainment.

Days can be spent trying out the many sporting activities or touring the small villages across from the island, where women, still dressed in traditional costume, braid handicrafts in straw and latanier.

65

FF3,250-5,340

à la carte

FF120

Honeymoon specials
Champagne welcome on arrival. Fresh flowers daily. Transfers to/from airport. Candlelit dinner at Le Gaiac, use of car during stay, sunset cruise, mementos. This package is based on a stay of four nights.

Sightseeing and leisure
Tours by jeep around the island. Shopping excursions to nearby Gustavia, sightseeing around the harbour, and yacht trips to neighbouring islands. Tennis, sailing, horseriding, Scuba diving, deep-sea fishing, windsurfing and snorkelling (the hotel provides flippers and diving masks).

St Kitts

flying time
London: 9 hrs
NY: 3 hrs
Miami: 4 hrs

when to go
Dec for Carnival
and for Christmas
celebrations.

currency
Eastern Caribbean
dollar, which is fixed
to US dollar.

language
English.

getting around
Flights to the other
islands depart about
six times a day, but
are often fully
booked. The local
inter-island 'bus' is
really the ferry. Taxis
are readily available,
but car hire provides
the most mobility.

The welcoming, laid-back classic old-Caribbean style of St Kitts will have you charmed as soon as you step off the plane.

There is a strong and vibrant West Indian culture here. The Indians called it 'Liamuiga', or fertile isle, but it was re-christened St Christopher (St Kitts for short) by Christopher Columbus in 1493.

Since then the island has been dubbed a fragment of Eden and you will find here, besides the amazing variety of flora and fauna, the finest collection of plantation house hotels in the Caribbean. Many are surrounded by sugar cane as they were 200 years ago, and they retain the grace and hospitality of the era, being quite small and run in the style of a private house, with guests meeting informally for drinks before dinner.

St Kitts has stunning beaches of black sand in the mountainous northern areas, but in the southern peninsula there are a number of good, long strips of golden-brown sand, usually deserted. The pace is restful here. Locals chat lazily under the shade of fig trees and visitors, after a few Caribbean beers, have the enviable choice of soaking up the Caribbean sun on the beaches or dozing away their afternoons in a hammock under the silky cotton trees.

Ottley's
Plantation Inn

PO Box 345
Basseterre
St Kitts

 St Kitts 10km

tel +869 465 7234
fax +869 465 4760

ottleys@specialhotels.com
www.specialhotels.com
ottleys@caribsurf.com
www.ottleys.com

Tour operators:
UK Caribtours, Kuoni

Lovingly transformed from the ruins of an old 18th-century sugar plantation, Ottley's Plantation Inn has risen from the depths of neglect to the heights of beauty. Family run, it snuggles in the foothills of Mount Liamuiga, a dormant volcano surrounded by acres of lush unspoilt rainforest, bright tropical gardens and rolling green lawns.

Accommodation is in the majestic Great House or one of the nearby stone cottages, in which Princess Margaret herself once stayed. The rooms are sensual and cool, decorated in colourful chintzes and tropical prints with polished wooden and wicker furniture. All have a balcony or private patio with spectacular ocean and mountain views.

The award-winning restaurant, The Royal Palm, is set into the old stone walls of the sugar mill house. and guests can discover the delightful New Island style cuisine, cooked and prepared with particular accomplishment and served in an *al fresco* setting.

You can laze around the spring-fed pool, sipping rum punches and enjoying the peaceful view of the surrounding tropical gardens, or venture out onto the cobbled trails of the property's own rainforest ravine – home to some of the island's green vervet monkeys. There are also daily shuttles to the beach and the historic city of Basseterre.

67

 US$220-450 (22)

 US$505-695 (5)

 US$60

 included

Honeymoon specials

For direct bookings, a package starting from US$2,125 for a seven-night stay is available. It includes airport transfers, champagne and flowers on arrival, all breakfasts, five dinners, Sunday brunch, deluxe island tour and your choice of a catamaran trip or rainforest hike.
Wedding packages are also available upon request.

Sightseeing and leisure

Visits to Independance Square, where slaves were once sold in the days of the working sugar plantation, Brimstone Hill and the capital, with its West Indian architecture. Batik demonstrations, carnival in December and music festival in June. Rainforest, volcano and historic tours and hikes. Spa services, swimming and watersports. Golf 20 mins away.

St Lucia

flying time
London: 8-9 hrs
Miami: 3-4 hrs
NY: 4-5 hrs

when to go
Feb for celebrating
Independence Day
and a real carnival
blast; May for the
jazz festival; Dec for
National Day.

currency
Eastern Caribbean
dollar, which is fixed
to US dollar.

language
English.

getting around
By local bus, taxi
or car. Ferries and
hopping planes
connect islands.
Yacht charters are
especially popular.

Swapped between the French and British no less than 14 times, St Lucia has a unique mix of Anglo-French culture.

One of the Caribbean's hottest destinations, it is a charmed isle – for her people, among the friendliest anywhere, the natural beauty of her hidden coves, her tropical abundance and her twin volcanic pyramids, or Pitons as they are officially known.

The majority of hotels are on the Leeward coast, facing the calm sea and the romantic orange glow of the sunset. Some of the charming smaller hotels offer seclusion in dramatic settings, tucked away in coves or in view of the Pitons.

The French heritage extends to the food, and West Indian ingredients take on a new life here in such Creole dishes as treacle and coconut chicken stew.

St Lucians delight in throwing a party and the island's nightlife is renowned for its liveliness, with every little town hosting its own weekly dance. The best-known party is the 'jump-up' on Friday nights in Castries, when clubs open their doors and let people – and speakers – spill into the street, both at full volume.

LeSPORT

Cariblue Beach
PO Box 437
Castries
St Lucia

✈ Hewanorra 90km

tel +758 450 8551
fax +758 450 0368

Contact:
+44 (0) 181 780 0800

sport@specialhotels.com
tropichol@aol.com
www.lesport.com.lc

Situated on the north-western tip of St Lucia, LeSPORT enjoys a crescent-shaped beach of soft sand on its doorstep. This all-inclusive resort is surrounded by lush tropical gardens of cascading bougainvillaea, sweet-scented *ylang-ylang* and gardenia. Here, the accent is on a harmonious body and mind, and while the senses soak up the natural beauty, every opportunity is afforded to shed the stresses and strains of the outside world.

The rooms are decorated in soothing pastel shades with white wicker furniture, four-poster beds and marbled bathrooms. Enjoy stunning sunsets from your private, sea-facing terrace.

The cuisine at LeSPORT is an experience that will tempt the gourmet, with international and regional dishes served at breakfast and lunch buffets. The *à la carte* dinner menu features local specialities such as grilled dorado with callaloo and crab risotto. Tao, the Pacific Rim seaside restaurant, will excite your tastebuds. Afterwards, enjoy limbo dancing and steel bands aplenty.

The romantic wedding gazebo is the ideal spot to exchange vows, and for a nominal fee, staff are happy to arrange everything from bouquets to champagne receptions, even a best man or maid of honour if required.

 US$225-300 (100)

 US$315-390 (2)

 included

 included

Honeymoon specials
Sparkling wine, fresh fruit basket, flower arrangement. Honeymoon massage by appointment.

Sightseeing
Craft market in the capital of Castries, working banana plantation tours, rain forest treks, botanical gardens, drive-in volcano and waterfalls. Jazz festival in early May.

Leisure facilities
Watersports, diving and snorkelling, tennis, golf, archery, fencing, cycling, gym with personal trainer, health and relaxation treatments (such as facials, salt loofah body buffs, aromatherapy, revitalising mineral bath, T'ai Chi, yoga, meditation, stress management and much more), fitness classes, plus board games.

Europe

IRELAND
Dublin

NORTH SEA

ENGLAND

ATLANTIC
OCEAN

London

Berlin

GERMANY

Paris

Prague

CZECH REPUBLIC

FRANCE   LIECHTENSTEIN   Vienna

Bern

SWITZERLAND   AUSTRIA

PORTUGAL   Madrid

ITALY

Rome

SPAIN

MEDITERRANEAN SEA

GR

MALTA

BLACK SEA

•Ankara

TURKEY

ns

CYPRUS •Nicosia

The crazy quilt of countries that comprises Europe fairly bursts with romantic honeymoon destinations to suit all tastes.

Here, dramatic landscapes have been softened by the patina of centuries. Only in Europe will your wanderings uncover such immense diversity. You will happen upon perfect hill towns amidst rolling vineyards, medieval abbeys cloaked in ivy, cosy 300-year-old thatched inns, the familiar sight of the ever-present London black taxi, white-washed structures overlooking bright blue waters and a Renaissance palace with gardens shimmering beneath the moon.

The rest is fine tuning. Looking for something hot, ancient and exotic? There's Turkey, Greece and all the Mediterranean Islands. Unspoiled green landscapes and a warm welcome? Try Ireland. Italy and France combine matured beauty, marvellous food, wine and art; while Austria and Switzerland offer alpine scenery and picture-postcard villages. Eastern Europe adds more than a hundred, long-forbidden surprises and delightful cities, while Scandinavia with its deep forests offers a retreat into nature.

Austria

flying time
To: Vienna/Salzburg
London: 2 hrs
NY: 9 hrs
Miami: 10 hrs

climate
There are four distinct seasons, with warm summers and cold winters with widespread snow.

when to go
Tourist areas are very busy July-Aug. Ski resorts operate Dec-April. From May-June, Sept-Oct it is quieter and good for touring.

currency
Austrian schilling. Credit cards, Eurocheques and traveller's cheques are widely accepted.

language
German. Many Austrians also speak some English, French or Italian.

getting around
By train, bus and tram. Scenic boat trips on lakes and the River Danube.

I f you are seeking a perfectly romantic setting for a winter honeymoon, Austria fits the bill.

The weeks leading up to Christmas see the streets come to life, bright with the lights of the Christkindl – Christmas markets that sell gifts and Christmas decorations, fresh local produce for the festive season, and warming cups of spicy *gluhwein*. And on New Year's Eve in Vienna, the grand Imperial Ball kicks off a season of lavish, glittering, full-dress balls that last throughout January and February.

On a snowy winter's day, you can escape the cold and join the locals over their coffee and cake in a Viennese coffeehouse such as the Cafe Sacher, which gave its name to the wickedly rich chocolate cake. Forget calorie-counting and fuel up on a hearty lunch of paprika-peppered *goulash*, and apple *strudel* with lashings of cream. Try the Austrian wines, too, which are as praiseworthy as many French or German varieties though lesser known.

Austrian ski resorts are renowned for their charm and *apres*-ski jollity. Most have as their centrepiece a pretty onion-domed church and a lattice of old-world streets lined with enticing shops and snug cafes. In the late afternoon, still in your ski gear, you can party to the music at a tea-dance and, after an ample dinner, try a sleigh ride or toboggan racing by moonlight. There are resorts to suit everyone, from fashionable

Kitzbühel, St Anton and Lech, to lively but less expensive Söll and Schladming.

In summer, the carpets of alpine flowers attract a more sedate kind of visitor. Others arrive for activity holidays. Hiking and climbing, hang-gliding, mountain-biking, horseriding, sailing, windsurfing and fishing are all popular, amid the spectacular mountain scenery of Austria's lakes and rivers.

While Vienna and Innsbruck are attractive, Salzburg is irresistible; a treasure trove of opulent, magnificently preserved Baroque buildings, splendidly situated between mountain peaks. It was in and around Salzburg that *The Sound of Music* was filmed and a half-day tour takes you round the locations where Julie Andrews and the children belted out the now familiar songs.

While some are humming 'Do Re Mi' or 'Eidelweiss', others are focused on 'The Magic Flute' or 'The Marriage of Figaro'. For Salzburg was, and still is, Mozart's city. You can visit the house where he was born in 1756, see the font in the cathedral where he was christened and hear his music in palaces, churches and concert halls. Several times a year the city revels in classical music festivals like the Mozart Week (January/February), the Easter Festival and the famous summer Opera Festival (July/August), which is always a sell-out. If you want to be part of it, book well in advance.

Arlberg Hospiz Hotel

Familie Werner A-6580
St Christoph, Tirol
Austria

✈ Innsbruck 100km
Zurich 210km

tel +43 54 46 26 11
fax +43 54 46 35 45

reservation@hospiz.co.at
www.specialhotels.com
www.hospiz.com

74   Member of:
Relais & Chateaux

The award-winning, family-run Hospiz, that dates back to 1386, offers a very warm welcome in a traditional Austrian ski resort. Situated in the village of St Cristoph, the smallest village on the Arlberg in western Austria, this skiing paradise benefits from its high altitude (1,800m) and enjoys snow from the end of November to the beginning of May.

Immediately opposite the hotel is access to the vast skiing area of St Cristoph, St Anton, Zurs, Lech and Stuben with 85 cable cars and lifts providing access to 260kms of groomed slopes and roughly 185kms of off-piste routes.

Aprés-ski, the fine food and excellent wines are waiting to tempt your palate in the early 19th century Hospiz farmhouse. Wines from five of the greatest French chateaux are available here. Soak up the sun on the terrace until it disappears and then retreat to the comfort of the crackling open fire to enjoy the local specialities such as roast wild duck with red cabbage. To relieve those post-ski aches and pains, rejuvenate yourself in the whirlpool and sauna or enjoy the sheer luxury of a massage.

🛏 ATS850-4,200

🛌 ATS850-5,600

🍽 from ATS450

☕ ATS225

Honeymoon specials
Glass of champagne on arrival, large in-room breakfast, special candlelit dinner.

Leisure facilities
Wellness centre which offers sauna, sunbed, spa, massage and indoor swimming pool.

Sightseeing
Situated on a mountain, there is some of the country's best skiing on the hotel's doorstep. Also, try snowboarding, horseriding, mountain biking, tobboganing, trekking, and horse-drawn sleigh rides. Close to the old city of Innsbruck and Lake Constanz.

Hotel Schloss Fuschl

A-5322 Hof bei Salzburg
Austria

✈ Salzburg 20km

tel +43 62 29 22 53/0
fax +43 62 29 22 53/1

fuschl@specialhotels.com
www.specialhotels.com
Reservation@schlossfuschl.at
www.schlossfuschl.com

Member of:
Leading Hotels of the World

Perched high above a lake of ice-blue waters, the Hotel Schloss Fuschl was built in 1450 as a hunting lodge for the Archbishops of Salzburg. From here great expeditions into the sublime landscape of mountains and lakes would begin. Today its rich past has not disappeared. Its unique atmosphere, decor and charm have been magically transformed into a luxury hotel, located in Austria's most beautiful landscape.

The spell cast by the breathtaking views from the bedrooms and suites has lured the likes of Clark Gable, Prince Charles and Gabriela Sabatini through the castle's enchanted doors. The magic is equally present in the restaurant's delicately prepared fish caught each day from the lake below. A beauty spa, nine-hole golf course and a host of sports activities from mountain biking (in real mountains) to cross-country skiing allows guests to work up a hearty appetite.

The hotel's public rooms are no less sumptuous than its private ones. The magnificent lounge, with vaulted ceiling, massive fireplace, antique furnishings and exquisite tapestries, is especially fine.

Nearby is Salzburg, Mozart's birthplace. To this day the city – as well as this grand hotel – is alive with the spirit of his beautiful and enchanting music.

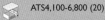 ATS2,100-6,800 (84)

 ATS4,100-6,800 (20)

🍽 Up to ATS 1,370 (3 courses)

☕ ATS195

Honeymoon specials
Packages are available upon request. Room upgrade on arrival subject to availability.

Leisure facilities
La Vie Beauty Farm using Shiseido products, holistic therapy, indoor swimming pool, sauna, Jacuzzi, tennis, 9-hole golf course. There is also a beach nearby.

Sightseeing
Salzburg is a charming city with many attractions on offer to the visitor. Among them are Mozart's birthplace, Festival Palace, Hellbrunn and Mirabell Castles, Bad Ischl and the Emperor's Villa, and boa trips on the Wolfgangsee.

Hotel Schloss
Mönchstein

Mönchsberg Park 26
A-5020 Salzburg
Austria

✈ Salzburg Int. 5km

tel +43 662 848 5550
fax +43 662 848 559

monchstein@specialhotels.com
www.specialhotels.com
salzburg@monchstein.at
www.monchstein.at

76

Member of:
Relais & Chateaux
Johansens

This enchanting castle hotel, above the rooftops of Salzburg in Mönchsberg Park, was originally built in 1358 to house the guests of archbishops and later became a popular venue for musical *soirées* by Haydn and Mozart. Hotel Schloss Mönchstein today has the reputation of being the 'Urban Sanctuary of the World' (Hideaway Report, USA).

Towers and turrets cloaked with ivy in summer and sparkling with snow in winter, renaissance-style furnishings and precious paintings adorn this splendid building. Most rooms are spacious and decorated in pastel shades with gilt-framed mirrors.

Authentic and international dishes are served in the award-winning Castle-Restaurant, Paris Lodron, which has outstanding views of the city below. Concerts take place every week in the Castle-Cafe, Maria Theresia, or on the garden terrace, Apollo.

A lift and a romantic 7-minute walk through the park links the hotel to the baroque buildings of the old town, and to concerts and entertainment.

The castle chapel, where brides and grooms have exchanged vows since 1531, still provides a perfect setting for a fairytale wedding. 'Salzburg's Wedding Wall', in front of the chapel, is covered in brass plates bearing the names of couples married inside. Receptions of up to 80 guests are catered for in the restaurant, cafe or castle grounds and staff can arrange cocktail parties and concerts.

 ATS2,900–6,500

 ATS5,400–30,000

🍽 ATS530–1,300

☕ included

Honeymoon specials

Wine and fruit on arrival. A sumptuous castle breakfast, candlelit gala dinner and palace concert. Room upgrade subject to availability. The package costs from ATS7,900 per couple and is based on a stay of two nights.

Sightseeing and leisure

The historic city of Salzburg, castles, lakes, mountains. Visits to Mozart's birthplace, Castle Mirabell and an underground glacier. Music festivals and events in the castle grounds and the city. Beauty treatments and massage by appointment. Tennis, golf and jogging. A full range of summer and winter sports nearby.

Thurnhers Alpenhof

A-6763 Zurs
Arlberg
Austria

tel +43 5583 2191
fax +43 5583 3330

✈ Innsbruck 150km

Open December-April

thurners@specialhotels.com
www.specialhotels.com

High in the Arlberg region of Austria, Zurs is one of the most exclusive ski resorts in Europe with slopes up to 2,800m above sea level. Centrally located in this serene white world is the rural architecture of the Alpenhof.

The hotel's owner is a collector of antiques and his love for things of beauty is reflected in both the public areas and in each of the 41 rooms. All have private bath or Jacuzzi and are beautifully furnished and bright.

When the day involves skiing, snowboarding or ice-skating, delicious, hearty cuisine is essential and the Alpenhof does not disappoint. Room rates include gourmet breakfast buffet, afternoon snacks, dinner of up to seven sumptuous courses and a fruit basket in your room.

Most guests spend their days on the slopes but even non-skiers can enjoy a trip to the Alpenhof. Fitness facilities are extensive and include a gym, indoor pool, sauna, steambath and solarium. Let the Alpenhof's in-house sport and activity trainer guide you down the road to better fitness while here.

In the evening, join the hotel in a romantic torch-lit hike, enjoy a gala cocktail event in the popular piano bar complete with open fire place or make new friends over a traditional fondue.

77

 ATS3,800-9,000 (24)

 ATS5,400-9,000 (17)

 included

 included

Honeymoon specials

Champagne, flowers, fruit basket in room on arrival. Plus free use of the wellness area which offers swimming pool, steambath, solarium and fitness facilities.

Sightseeing and leisure

Snow-covered landscape, beautiful mountain world of the Arlberg region, small Austrian villages, skiing paradise with 180km of prepared ski pistes. The hotel offers indoor pool, sauna, steambath, solarium, and even a cinema.

Czech Republic

flying time
To: Prague
London: 2½ hrs
NY: 9 hrs

climate
Warm, showery summers and cold snowy winters. July is the hottest month and Dec-Feb see temperatures below freezing.

when to go
Prague can be visited year-round but it can be crowded in summer. More rural areas are best visited in summer unless you want to take advantage of the ski areas in the Krkonose Mountains, which should be visited Dec-Feb.

currency
Czech crown.

language
Czech although German and English are widely spoken.

getting around
Prague is a walking city but trams and a good metro system offer respite to the weary traveller.

The Czech Republic welcomed few tourists until 1989 when its borders finally opened to the outside world. Today, some 17 million visitors a year appreciate the beauty and mystery of this unspoilt land which adjoins Austria, Germany, Poland and the Slovak Republic.

Most come to view the incredible architecture of the capital, Prague. Buildings from Gothic to Cubist dot the winding lanes and in the new town – Nove Mesto – a youthful vibrancy buzzes through the tiny cafes and individualistic shops. This is also Prague's entertainment and cultural hub home to excellent centres of music, theatre and art.

Outside of Prague the 79,000 square kilometres of the Republic is relatively undiscovered by tourism but should not be ignored. As well as many historical cities and castles, highlights include taking the waters in the Victorian spa town of Karlovy Vary or the picturesque train ride to the sleepy village of Krivoklat. In winter, ski the peaks of the Krkonose Mountains. And in summer months, cool off in the glacial lakes of the Sumava or the mysterious caves of Punkevni. But all year-round, don't miss the chance to sit back and watch the world go by with a glass of the world famous Czech beer.

Hotel Hoffmeister

Pod Bruskou 7
Klarov 11800, Prague 1
Czech Republic

✈ Prague 19km

tel +420 2 5731 0942
fax +420 2 5732 0906

hoffmeister@specialhotels.com
www.specialhotels.com
hotel@hoffmeister.cz
www.hoffmeister.cz

Tour operators:
UK & US Utell

Member of:
Relais & Chateaux
Johansens

Malà Strana is known as the 'romantic sector' of Prague and nestled in the midst of its 17th century buildings, at the foot of old castle steps lies Hotel Hoffmeister. A traditionally fronted building, the hotel is within easy reach of all of Prague's most important cultural sights and the main shopping areas.

The 38 rooms and four suites are ornately decorated in a variety of colour schemes and all offer high standards of comfort and refinement. Each has climate control, satellite TV and mini bar.

The hotel offers two opportunities for diners; its full service restaurant 'ADA' excels at both Czech and international cuisine and the Cafe Ria is perfect for light meals or dining *al fresco* during Prague's warm summer days. Finally, don't miss the chance to sample a fine bottle of Moravian wine from the extensive local and international cellar held by the hotels' Bar Lily.

The walls of the public areas are lined with the work of artist – and the father of the hotel's owner – Adolf Hoffmeister. His caricatures of cultural icons like Salvador Dali, John Steinbeck and Jean Cocteau adorn the walls and provide the perfect backdrop to your stay in Prague, which is renowned for its art, not to mention beauty, culture and history.

83

 US$165-223* (36)

 US$205-395* (5)

 US$50-100

 US$10

Honeymoon specials
A three-night stay in the honeymoon suite US$1,200*, which includes Sekt and flowers on arrival, breakfast room service, one candlelit gala dinner with live music in hotel restaurant (drinks excluded), plus private guided tour of Prague.

* Plus tax of 22%.

Sightseeing and leisure
Prague is the cultural centre of Czech Republic with many theatres, operas, concerts and galleries within easy reach of hotel. There is also a nine-hole golf course in Prague and an 18-hole layout 40km away. Excellent fitness and leisure centre nearby; arrangements in beauty facilities on request.

France

flying time
To: Paris
London: 1 hr
NY: 8 hrs
LA: 12-13 hrs

**climate/
when to go**
July-Aug are the
warmest months and
the liveliest time,
with plenty of special
events. Book well in
advance and at
Easter. June-Sept
offer more peace
and nicer weather.
The south is warmer
May-Oct, while the
north coast has
similar weather to
southern England.

currency
French franc.

language
French.

getting around
There are airports in
all the main areas.
The rail service is
one of the best in
Europe, and there
are a number of
good *autoroutes*.
From Britain, use the
Chunnel or any of
the innumerable
ferry crossings daily.

From the grandeur of Paris to the warm rustic pleasures of south-west France, from the windswept rocks of Brittany to the star-studded resorts of the Côte d'Azur, France is a country to set you dreaming.

The coastline is spectacular for much of its length, with some of the best sandy beaches in Europe. Inland, there are chateaux galore, many turned into luxurious hotels where you can sleep in a bedchamber made for a lord and his lady. Vineyards beautify many of the provinces. Champagne, Bordeaux and Burgundy, with their pretty hill-top villages, count among the most famous wine areas in the world.

While the western half of France undulates softly towards the Channel and the Atlantic, the eastern half is marked by magnificent mountains. In the foothills of the Vosges and Jura ranges you can go skiing and hiking in the mighty Alps which border Switzerland and Italy.

The Alps form the eastern boundary of that earthly paradise, Provence. The most famous slice of the Provencal coast is known by the dreamy title Côte d'Azur. Here there are watersports, wonderful restaurants and glitzy casinos aplenty to be found in the glamour-rich, *tres chic* resorts of St-Tropez, Cannes, Nice and Monte-Carlo.

Information & Reservations
UK 0870 606 1296
INT. +44 870 606 1296

Moyenne Corniche
Rue de Barri
06360 Eze-Village
Alpes Maritimes
France

✈ Nice 20 km

tel +33 492 10 66 66
fax +33 493 41 06 72

chevre@specialhotels.com
www.specialhotels.com
www.chevredor.com

Member of:
Relais & Chateaux

Located on a hillside in the striking and beautiful Côte d'Azur, the Chateau de la Chevre d'Or dramatically overlooks the Mediterranean. From its 1,200ft vantage point, and from every room, you can enjoy the unforgettable panoramic view.

With just 30 rooms and suites, the castle is like taking a step back to a romantic bygone age. Some are in the very head of the impressive signioral residence, some scattered among the village with its stone-walled houses. In all, the lush furnishings create an air of homely elegance.

There are three restaurants here. Dine on *haute cuisine* and vintage wine in the five-star La Chevre d'Or, traditional fare in the Le Grill de Chateau or try the newly opened L'Olivier. A gentle stroll brings you to the hotel's sister restaurant in the village.

Days can be spent exploring the tiny streets of Eze or perhaps Nice or Monte-Carlo.

For relaxation, try the hotel pool with its lovely vista – or take a trip down to the beach and the azure sea that dominates the view from the hotel. It's only a very short drive away.

85

 FF1,550-3,800 (22)

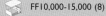 FF10,000-15,000 (8)

 FF280-580

 FF120

Honeymoon specials
A VIP welcome for newly-weds. Upgrade on availability.

Sightseeing and leisure
Monte-Carlo Golf Club is nearby. Because of its location on the Côte d'Azur a huge range of leisure activities are available (watersports, tennis, health and beauty spas) all of which can be arranged by the hotel. Sightseeing and other attractions are equally numerous including the nearby cities of Nice and Monte-Carlo.

Hotel Royal
Domaine du Royal Club

BP 8
74502 Evian Les Bains
France

✈ Geneva 45km

tel +33 450 26 85 00
fax +33 450 75 61 00

evian@specialhotels.com
www.specialhotels.com
www.evian.com/domaine/

Tour operators:
UK Elegant Resorts
US Spa Finders

86

This splendid Belle Epoque hotel with its stunning colonnades, domes, rotundas and frescoes, grandly overlooks Lake Geneva and is surrounded by 42 acres of magnificent parkland.

The Hotel Royal was built on a grand scale in 1907 in honour of Edward VII. Rooms are very spacious, light and airy and furnished with antiques and large brass beds. All have luxurious and large en suite marble bathrooms, private terraces and wonderful views over the lake or park. As one would expect, service is discreet and attentive.

In the resort's nine restaurants, you can choose from an array of dishes spanning five continents or more traditional fare inspired by local produce.

The famous spa town of Evian has always been conducive to rest and recuperation. In keeping with this tradition, the hotel's own world-renowned spa, the Better Living Institute,

 FF730-3,280 (123)

 FF 1,540-12,000 (31)

 FF110-480

 FF115

Honeymoon specials
VIP treatment for honeymooners includes flowers, fruit and complimentary champagne.

Wedding package: VIP welcome treatment of flowers, fruit and champagne in the room, suite accommodation for the wedding night (50 minimum guests), continental breakfast and champagne. More details available on request.

Evian

provides a huge range of revitalising treatments and special health programmes.

The geographic location of this grand hotel provides a wide range of leisure opportunities. You can play tennis, try archery, and golfers have free access to the Evian Masters' course with amazing panoramic views over the lake.

The Casino Royal Evian is a great venue for evenings where guests can try their luck on the tables, enjoy a meal in the restaurants or dance the night away in the Flash night club.

Wedding receptions of up to 250 guests are catered for in the chalet-style Hotel Ermitage, in the Chalet du Golf overlooking the course, or in the Royal Casino's splendid reception rooms, the Orée du Lac and the Coupole.

Leisure facilities

Free and unlimited access to the sport and leisure facilities of the Domaine, including 18-hole golf course (two consecutive nights minimum), tennis courts, 'Oxygen' track, archery, squash and climbing wall. The hotel also has its own fitness centre, indoor and outdoor swimming pools, sauna, Turkish Bath and Jacuzzi.

Sightseeing

Ladies professional golf tournament in June; Evian Music Festival in July. A good range of exhibitions, and museums are nearby. Trips across Lake Geneva. Visits to the historic and picturesque cities of Annecy, Lausanne and Geneva.

Information & Reservations
UK 0870 606 1296
INT. +44 870 606 1296

Château Eza

F-06360 Eze Village
Côte d'Azur
France

✈ Nice Int. 20 mins

tel +33 4 93 41 12 24
fax +33 4 93 41 16 64

eza@specialhotels.com
www.specialhotels.com
chateza@webstore.fr
www.slh.com/chatueza/

Tour operators:
UK Elegant Resorts

Member of:
Small Luxury Hotels

Clinging to the walls of the medieval village of Eze, more than 1,300 feet above the sparkling waters of the Mediterranean Sea, the Château Eza is an enchanting, romantic and secluded hotel.

In a part of the scenic and ultra-stylish Côte d'Azur that few know even exists, the hotel is a glorious castle of stone on a narrow cobbletsone street, too small even for modern cars.

To reach this castle hideaway which honeymooners will absolutely love, donkeys await at the bottom of the hill to carry guests up the walkways to a palace that is fit for royalty – indeed this château was once home to H.R.H. Prince William of Sweden.

The medieval feel extends to the 10 bedrooms, all reached along stone passageways and via ancient stone steps. Each room is totally individual but all have been newly decorated and include modern day luxuries while some have charming fireplaces, private balconies and breathtaking views.

Voted the second most romantic restaurant in the world, Château Eza offers indoor glass dining or outdoor terraces above the cliff with spectacular, sweeping views along the coast. The gourmet food on offer is created by Nice native Thierry Bagnis who searches the local markets to bring only the finest food to the table. Truly a delight.

 FF2,000-3,300 (7)
 FF3,300-3,800 (3)
 on request
 included

Honeymoon specials
Complimentary champagne, fruits and flowers on arrival. Information on other packages available upon request.

Sightseeing and leisure
Monte-Carlo Golf Club 5km away, another 30 courses within an hour's drive of the hotel. For sightseeing, Monaco, Monte-Carlo, Nice and Cannes are all within easy reach. Don't forget about the Cannes Film Festival in May. Also, extensive leisure facilities nearby.

Hotel du Palais

l'Avenue de l'Impératrice
64200 Biarritz
France

✈ Biarritz 3km

tel +33 5 5941 6400
fax +33 5 5941 6799

palais@specialhotels.com
www.specialhotels.com
manager@hotel-du-palais.com
www.hotel-du-palais.com

Member of:
Leading Hotels of the World

Biarritz, set in a dramatically beautiful landscape at the foot of the Pyrenees, has for centuries courted the rich and famous. The Hotel du Palais, formerly the summer residence of Napoleon III and Empress Eugenia, dominates the town and is a splendid example of Second Empire architecture, blending sumptuousness with both elegance and restraint. The hotel has been painstakingly restored to combine luxury with period charm.

The bedrooms are especially refined, being individually decorated in light shades, with flowing drapes and period antiques. Most are ocean facing with calming views of the sandy beaches.

Classic French cuisine and mouth-watering regional specialities are served in the hotel's two stunning restaurants: the palatial La Rotonde and the more intimate Villa Eugénie.

Visitors can explore the rolling hills and the small fishing villages surrounding Biarritz, with their pretty brightly painted houses and many bustling markets, which characterise the Basque region.

Sports facilities are unusually comprehensive. The town's busy casinos and inns also provide a stimulating variety of evening entertainment.

89

 FF1,200-2,850 (134)

 FF2,500-6,350 (22)

 from FF295-395

 from FF140

Honeymoon specials
Flowers, fruit basket and perfume on arrival. Double room with sea view, continental breakfast and dinner to be taken overlooking the ocean. The package costs from US$420 per couple per day.

Sightseeing and leisure
Romantic walks to Musée del al Mer. Trips to picturesque villages over the Spanish border and prehistoric caves. Tapas-style gala evenings in a Basque farmhouse. Music festivals year-round. Swimming pool, sauna, fitness club, all watersports, beach diving, tennis, riding. Golf on the 100-year-old Phare golf course.

Hotel Martinez

73 La Croisette
06406 Cannes
France

✈ Nice 25km

tel +33 92 98 73 00
fax +33 93 39 67 82

martinez@specialhotels.com
www.specialhotels.com
www.martinez@cannes-hotels.com

Tour operators:
UK Elegant Resorts
Cresta Holidays

90

Member of:
Concorde Hotels
Leading Hotels of the World

Home to the famous film festival, Cannes on the French Riviera is France's answer to Hollywood. Commanding grand views over the city and the bay on the famous Croisette Boulevard is the Hotel Martinez, an Art Deco Palace which has kept all of its '20s and '30s glamour and style with spiral staircases, piano bar and hotel staff in crisp white linen.

The glitz is carried through to the 400 or so spacious, sun-filled rooms and suites. Wooden walnut furniture, Art Deco carriage clocks and fireplaces, stylish lamps and bold print wallpapers and bedspreads make the Martinez a supremely elegant place to stay, continuing the tradition of Cannes as one of the playgrounds of the rich and famous from around the world.

The hotel's Palme d'Or restaurant has a deservedly high reputation, noted for its 1930s furniture including black lacquered armchairs covered in pearl-grey and maroon and using period silverware and glassware. The cuisine is international with regional provençal recipes such as bouillabaisse also on the menu.

For those who want to arrive in style, a pier with stylish pink parasols and sun-loungers stretches out into the azure waters of the Mediterranean. And for true glitz, a Los Angeles-style palm-fringed pool with a private beach, are available for not only sun-seekers among you, but star-gazers alike.

 FF1,250-4,800 (393)

 FF2,750-15,000 (24)

 from FF360

 FF145

Honeymoon specials
Package rates from FF1,100-2,600* per room per night depending on the season and including taxes and services except local taxes. Access to private beach, buffet breakfast. Rates available for limousine or helicopter transfers and menus at the gourmet restaurant La Palme d'Or. Minimum stay of two nights.
*Not valid during festival periods.

Sightseeing and leisure
Cannes Film Festival in May, Fireworks Festival in July and August. Trips to museums, Provencal markets, Grand Canyon du Verdon and Grasse (home to France's scent trade). Beauty salon, pool, extensive watersports.

Hotel Royal Monceau

37 Avenue Hoche
75008 Paris
France

✈ Orly 30km
Roissy 35km

tel +33 1 42 99 88 00
fax +33 1 42 99 89 90

Toll free:
UK 0800 868 588

monceau@specialhotels.com
www.specialhotels.com
royalresa@jetmultimedia.fr

91

A child of the 1920s, this lavish hotel is just a stone's throw from the Arc de Triomphe, yet has managed to maintain an unpretentious and tranquil atmosphere and is ideal for honeymooners.

The property is imbibed with the spirit of the Roaring Twenties with antique furniture, chandeliers, fabulous flowers and a timeless elegance. In fact, marble bathrooms and spacious rooms are the hallmark of the accommodation.

And it offers a choice of two fine restaurants.

Sample French gastronomy at its best in a garden of flowers or indulge in the delights of Italian cuisine surrounded by Venetian decor, named one of the best Italian restaurants in Paris.

Relax in the heated indoor swimming pool, enjoy a sauna, a steambath and a massage or take some exercise in the hotel's gym before exploring the wonders of Paris from the Eiffel Tower to the Louvre gallery and the sumptuous shops along the Champs Elysées and Faubourg St Honoré.

🛏 FF2,750-3,750 (189)

🛋 FF4,300-19,000 (40)

🍽 FF290-600

🍵 from FF155

🍷 Ⓢ

Honeymoon specials

'Heavenly Honeymoon Package' from 1/1-26/12/99 costs from FF3,100-4,300 depending on room type. It includes: room upgrade if available, American breakfast, flowers, fruit, chocolates and champagne on arrival, bottle of wine for any meal taken in hotel's restaurants, free use of spa, fitness centre, embroidered bathrobes, plus voucher for one night stay in a Kempinski Hotel on first wedding anniversary.

Sightseeing and leisure

Arc de Triomphe, Champs Elysées, Louvre, Grand Palais and Orsay museums. Shopping, theatre, opera.

Germany

flying time
To: Frankfurt
London: 1-2 hrs

**climate/
when to go**
The weather can be
unpredictable and it
can rain at any time.
May-Oct are the
best months. July
temperatures
average 18°C in the
lowlands and 20°C
for more sheltered
southern parts. Ski
fans will enjoy the
cold conditions
from Dec-Mar.

currency
Deutsche mark.
The Euro will be
accepted once bank
notes are printed.

language
German although
English is widely
spoken.

getting around
A good network of
internal flights, high
speed train links and
coach services. Good
taxi and bus services
in cities. Car hire is
best way to tour and
see the countryside.

92

Germany is a stunning mix of old world romance and modern day glitz with the wooded mountains of Bavaria dotted with fairytale castles contrasting nicely with the cosmopolitan buzz of the cities.

Hansel and Gretel houses wait to be discovered in picturesque countryside valleys where rolling hills are covered with vineyards and which give way to magnificent mountains, perfect for walking in summer months and skiing in winter.

Explore the myriad of old streets filled with ancient burgher houses and vaulted cloisters in the old towns and cities before bursting out into 1990s splendour as new architects transform the modern cities.

The post-war history of Berlin is as fascinating as that of centuries gone by while other cities like Hamburg and Bonn have developed into Europe's finest with every form of entertainment on offer from opera to pop concerts or ballet to street performance.

Indulge in the luxury of a spa treatment in one of Germany's famous spa towns. Pamper yourself like never before and then enjoy the glitz and glamour of these big name resorts.

The magic of Germany will never cease to amaze. Whatever you want you can find it here between the glistening waters of the North Sea and the Baltic to the north, and Switzerland and Austria to the south.

Kempinski Hotel Atlantic

An der Alster 72-79
20099 Hamburg
Germany

✈ Fuhlsbuttel 12km

tel +49 40 28 88 0
fax +49 40 24 71 29

kempinski@specialhotels.com
www.specialhotels.com

93

Opened in 1909 for ocean liner passengers, this grand hotel retains the charm and elegance of yesteryear while maintaining its well-earned reputation for exquisite hospitality.

Overlooking the picturesque Alster Lake, this hotel remains in the heart of the city's social life and hosts numerous grand balls throughout the year. But it is also the perfect choice for those looking for a romantic honeymoon hideaway. The service here is discreet and impeccable and staff have retained that special personal touch which has always set this hotel apart.

Turn-of-the-century styling means high ceilings and spacious rooms with either sweeping views of the lake or of the hotel's inner atrium courtyard. The seafaring theme is continued in the elegant and sumptuous suites, each named after celebrities with a special link to the Atlantic.

Right in the heart of the city, it is just a brief stroll to the stylish shopping district of Hamburg and just a short journey to most of the city's many cultural sights and attractions, including theatres and ballet.

Also, treat yourself to a visit to the city's botanical gardens and zoo while here. You may even be interested in the famous nightlife of St Pauli and the Reeperbahn which are within easy reach.

 DM375-525 (242)

 DM795-2,100 (12)

🍽 DM75

☕ DM34.50

Honeymoon specials

A number of wedding and honeymoon specials are available from DM599 which includes a lake-facing room or suite, wedding breakfast served in the room, a bottle of champagne, flowers and a surprise from the patisseries as a welcome gift.

Sightseeing and leisure

The hotel offers massage, solarium, golf course, tennis, jogging path and cycle rental. Locally there are many things to see and do around Hamburg, such as boat rides on the Aster, modern musicals as well as classical opera and ballet performances.

Greece

flying time
To: Athens
London: 3 hrs
NY: 10-11 hrs
LA: 13 hrs

climate/ when to go
The 'season' opens with the celebration of Greek Easter. Beautiful wildflowers in the spring are followed by long hot summers; and you can often swim until mid-Oct.

currency
Greek drachma. Traveller's cheques and cheque cards are useful, but for travel on the more remote islands, you will need drachma.

language
Greek but most everyone speaks some English.

getting around
Car hire is not too expensive, but take care on the winding mountain roads. And remember to get car insurance. Many islands have direct flights to Athens.

There is nothing like Greece and its stunning islands to make the rest of the world seem blurred, hesitant and grey.

In the translucent light, the Aegean is the bluest of seas, Greek houses are the most dazzling white, the harbours and their sunlit boats shimmer brilliantly and there is no scent so heady as Greek mountain herbs and pines on a beautiful summer's day.

The intensity of the Greek present makes a striking contrast with the haunting beauty of its ancient monuments, and nowhere more so than in Athens, where the Parthenon overlooks the exuberant capital. From Athens, it is easy to reach idyllic Delphi, sacred to Apollo, or see a play at the ancient and mysterious theatre of Epidauros. Also from Athens you can hire a boat and sail to literally hundreds of secluded islands which come in an astonishing variety.

Some are lush and forested, some rolling with rows of agricultural crops, others stark, rockbound, almost biblical, crags rising out of the Aegean.

Just over a hundred islands are inhabited, and all but a very few have excellent sugary-white beaches, lapped by the cleanest, warmest, most transparent seas to be found anywhere in Europe.

For sheer romance, it's the idyllic getaway destination.

Elounda Mare

72053 Elounda
Crete
Greece

✈ Heraklion 70km

tel +30 841 41102
fax +30 841 41307

elounda@specialhotels
www.specialhotels.com
www.relaischateaux.fr/elounda

Tour operators:
UK Elegant Resorts
Best of Greece

Member of:
Relais & Chateaux

96

The gorgeous island of Crete, legendary birthplace of ancient Greek myth, was once home to King Minos and his dark labyrinth. The Elounda Mare is a secluded little world that enjoys a privileged position overlooking the coastline of Mirabello Bay and the mountain range of Sitia.

The bungalows of Elounda Mare are the perfect place for newly-married couples seeking serenity and seclusion. Each one follows Cretan tradition, blending whitewashed walls with local beige and grey stone and marble. All rooms are furnished with locally crafted dark wood, Grecian folk art and tapestries in rich colours. Wide windows lead onto private terraces, each fitted with a swimming pool.

Beginning the day with breakfast from a rich buffet, guests can watch the fishing boats haul in the catch of the day. A few hours later this fresh fish is served at the Yacht Club. Crowning the small harbour and sandy beach, the Yacht Club also forms the venue for traditional Greek evenings with food, music and dance. The more intimate Old Mill restaurant offers a refined menu with a fine selection of Greek and French wines.

The hotel has a private chapel in the grounds and is happy to take care of any arrangements necessary for a perfect wedding.

🛏 Dr42,000-147,000

🛏 Dr57,000-280,000

🍽 US$35-100

☕ included

Honeymoon specials
Sparkling wine, fruit and flowers in room on arrival. Room upgrade subject to availability.

Leisure facilities
Sailing, Scuba diving, tennis, massage, aromatotherapy, sauna and steam bath available. A 9-hole, par-3 golf course and gym are nearby.

Sightseeing
Crete is packed with historic attractions including the archaeological remains at Knossos and Tahe Heraklion museum. As well as these, restaurants, markets and breathtaking scenery abound.

Kivotos Clubhotel

Ornos Bay
Mykonos 84600
Greece

✈ Mykonos 3km

tel +30 289 24094
fax +30 289 22844

From 15 Oct-30 April 2000 contact:
tel +30 172 46766
fax +30172 49203

kivotos@specialhotels.com
www.specialhotels.com

Member of:
Small Luxury Hotels

Kivotos Clubhotel is a luxurious resort overlooking the magnificent Bay of Ornos.

Though new, the Kivotos revels in old-fashioned traditions of service and hospitality, treating all its guests as VIPs. Champagne and a fruit basket await guests in their room on arrival, compliments of the house. The comfortable and spacious rooms benefit from sea views as well as a whole batch of modern amenities including video and colour television. Every guest will feel pampered and at home.

As well as barbecues around the pool, there are two dinner restaurants that offer a variety of top-quality cuisine: La Medusse, with its subtle mix of Greek and French dishes, and Mare, with a gourmet Italian seafood menu. Alternatively, a range of picnics can be made up to be taken on excursions to Delos and other golden sandy beaches on the island.

For a truly romantic experience, honeymooners may wish to avail themselves of the hotel's yacht, the Prince de Neufchatel. Available for a daily or weekly cruise, the yacht has spacious teak decks (ideal for sunbathing) and elegant suites with private bathrooms. On board, an experienced crew of three tends to passengers' every need, 24 hours a day.

97

🛏 DRS46,000-98,000 (30)

🛏 DRS90,000-196,000 (10)

🍽 DRS7,500-10,000 per person

🍷 included

🍾

Honeymoon specials
Flowers and complimentary champagne on arrival. Room upgrade when available.

Leisure facilities
Sauna, pool, squash, fitness centre, massage and Jacuzzi.

Sightseeing
Archaeological museum, Hora, the Little Venice, Castro, Panagia Paraportiana, Super Paradise, the island of Delos. The area surrounding Kivotos is full of ancient history and archaeological sites to explore.

St Nicolas Bay

PO Box 47
GR 72 100 AG Nikolaos
Crete
Greece

✈ Heraklion 69km

tel +30 841 25041
tax +30 841 24556

nicolas@specialhotels.com
www.specialhotels.com

Open April-October

98

Encircled by emerald green gardens, this five-star deluxe bungalow hotel is a haven of tranquillity between sea and sun, just two kilometres from the lively town of Aghios Nikolaos.

Nestling among olive, lemon and orange trees, each of the open-plan bungalows and suites are elegant and decorated to a very high standard. Junior and bungalow suites all have private pools, sun terraces and stunning sea views.

Many choices await you for dining. Labyrinthos and the Club House restaurants offer informal buffet breakfast and dinners; the beachfront Blue Bay offers *à la carte* lunch; and for those romantic evenings visit the poolside Minotaure or beachfront Kafenion for dining under the stars. Seafood is a speciality of both establishments. Pre or post-dining, relax in the air-conditioned comfort of the hotel's two cocktail bars or simply explore the spacious, cool public areas.

Just a short walk away from the swimming pool you come to the hotel's secluded sun drenched bay. Sunbeds and umbrellas are provided or if you prefer to keep active, diving, canoeing, waterskiing and windsurfing are available. A short walk also brings you to the town of Aghios Nikolaos with cafes, shops and nightlife to keep you entertained.

US$150-270 (57)

US$246-435 (46)

US$18-36

included

Honeymoon specials

Champagne, flowers and basket of fruit on arrival. Complimentary room service breakfast any time. Upgrade to superior room depending on availability. Honeymooners also have complimentary use of the steambath, sauna and Jacuzzi at the fitness centre.

Sightseeing and leisure

Local attractions include Byzantine churches and monasteries, the museum of Minoan Civilisation, Palace of Knossos and Phaistos. At the hotel's private beach there is a watersports centre, plus you can hire a cabin cruiser for private sea excursions. The hotel also boasts indoor and outdoor pools, fitness centre, gym, steambath, Jacuzzi and massage, among other facilities.

Information & Reservations
UK 0870 606 1296
INT. +44 870 606 1296

Santa Marina Hotel

Ornos Bay, GR-846 00
Mykonos
Greece

✈ Mykanos 4km

tel +30 289 23220
fax +30 289 23412

santa@specialhotels.com
www.specialhotels.com
www.santamarina.com
www.santa-marina.gr
info@santa-marina.gr

Tour operators:
UK Amathus, Gullivers
US Zeus, Homeric

Mykonos, a glittering jewel in the Aegean Sea, is home to Santa Marina, which sits on a hilltop overlooking Ornos Bay. A 20-acre complex of whiter than white dwellings, set in lush gardens dotted with pools and terraces, close to sandy beaches and clear waters, the resort is an ideal place to soak up the sun and relax.

Each of the 90 rooms and suites has its own atmosphere, none more so than the delightful Cycladic windmill which has been converted into a three-storey suite. All are furnished in contrasting yet complementary colours with soft furnishings and cooling stone floors. Fling the windows open or step out onto the private terrace to let in the sea breezes and enjoy breathtaking views.

For guests who want a little more than a warm dip in the Mediterranean, a variety of sports are on offer such as waterskiing, Scuba diving and tennis. For the even more active there is a health club and spa to really work up an appetite.

Two restaurants, one overlooking a charming cove, the other poolside, offer a fine variety of international cuisine. Being close to the sea, freshly-caught seafood is always on the menu.

99

 US$160-340 (60)

 US$215-640 (30)

US$30-60

US$10

Honeymoon specials

Complimentary fruit and wine on arrival. Room upgrade when available.

Leisure facilities

Aesthetic Institute, beauty treatments and massage. Gymnasium with swimming pool, sauna, Jacuzzi and steambath. Two tennis courts and private beach.

Sightseeing

Ancient island of Delos, religous centre for the ancient Greeks, which takes half an hour by boat. There are also shops, bars, restaurants and clubs nearby.

Italy

flying time
To: Florence, Milan, Rome
London: 2-3 hrs
NY: 9-10 hrs
LA: 13-14 hrs

climate
Pleasant but variable. It rains as much in Rome as in London in winter. Summer is hot and dry in the south; humid and hot in the northern lowlands; the Alps stay cool; the coast is refreshed by breezes.

when to go
Year-round, with festivals all summer and cultural events throughout the winter. For scenery, you can't beat spring and early autumn.

currency
Italian lire.

language
Italian though English is widely spoken.

getting around
There are numerous regional airports, and efficient train and bus networks throughout the country, even in small coastal regions.

The Italians have no false modesty. 'Ours is the most beautiful country in the world', they tell you. And who can argue?

From the snowy northern Alps to the lacy almond groves of Sicily in the south. From the long, liquid sapphire lakes of Como, Garda and Lugano to the sublime and glitzy Amalfi Coast, playground of Roman Emperors. Italy is sensuous, sumptuous and blessed.

Mountains fall sheer into the sea, lakes glimmer amid vineyards and castles, and each hill wars a cape of olive groves and a medieval town on top like a hat.

Nowhere else will you find such a concentration of art. The country is roughly the size of Britain but contains half of the greatest art in the entire world.

The Uffizi Gallery in Florence alone houses more work by Michelangelo than anywhere else in Italy, along with important works by Boticelli, among others.

Italy was the first country in Europe to recover after the Dark Ages, and the Italians used this headstart to build dream cities such as Venice, Siena, Naples and Rome. They softened the wild contours of the land with villas and beautifully structured, romantic gardens.

Best of all, the Italians learned to cultivate pleasure and delight to a unique degree. Thanks to all the wine cellars and rambling vineyards, well-preserved castles and farmhouses among fields of lavender, there are characterful hotels a plenty. Elegance and grace fill every detail here, from designer clothes to the tomato-rich sauces of a hearty Tuscan stew. Beauty is more than skin deep in Italy; it is a way of life.

Albergo Pietrasanta

Palazzo Barsanti Bonetti
Via Garibaldi 35
55045 Pietrasanta (Lucca)
Italy

✈ Pisa 25km
Florence 90km

tel +39 05 84 79 37 26
fax +39 05 84 79 37 28

albergo@specialhotels.com
www.specialhotels.com

102

Tour operators:
UK Elegant Resorts

Member of:
The Charming Hotels
Hospitality in Historical Houses

This small, exclusive hotel occupies Palazzo Barsanti Bonetti, a 17th-century building that is one of the most important in this very historical centre of Pietrasanta. Its secluded and private, atmosphere is home-like which makes staying here a unique and unforgettable experience.

All rooms are equipped with air conditioning, satellite television, minibar and are decorated with a magnificent array of original frescoes.

Pietrasanta is only a few miles away from the major sites of historical and artistic interests in Tuscany, providing the perfect destination for that sleek cultural break in the sunshine.

Take time to explore the area, visiting the many monuments and cathedrals before heading for the seaside to relax on the beach.

 ITL300,000-430,000 (8)

 ITL450,000-590,000 (10)

 ITL40,000-70,000

 included

Honeymoon specials

Welcome drink, Tuscany wine and local biscuits, roses in the room on arrival, breakfast in the room or in the conservatory until 2pm. Room upgrade subject to availability. Candlelit dinner. If stay is longer than seven nights, one night will be free of charge.

Sightseeing and leisure

Situated in northern Tuscany, you can take excursions to typical Tuscan villages nearby, boat trips to the romantic area of Cinqueterre, Pisa, Lucca. At the hotel, facilities include gym and bicycles. Nearby are a swimming pool, tennis, golf and watersports.

Grand Hotel Cocumella

Via Cocumella 7
80065 Sant Agnello
Italy

✈ Naples 50km

tel +39 081 878 2933
fax +39 081 878 3712

cocumella@specialhotels.com
www.specialhotels.com
hcocum@tin.it

Tour operator:
UK Elegant Resorts

Member of:
Small Luxury Hotels

Once a Jesuit monastery and still a haven of peace and tranquillity, the Grand Hotel Cocumella lies a 15-minute walk from Sorrento's busy main square.

The name of the hotel is said to come from its favourable position in beautiful gardens and for the fertility of its orange and lemon orchards. Another theory is that it was named after the vases that were used for collecting spring water produced here. The roman cistern used to provide water for many houses in the area but today has been converted into a conference room.

The antique cloister has been transformed into a stunning and atmospheric dining room while the annexed chapel is used for concerts which are held regularly throughout the summer.

The ambience of days gone by still pervades in the 60 bedrooms, all individually decorated with original furnishings, but also well equipped with

modern day amenities for the utmost comfort.

The hotel boasts two restaurants as well as a terrace overlooking the grand Bay of Naples and a swimming pool hidden in the beautiful gardens along with a tennis court. And to explore the famous Amalfi coastline, take a trip on the hotel's 30m sailboat, the Vera, which was built in 1880.

103

🛏 ITL450,000-570,000

🛎 ITL600,000-920,000

🍽 on request

☕ included

💍🍾

Honeymoon specials
Room upgrade depending on availability. Italian Spumante, fresh fruit and flowers on arrival.

Leisure facilities
Swimming pool, seaside solarium, tennis, private chapel for concerts, tennis.

Sightseeing
Naples, Pompei, Positano, Amalfi, Vesuvius, Cocumella's own tall ship 'Vera', built in 1880 and used for day cruises along the Amalfi Coast and to Capri.

Grand Hotel
Excelsior Vittoria

Piazza Tasso 34
80067 Sorrento
Italy

✈ Naples 60km

tel +39 08 18 07 10 44
fax +39 08 18 77 12 06

excelsior@specialhotels.com
www.specialhotels.com
www.exvitt.it

Tour operators:
UK Abercrombie & Kent

104

Member of:
Charming Hotels

The Excelsior Vittoria is a supremely elegant 19th-century building perched gloriously high above Sorrento on the dramatically beautiful Amalfi coast. The hotel was built in 1834 on the sight of a Roman villa and in the impeccable gardens and orange grove where archaeological treasures have been found, some of the original columns can still be seen.

Eighteenth-century frescoes, handsome vaults and mouldings and antique furnishings characterise the elegance and refinement of this beautifully maintained hotel, which has been owned by the Fiorentino family for more than 160 years.

Most rooms have antique iron beds, spacious marble bathrooms and splendid sweeping views over the Bay of Naples.

Guests can dine *al fresco* against the impressive backdrop of Mount Vesuvius or enjoy traditional Italian and Neopolitan dishes under the majestic painted ceilings of the Vittoria dining room. This grand banqueting room and the adjoining reception hold up to 350 guests and provide a splendid venue for a wedding party.

Visitors can sip cocktails on the terrace, enjoy a moment of meditation in the reading room, swim in the hotel pool or take a cruise along the coast.

ITL486,000-619,000 (95)

ITL789,000-2,000,000 (15)

ITL75,000

ITL15,000

Honeymoon specials
Flowers and Italian champagne on arrival.

Sightseeing and leisure
A private lift links the hotel to the lively port of Sorrento. The archaeological treasures of Naples, Pompeii and the natural beauty of the surrounding area and islands – Capri, Positano, Ravello, Amalfi, Ischia – are within easy reach.

Information & Reservations
UK 0870 606 1296
INT. +44 870 606 1296

San Marco 2159
30124 Venice
Italy

✈ Marco Polo 12km

tel +39 41 520 0477
fax +39 41 523 1533

europa@specialhotels.com
www.specialhotels.com
www.sheraton.com

Hotel Europa & Regina

Situated directly on the banks of the Grand Canal and just yards from St Marks Square this five star resort offers unrivalled location and luxury. As your gondola sails gently up to the door you realise you are in the heart of one of the world's most special cities.

Precious marble, elegant damasks and detailed stuccowork characterise the grand communal areas while each of the 185 rooms offers the height of sumptuous comfort. Lush furnishings, plump pillows and crystal chandeliers are present in all the rooms – while the deluxe suites look out over the Grand Canal, surely one of the most famous sights in the world.

No visitor to Italy wants to miss out on dining, and with the hotel's La Cusina restaurant on site you are treated to some of the finest meals in Venice – and one of the most amazing views. The dining terrace is located directly overlooking the gondolas plying their trade along the canals.

Venice truly is the city of lovers and with its prime location, Hotel Europa & Regina makes it easy to visit all the sights. On summer days when you need to just relax, take a trip to the hotel's private beach and sports facilities in the nearby Venice Lido – the perfect place to while away a sunny day.

 ITL700,000-1,023,000 (168)

 ITL1,749,000-2,700,000 (17)

 ITL180,000

ITL71,500

Honeymoon specials
Fruits and flowers in the room on arrival.

Sightseeing and leisure
The romantic city of Venice is minutes away and offers wonderful shopping trips, gondola trips, markets, buzzing cafes and restaurants plus famous art galleries. Leisure and beauty facilities are at Venice Lido, which is near to the hotel, and can be arranged for you.

Hotel Santa Caterina

SS Amalfitana 9
84011 Amalfi
Italy

✈ Naples 70km

tel +39 08 98 71 012
fax +39 08 98 71 351

caterina@specialhotels.com
www.specialhotels.com
s.caterina@starnet.it

106

This stunning hotel, looking like a huge wedding cake on top of a mountain, was built at the turn of the century to be a resort for the artistic, cultural and political figures of the day. Surrounded by marvellous gardens and terraces, with glorious views of the Amalfi coastline and its own private beach, the hotel is as stunning now as it was then and no one can help but feel important when they step into its gracious, marbled reception hall.

The rooms and suites are light and airy with large beds and their own seating areas. All suites have their own Jacuzzi, lounge and private gardens with ivy-clad trellises. There is even a beautiful and romantic honeymooners cottage in which to stay.

While guests enjoy the panoramic views, they can sample the first-class international cuisine, lovingly served in the elegant restaurant. In the evenings there is guitar and mandolin music or the tinkling of ivory in the Piano Bar to lend an additional atmosphere to the already compelling scene.

Nearby are some unforgettable destinations to visit, including Sorrento, Ravello, Positano, Capri and Pompeii, while Amalfi, a thriving, bustling, fun-packed coastal resort, is right on the hotel's doorstep.

 ITL390,000-590,000 (50)

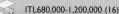 ITL680,000-1,200,000 (16)

 ITL95,000

 included

Honeymoon specials
Champagne and flowers in room on arrival.

Sightseeing and leisure
Two lifts connect the hotel with a swimming pool and private beach with platform to admire the sea's dazzling colours. Sunbeds, umbrellas and bar service available.

Hotel Villa Cipriani

Via Canova 298
31011 Asolo (Treviso)
Italy

✈ Venice 65km

tel +39 04 23 52 34 11
fax +39 04 23 95 20 95

cipriani@specialhotels.com
www.specialhotels.com
www.sheraton.com

Tour operators:
UK Elegant Resorts
Abercrombie & Kent

Depending when you arrive at the Hotel Villa Cipriana your first impressions will vary. The property prides itself on its incredible gardens and as the seasons change so do the sights and smells that regale your senses. Is spring with its beds of tulips most beautiful? Or does that prize go to summer when the gardens cascade with roses of every imaginable hue?

Flowers and fruit are also found in every room complementing the pastel colours that combine perfectly with beamed ceilings and terracotta tiled floors to create feelings of space and warmth.

The hotel restaurant is internationally renowned and frequented by guests and celebrities alike. The local Venato fare is famed and dishes are made with seasonal local vegetables including asparagus and Porcini mushrooms; and tenderloin from the pastures of nearby Montello. Before dining, indulge in an aperitif, perhaps one of the peach *Bellinis* that have for so long been a speciality of the house.

Hotel Villa Cipriani overlooks the old walled city of Asolo, famed for its artistic and archaeological history. However, just a short distance away are some beautiful and charming towns including Treviso, Bassano del Grappa and, of course, Venice, one of the most romantic cities in the world.

107

ITL328,000-704,000 (31)

ITL150,000-220,000

ITL32,000-59,000

Honeymoon specials
Italian Spumante and fruit basket on arrival.

Sightseeing and leisure
A local antique market is held every second weekend except during the months of July and August. Day trips to romantic places such as Marostica, Venice and Verona should not be missed. The hotel can assist in arrangements and with tickets to special events, such as operas in Verona.

Il Melograno

Masseria Torricella 345
70043 Monopoli (Bari)
Italy

✈ Bari 60km
Naples 290km

tel: +39 08 06 90 90 30
fax: +39 08 07 47 908

melograno@specialhotels.com
www.specialhotels.com
melograno@melograno.com
www.melograno.com

Member of:
Relais & Chateux

108

This elegantly restored and beautifully placed hotel is built on a 16th-century 'Masseria' – a fortified farmhouse – which was originally built as a defence against Saracen and Byzantine invaders.

The Il Melograno is now a charming five-star hotel, offering comfortable and luxurious surroundings. The bedrooms, 33 rooms and four suites, are nestled around a central piazza and each has an individuality combining old world style with modern comforts. They are spacious and beautifully decorated, furnished with antiques personally chosen by Camillo Guerra, the hotel's owner.

The two restaurants offer a variety of local dishes.

The Il Ristorante Melograno specialises in the Pugliese version of the delicious Mediterranean cuisine using home-grown produce and hand-made pasta. Meanwhile, the newly opened La Peschiera is a quiet and secluded restaurant built on the foundations of an old fishery located at the private beach six kilometres from the hotel.

Also on the hotel's doorstep are many remains of the old town. Visit the ancient Egnatia and Byzantine ruins as well as the charming cathedrals. The busy local market should not be missed, where visitors can enjoy traditional specialties, including espresso in an open-air cafe.

 ITL360,000-600,000 (33)

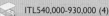 ITL540,000-930,000 (4)

🍴 ITL80,000

☕ ITL25,000

Honeymoon specials
Complimentary fruit and Spumante on arrival. Honeymooners receive one night free when staying 14 nights or more.

Leisure facilities
Two floodlit tennis courts, outdoor pool, indoor heated pool for use during the winter months. In summer, Il Melograno has a private beach club 7km away for guests.

Sightseeing
There is a weekly market on Tuesday where you'll find clothes, pottery, local crafts and all types of regional food. The opera festival in Martina Franca is held in July and August and is well worth a visit. Also, the ruins of ancient Egnazia, the Caves of Castellana and Trulli of Alberobello can be reached within half an hour by car.

La Posta Vecchia

Palo Laziale
00055 Ladispoli
Italy

✈ Rome 20km

Tel +39 06 99 49 501
Fax +39 06 99 49 507

vecchia@specialhotels.com
www.specialhotels.com
www.lapostavecchia.com

109

A wealth of history awaits guests to this magnificent villa just a few miles from Rome. Indulge in the fantasy of staying as the guest of an aristocratic family and slip into the relaxed atmosphere of this 17-bedroom hotel.

Surrounded by 125 acres of wildlife park and overlooking the azure Mediterranean, the villa is rumored to be on the site of the original home of Emperor Tiberus. True or not, no visit is complete without a look in the hotel basement where 2,000 years of history lies in wait. And unlike most hotels, La Posta Vecchia boasts its very own museum.

But above ground, too, this hotel is special with its stunning indoor pool complete with ocean views, lounge with deep, comfortable sofas and book-lined walls, and a general 'family house' atmosphere. Large bedrooms with beautifully stylish furnishings and luxurious wall hangings are also the norm.

Let a guide take you on private viewings of some of the world's most famous cultural sites, including the Sistine Chapel, or take a romantic champagne picnic to Ostia Antica. Alternatively, workout with the hotel's trainer or indulge in holistic and Shiatsu massages or simply relax by the ocean. The choices are yours.

ITL775,000-990,000 (9)

ITL1,550,000-2,380,000 (8)

from ITL140,000

included

Honeymoon specials
Bottle of Italian Spumante and fresh flowers on arrival. Room upgrade depending on availability.

Leisure facilities
Indoor swimming pool, Shiatsu massages on request.

Sightseeing
Champagne picnic to Ostia Antica, Etruscan and Roman archaeological areas, the museums and historical delights of Rome only 30 minutes away.

Le Silve Di Armenzano

Loc Armenzano
Assisi
Italy

✈ Assisi 12km
Rome 187km

tel +39 075 801 9000
fax +39 075 801 9005

armenzano@specialhotels.com
www.specialhotels.com

110

Umbria is one of Italy's most picturesque regions and from its position deep in the countryside hotel Le Silve offers stunning views. It also offers the ultimate in seclusion. Tucked at the base of the mountains, the meadows and woodlands surrounding the hotel are inhabited only by horses and deer.

The 10th-century inn contains an intimate number of rooms – 19 to be exact – and each is furnished with a mix of wood, stone tapestry and antiques. All have incredible views over the countryside and/or the hotel pool and many offer terraces complete with a rocking chair to let you while the time away.

Handmade pasta and freshly baked bread are the specialities of the hotel's rural restaurant and dining *al fresco* is always an option on those warm and enviable Italian evenings.

Le Silve prides itself on offering a simple and relaxing holiday for honeymooners. You can take a romantic walk or horseback ride through the fields. Or take a drive to wander around the incredible basilica in nearby Assisi. The city of Rome is also an easy day trip away meaning every stay offers you the perfect combination of urban sophistication and quaint countryside charm.

 ITL150,000-230,000 (15)

 from ITL300,000 (4)

ITL60,000

ITL15,000

Honeymoon specials
Fruit and chocolates in room on arrival.

Sightseeing and leisure
Situated close to beautiful Assisi with its centuries-old churches and squares. Horseriding and walks through the surrounding countryside. There is mini-golf nearby.

Romantik Hotel Poseidon

148 Via Pasitea
84017 Positano
Italy

✈ Naples 60km

tel +39 08 98 11 111
fax +39 08 98 75 833

romantik@specialhotels.com
www.specialhotels.com
poseidon@starnet.it
www.starnet.it/poseidon

Tour operators:
UK Italian Expressions

Few swimming pools offer a view like that afforded by the freshwater oasis of the Romantik Hotel Poseidon. Its location high up in the Amalfi hills commands an idyllic view over the so-called 'vertical village', the tiny hillside town of Positano.

The hotel began life as a private home and at first glance still appears to be purely a beautiful villa surrounded by luscious greenery. However, inside you experience all the service and amenities of a first-class establishment. Each of the hotel's 48 rooms and two suites are furnished tastefully with terracotta floors and simple accessories and offer private terraces with outstanding views of the bay.

The on site restaurant La Terraza del Poseidon offers fine cuisine and on balmy summer nights you can dine on the vast bougainvillaea-clad terrace with its splendid views. In 1997 the hotel opened the Laura Elos Beauty Centre offering personalised treatments and a fully equipped gym.

With beautiful, historic sights such as Capri, Amalfi and Pompei just a few miles away, Positano deserves its title as a 'tiny corner of paradise' and the Romantik Hotel Poseidon is the perfect place from which to enjoy this beautiful unspoilt town.

111

 ITL290,000-410,000 (46)

 ITL550,000-720,000 (3)

 ITL70,000

included

Honeymoon specials
Complimentary champagne and flowers on arrival.

Leisure facilities
Laura Elos Beauty Center for body and face treatments, massage, Turkish bath, outdoor swimming pool, gym.

Sightseeing
The hotel can arrange excursions to the beautiful areas around Pompei, Amalfi, Ravello, Naples, Paestum and the island of Capri. All are within easy reach by road or sea transport.

Liechtenstein

flying time
To: Zurich
London: 1 hr
NY: 8 hrs

**climate/
when to go**
In summer, for
romantic walks
through wildflower
meadows and
vineyards. In winter,
for skiing, ice-skating
and tobogganing at
Steg and Malbun.

currency
Swiss franc.

language
German, though
English is widely
spoken.

getting around
Taxis are expensive
so the best option is
to rent a car. Zurich
is just 90 miles away.

One of the smallest countries in the world, Liechtenstein lies in the heart of Europe, sandwiched between Austria and Switzerland, with which it is so closely linked that you cross the border without knowing it.

Its 65 square miles comprise lowlands, including part of the fertile Rhine Valley, and alpine valleys in the shadow of jagged peaks. Visitors to this charming enclave enjoy the novelty of being in a country seemingly without borders, with no armed forces, and with almost as many international companies and corporations registered here as there are residents. For Liechtenstein, like Switzerland, enjoys banking secrecy, a favourable tax regime and a healthy economy. Standards are high, and prices reflect this.

For honeymooners, however, this is a place to relax, surrounded by clear air and magnificent scenery, and there is a good range of hotels, guest houses and chalets. The quaint capital of Vaduz, where the ruling prince lives in a medieval castle, has attractive shops and a couple of good museums.

Beyond Vaduz, the countryside gives way to forests and vineyards, whose products are surprisingly good, especially Vaduzer, a red wine. The villages, which are scattered among hills and orchards, are especially charming, and best explored on foot.

Park Hotel Sonnenhof

Mareestrasse 29
FL-9490 Vaduz
Liechtenstein

✈ Zurich 120km

tel +41 75 232 1192
fax +41 75 232 0053

sonnenhof@specialhotels.com
www.specialhotels.com
www.integra.fr/relaischateaux/
sonnenhof

Closed Christmas-mid-Feb

Member of:
Relais & Chateaux

The district of Vaduz, home to the Prince of Liechtenstein, is rich in natural beauty and cultural heritage. The Park Hotel Sonnenhof is located on the edge of extensive woods and vineyards with spectacular views overlooking the upper Rhine Valley and Swiss Alps beyond.

This is a family-owned hotel and the staff are extremely friendly and welcoming. The rooms are all light and airy with balcony or terrace and splendid views of Vaduz castle. Each is equipped with a television, radio, safe and minibar.

In the restaurant, guests can indulge in a wide selection of traditional dishes, and a choice of fine wines from the hotel's own vast wine cellar.

Park Hotel Sonnenhof is a haven of peace and tranquillity and serves as an ideal base for avid hikers. Well-marked trails lead visitors through remote countryside and romantic valleys. Guests can also take advantage of the health club with its indoor swimming pool, solarium and sauna.

The charming town of Vaduz offers a lively programme of sports and festivals throughout the summer months, becoming a thriving and exciting skiing centre in winter.

113

 US$250-350 (17)

 US$320-440 (12)

 US$60-125

 included

Honeymoon specials

Flowers and wine on arrival. One free entrance to thermal baths in Bad Ragaz and the national museum nearby. Specially decorated honeymoon table for dinner. This package is valid for a minimum stay of three days.

Sightseeing and leisure
Excursions by horse-drawn carriage to historic sights, local wine areas and thermal springs of Bad Ragaz. Hikes in alpine forests and mountains featured in the filming of *Heidi*. Swimming, surfing, sailing, golf, riding, squash, tennis, cycling, paragliding and skiing nearby. Health and beauty salons.

flying time
Between 1-2 hrs
from London to
any of the islands.

climate
The mild Med makes
it a pleasure to visit
summer or winter.
Generally the
summers are hot
and dry with warm
and wetter winters.

currency
This varies from
island to island and
includes the French
franc, Italian lire,
Spanish peseta,
Maltese pound.
Credit cards and
traveller's cheques
are widely accepted.

language
French, Spanish,
Italian and Maltese.
English spoken in
resort areas.

getting around
Ferries ply their
trade between
islands. On land, taxis,
buses and car hire
are available.

The azure blues of the Mediterranean Sea, white, sandy beaches, olive groves, vineyards and sunshine are the hallmarks of this region, located between Europe and Africa.

The Med islands that lie scattered across this region are hugely varied in style, not only because of the different geography but because of the different cultural backgrounds of their peoples. The French, Italians, Spanish and Maltese all lay claim to some of the islands, colouring each territory with their own characterful, distinctive styles.

But whatever the differences, the friendly welcome, stunning scenery, excellent cuisine, top-class resorts and a sense of rich history is common to all whether you choose to visit the island of Malta, explore the Balearics, discover Corsica or simply relax in Sardinia.

Explore the huge mountains and deep river gorges of these islands, gaze upon the olive groves, wander through heavily scented forests of pine, beech and chestnut or kick-back on the gorgeous sugary white sand beaches that follow the coastlines for miles.

Discover centuries of mysterious European history in ancient towns and cities, medieval forts and dramatic cliff-top castles, or indulge yourself in the array of fine cuisine and local wines.

Enjoy the Mediterranean from lazy swims in secluded coves to deep-sea fishing, Scuba diving or paragliding above the waters with views of the islands around.

Le Maquis

20166 Porticcio
BP 94, Corsica
France

✈ Ajaccio 10 km
tel +33 4 95 25 05 55
fax +33 4 95 25 11 70

maquis@specialhotels.com
www.specialhotels.com
www.slh.com

Tour operators:
UK Elegant Resorts

Member of:
Small Luxury Hotels

Corsica, the fourth largest island in the blissful waters of the Mediterranean Sea, is renowned for its abundance of wild flowers and the incredible diversity of its landscapes – from gorges and mountains to forests of pine, beech, birch and ancient fields of sun-drenched crops. The maquis herbs of thyme, marjoram, basil and rosemary flavour the air as well as the cooking and are found everywhere. There is, however, only one Le Maquis, a magnificent hotel set on its own sandy beach commanding outstanding views across the bay.

Truly Corsican, Le Maquis' whitewashed walls, shutters and terracotta roofs soak up the warm sunshine. Inside, the hotel's spacious rooms and suites with their stone floors and antique beams are gently cooled by fresh sea breezes. The hotel has a rustic charm, more like a country house than a hotel, with open fireplaces and high vaulted ceilings. This is combined effortlessly with more modern pleasures such as refined dining, two swimming pools and a floodlit tennis court.

Nearby is the lively waterfront town of Ajaccio with its many bars, cafes, restaurants and shops. Napoleon Bonaparte was born at Ajaccio in 1769. Given the blessings of the island's charms, it's a wonder he ever left.

115

 FF600-2,600 (17)

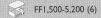 FF1,500-5,200 (6)

⌾ from FF250

☕ FF80

Honeymoon specials
Champagne and fruit basket on arrival. Room upgrade subject to availability.

* Please note there is a five night minimum stay from 1 May-1 October 1999.

Leisure facilities
Hair dresser on site. Thalassotherapy centre nearby which hotel can provide details on.

Sightseeing
Bonifacio is just a few hours' drive away and there is much to see and do in that area – play golf at Sperone Golf Club being one of them. Nearer to Le Maquis are many bars, restaurants and shops in Ajaccio, not to mention the rugged natural beauty of the surrounding coastline and countryside. There are fantastic walks within a short distance from the hotel.

Na Xamena
Hotel Hacienda

07815 San Miguel
E 07815
Ibiza
Spain

✈ Ibiza 25km

tel +34 971 334 500
fax +34 971 334 514

xamena@specialhotels.com
www.specialhotels.com
htl.hacienda@vlc.servicom.es

Open Apr-Dec

116

Member of:
Relais & Chateaux

The north-west of the island of Ibiza, with its scattered white fincas and coastal belt of coves, is an area of outstanding natural beauty. Na Xamena Hotel Hacienda sits high up on an impressive clifftop, tucked into pine forests. This privileged setting gives the hotel magical views and a sense of space and isolation, also echoed in the building's simple and elegant design.

The rooms combine a modern Zen style with traditional antiques from the Pacific islands. Many have a whirlpool bath and afford spectacular views overlooking the sea, with an unforgettable sunset.

Each has mini bar, satellite television and safe.

The three restaurants here offer totally different experiences: the poolside Las Cascadas, serving fine local Mediterranean cuisine; the grill for a more informal lunch on the terrace with breathtaking views of the cliffs; and the gourmet restaurant, Sueño de Estrellas, for a romantic candlelit dinner.

Terraces provide secluded spots where couples can relax and unwind. For the more energetic, the hotel is within easy reach of sandy beaches and lagoons offering a range of waterports, and the busy and exciting nightlife of Ibiza town.

🛏 PTS25,700-47,600* (50)

🛏 PTS34,100-117,000* (10)

🍴 PTS7,100*

☕ PTS2,400*

🌀 🍾

Honeymoon specials
Spanish champagne and fruit in the room on arrival.

Sightseeing
A 20-minute drive from the centre of Ibiza. Sandy beaches and coves. Concerts, exhibitions, performances in traditional costume.
*VAT not included.

Leisure activities
Indoor and outdoor swimming pools, mountain biking, tennis courts. Well-being zone with massage, Turkish bath and sauna. All watersports, golf and riding nearby.

La Residencia

Son Canals S/N
07179 Deia
Mallorca

✈ Palma 45km

tel +34 971 639011
fax +34 971 639370

residencia@specialhotels.com
www.specialhotels.com
laresidencia@atlas.iap.es

Tour operators:
UK Elegant Resorts
Western & Oriental

Tucked away amid 30 acres of aromatic olive and citrus groves and with stunning views of the surrounding mountains and village, La Residencia is a hotel of distinction designed for those with a love of luxury, excellent hospitality and truly personal service.

Hidden away in the Majorcan hill village of Deia, the hotel is an oasis of luxury and charm. Its candelabra-clad, ultra-romantic restaurant, El Olivo, has achieved award-winning status and has become famous across Spain as one of the best that the country has to offer, while Son Fony offers a more informal choice.

La Residencia is also the perfect place to pamper yourselves with the Virgin Touch Beauty Salon offering a full range of treatment from massages and aromatherapy to hydromassage and stress alleviation treatments.

For sports lovers, the hotel's tennis coach will help improve your game while the hotel works closely with some of the island's finest golf courses, including Son Vida and Bendinat.

And for those who can tear themselves away from this haven, the island is full of surprises from sightseeing locally in the quaint little villages and in Palma, to wine tasting and a visit to an olive press.

117

🛏 PTS17,500-62,500 (64)

🛏 PTS49,500-130,500 (3)

🍽 PTS6,000-11,000

☕ included

🍷 Ⓢ

Honeymoon specials
Complimentary Cava and flowers in room on arrival. Room upgrade depending on availability.

Leisure facilities
Two outdoor swimming pools, two tennis courts, Virgin Touch Beauty Salon on site, hydrotherapy, steamroom. There are also three golf courses within an hour's drive.

Sightseeing
Shopping and cathedrals in Palma, Valdemossa Monastery, Deia village, excursions to Son Marroig museum, local bustling markets.

Ta' Cenc

Sannat
Vct 112
Gozo
Malta

tel +356 556 819
fax +356 558 199

✈ Malta 15 min by helicopter

tacenc@specialhotels.com
www.specialhotels.com

Tour operators:
UK Gozo Holidays
US Hideaways

18

Situated in a private estate with spectacular views over the sea, Ta' Cenc is Gozo's most imaginative hotel. And one that the readers of Condé Nast *Traveller* obviously like as they voted it the 21st Best Hotel in the World in the 1998 ranking.

Crafted from local limestone, its intricate design reflects perfectly the rugged nature of the Gozonian landscape. Most sought after are the nine Trullo-type rooms, which each have two bedrooms and a private terrace. However, other bedrooms and guest bungalows offer high levels of comfort in a modern spacious design.

Delicious herbs from their own vast garden flavour the imaginative cuisine in the Il Carrubo restaurant which offers both *à la carte* and *table d'hote* menus. For lighter meals, dine at the snack bar which is situated between the hotel's two freshwater swimming pools.

A short shuttle journey takes you to their private beach, the romantic rocky inlet of Kantra Beach. Sun loungers, sports facilities and a reading room help pass time on land, but the crystal clear waters of the bay will entice even reluctant water babies.

Exploring this 14km by 7km island is easy and sights include quaint villages, bustling markets and no fewer than 44 beautiful churches.

US$109-176
US$76-135 (83)
US$29-45
US$15

Honeymoon specials
With a stay of seven nights, you get one free night. On second day only, you receive free car hire and flowers, fruit and champagne in room.

Sightseeing and leisure
On Sundays during the summer, each village celebrates its own feast dedicated to the patron saint of that village. Also nearby are temples – in Xaghra – which are the oldest free-standing pre-historic temples in the world. Leisure and beauty facilities nearby and available on request.

Forte Village Resort

09010 S Margherita di Pula
(Cagliari)
Sardinia

✈ Cagliari 45 mins

tel +39 07 09 21 516
fax +39 07 09 21 246

forte@specialhotels.com
www.specialhotels.com
www.fortevillageresort.it

Tour operators:
UK Citalia
US Spa Finders

Picture an island paradise with a choice of seven beautiful and unique hotels and a range of bungalows. Imagine tropical gardens, blue sea, powder beaches, stunning sunsets, gourmet cuisine and every facility you could possible dream of. Welcome to the Forte Village Resort.

This 25-hectare complex offers a mind-boggling selection of accommodation. Whether you're looking for that perfect beach setting or the freshness of the forest, there's something for you, all offering seclusion and class. Sixteen restaurants give you the opportunity to sample a huge range of Italian delicacies where super-fresh fish and pasta abound, with lobster a famous speciality.

If activity is what you're looking for, you can play to your heart's content. Choose from tennis (17 courts), golf (at Is Molas), aerobics, volleyball or even football. There's also the Thermae del Parco Health Club & Spa to enjoy. Sun worshippers can while away the hours on the beautiful beach or take to the water with windsurfing, waterskiing, sailing and Scuba diving all right on the doorstep.

The Piazza Maria Luigla offers entertainment aplenty with cafes, shops, disco evenings and concerts. Or if you really feel the need to explore further, a wide range of excursions are available.

119

ITL285,000-2,190,000* (698)

 included

 included

Honeymoon specials

Flowers and fruit on arrival (champagne on request). Limousine transfer on request, plus personalised check-in.

There are seven hotels here with a variety of rooms, suites and bungalows, so these prices are merely a guideline. Phone for specific hotel rates.

Sightseeing and leisure

Beaches and boat trips to Tuaredda and Su Giudeu in the Bay of Chia. Excursions to the Phoenician-Roman city of Nora and to Caloforte. The hotel offers tennis, swimming pools, squash, football, volleyball, go-karts, watersports, spa with beauty facilities and fitness centre, plus the Piazza, for discos, concerts, cafes and more.

Portugal & Madeira

flying time
To: Faro, Lisbon or
Funchal for Madeira
London: 2-4 hrs
NY: 7-9 hrs

climate
The mainland is
warm and dry May-
Sept. The northern
part of the country
is cooler and wetter,
as is winter.
Madeira is mild and
sub-tropical with
temperatures at a
steady 17°-30°C.

when to go
Portugal is lovely
anytime, but Carnival
(Feb-Mar) is a real
treat. Madeira
celebrates New Year
with gusto from early
Dec, but hotel prices
tend to rise.

currency
Portuguese escudo.

language
Portuguese. On
Madeira English is
widely spoken.

getting around
Taxis are cheap.
Buses are generally
faster than trains. On
Madeira a car is best
for touring.

Portugal is a gentle land, with a warm and welcoming people. It's a small country, tucked away at the end of the Iberian peninsula, with a long Atlantic coast, a proud history and a thrilling, diverse landscape.

The remote northern interior is hauntingly beautiful. Lisbon, the capital, has all the verve of a modern metropolis, with a charming medieval mantle of churches, forts and staggeringly beautiful palaces.

The Algarve in the south is famed for glorious beaches, little fishing villages and fabulous golf courses that regularly attract world-wide praise.

And washed by the waters of the Atlantic, the tiny, steep-sided island of Madeira is a miniature paradise. For those who love nature, the dramatic, lush terrain and exuberant flora of this little island provide a romantic and uplifting honeymoon setting.

Portugal is not an expensive place to visit. Life is simple, but standards are high, and good value can be relied upon, especially where food is concerned. Fresh seafood and salads, fine olive oil, garlic – then more garlic – are the hallmarks of Portuguese cuisine. Simply prepared, and in abundant quantities, the food is an ideal match for the country's crisp, white wines.

The whole region is incredibly picturesque. A little exploration away from the tourist trail reveals isolated beaches, hillside settlements, lush valleys with trickling streams and lots and lots of fragrant eucalyptus and pine-studded mountains.

121

Hotel La Reserve

Santa Barbara De Nexe,
8000 Faro, Algarve,
Portugal

✈ Faro 10km

tel +351 89 99 94 74
fax +351 89 99 94 02

reserve@specialhotels.com
www.specialhotels.com

Quietly hidden within 10 lush acres of parkland in the beautiful green hills of The Algarve's Santa Barbara de Nexe, Hotel La Reserve offers the perfect combination of spatial surroundings, seductive scenery and gourmet cuisine. Each of the 20 luxurious suites has a south-facing distant sea view and private terrace. Pale colours and simplistic furnishings create a clean uncluttered decor with no compromise on comfort.

Evening's place you perfectly to enjoy one of The Algarve's premier dining experiences as Restaurant La Reserve is renowned as the area's finest eatery. After dining retire with a drink to the romantic,

walled patio surrounded by La Reserve's signature blooms or relax in the stylish and elegant marble surroundings of the bar itself.

Daytime, La Reserve offers you a wealth of experiences that exploit The Algarve's year-round sunny climes. Relax by the large swimming pool, wander through the beautiful gardens or work up an appetite on the tennis court. Golf can also be arranged at any of the area's top courses.

If you can tear yourself away, just a short drive brings you to the shopping and interesting sights of the nearby town of Faro, or to the cool, calm waters and golden sands of the coast.

🛏 ESC28,000-40,000 (12)

🛏 ESC30,000-44,000 (8)

🍽 ESC10,000

☕ included

🍸 🌀

Honeymoon specials
Champagne, flowers and fruit on arrival.

Leisure facilities
Tennis and swimming pool on site. Beauty facilities and horseriding nearby. Also, within easy reach are fine golf courses such as Vale do Lobo, Vila Sol and the three courses at Vilamoura.

Sightseeing
Bustling local markets, excursions to Faro other towns and historical places of interest, and local pottery shops.

Hotel Quinta do Lago

Quinta do Lago
8135-024 Almancil
Algarve
Portugal

✈ Faro Int. 20km

tel +351 08939 6666
fax +351 08939 6393

quinta@specialhotels.com
www.specialhotels.com
hqdlago@mail.tlepact.pt
www.orient-expresshotels.com/

Tour operators:
UK Elegant Resorts

Member of:
Leading Hotels of the World
Orient Express Hotels

123

This luxurious hotel is situated on the dramatic Algarve coastline beside a tidal estuary in the exclusive Quinta do Lago estate, with its undulating hills, pinewoods and championship golf courses.

All rooms are spacious and furnished in light, natural wood and pastel shades. Most rooms enjoy views across the gardens to the Atlantic Ocean beyond. All have balconies opening onto terraces.

Guests can enjoy cocktails in the Laguna Bar before dining in one of two restaurants offering traditional Portuguese cuisine and Venetian specialities, or al fresco on the poolside terrace where fish, shellfish and meat are barbecued daily.

A romantic wooden footbridge over the Ria Formosa Estuary links the hotel to the pretty beaches and a wealth of sports activities.

The hotel is ideally placed for exploring the spectacular Algarve countryside or perhaps cruising along the still, clean waters of the River Guadiana, and ending the day with typical Portuguese dancing.

The 17th-century baroque church of São Lourenço, decorated with astonishingly beautiful tiles, or azulejos, provides a romantic setting for a wedding. Buffets and cocktail parties for up to 200 can be arranged in the elegant São Lourenço room or on the extensive hotel lawns.

 ESC33,000–71,000 (141)

 ESC80,00–275,000 (9)

 ESC7,000

 included

Honeymoon specials

Champagne and strawberries on arrival. Horseriding or massage. Champagne cocktail followed by candlelit dinner. A guided visit to picturesque Loulé market and the St Lourenço church. A day's car hire. The package costs from ESC178,500 per couple based on a stay of three nights.

Sightseeing and leisure

Romantic walks around the Ria Formosa Estuary and bird sanctuary. Excursions to towns of Silves, Faro and Olhão. Jeep safaris. Visits to local Portuguese potteries. Swimming pools, floodlit tennis courts, health club. Bike hire, clay pigeon shooting, deep-sea fishing and all watersports available close by. Three golf courses on the estate.

Lapa Palace

Rua do Pau de Bandeira
No 4
1249-021 Lisbon
Portugal

✈ Lisbon 10km

tel +351 1 395 0005
fax +351 1 395 0665

lapa@specialhotels.com
www.specialhotels.com
reservas@hotelapa.com
www.orient-expresshotels.com

124

Tour operators:
UK Elegant Resorts

Member of:
Leading Hotels of the World
Orient Express Hotels

Lisbon is one of Europe's most sophisticated and architecturally beautiful capitals. Set on a hill, close to the majestic River Tagus, travellers will find the ornate elegance of the Lapa Palace the perfect base for exploration.

Marble stucco, carved wood and richly patterned tiles reveal a stately beauty few modern resorts can hope to offer – yet the hotel was only opened a few years ago, in 1992. The six public rooms are lavishly decorated, a theme that runs throughout the 94 guest rooms, which includes poolside accommodation as well. Each is individually decorated and feature decor ranging from 18th-century classical designs to Art Deco chic.

The beauty is carried throughout and Lapa Palace boasts stunning gardens to wander round. The Embaixada restaurant is equally well-appointed and features traditional Portuguese and international cuisine served in bright, airy surroundings.

Also close to the hotel are Lisbon's most famous sights. The Torre de Belém, Castelo Sao Jorge and the ornate Jerónimos monastery. However to truly get a sense of this quietly beautiful town, you need only walk for a while in its quiet streets or soak up the silence in one of it's characterful, palm-fringed 18th-century squares.

🛏 ESC68,400-87,400 (86)

💰 ESC84,800-103,800 (8)

🍽 ESC7,500

☕ ESC2,800

🎰 ♿ 🍾 🕶

Honeymoon specials

Three or seven nights deluxe accommodation, daily American breakfast, fruit, flowers and port on arrival, welcome cocktail, champagne, one á la carte lunch or dinner in the restaurant (exc. drinks), one candlelight dinner in room (exc. drinks), day's sightseeing tour in limo, use of health club, transfers. From ESC68,400 per room per night.

Sightseeing and leisure

Indoor heated pool, health club with Scottish bath, Turkish bath, sauna, solarium, outdoor pool. Nearby is Lisbon, Belém Tower, Jerónimos, Expo '98 facilities now known as Nations Park. Golf on five championship courses can also be arranged.

Reid's Palace

Estrada Monumental 139
9000-098 Funchal
Madeira

✈ Santa Cruz 22km

tel +351 91 71 7171
fax +351 91 71 7177

UK sales office:
tel +44 (0) 171 805 5059
fax +44 (0) 171 805 5931

reids@specialhotels.com
www.specialhotels.com
reidshotel@mail.telepac.pt
www.orient-expresshotels.com/

Member of:
Leading Hotels of the World
Orient Express Hotel Group

Madeira's grandest deluxe hotel sits on the outskirts of Funchal, perched on a clifftop overlooking the bay, where hanging vines jostle for room with displays of geraniums, hibiscus and salvias. This is the perfect hideaway for those in search of peace and relaxation whilst enjoying a magnificent sub-tropical climate.

Built in 1891, this Mediterranean-style hotel, which combines old world charm with luxurious facilities, has always been a favourite of royalty and celebrities. Edward VIII, Sir Winston Churchill and Fulgencio Baptista are among those who have passed through its doors. All rooms are spacious, light and airy, and some, such as those in the recently restored Garden Wing and main building, have deluxe marble bathrooms.

There are five restaurants including the turn of the century main dining room, Les Faunes (seasonal), where guests can savour fine French cuisine while enjoying panoramic views of the harbour. The Trattoria Villa Cliff, set against an open-air backdrop, and Brisa do Mar (seasonal) provides a romantic setting for *al fresco* dining.

Activities abound at Reid's – from sunbathing to watersports, tennis, and a health centre with saunas and massage – there's something to suit every taste.

125

 ESC58,000–95,000 (130)

 ESC102,000–320,000 (32)

 ESC8,100

 included

Honeymoon specials

Half bottle of champagne, fruit, flowers in room on arrival. Also, complimentary mini bar (soft drinks and beer). Room upgrade subject to availability.

Sightseeing and leisure

Historic town of Funchal and old churches to explore. Levada walks and mountain-hiking 6,000ft above sea level. Madeira Night once a week in hotel and sunset cruise. Golf at nearby Palheiro and Santo da Serra courses (30% discount for Reid's guests). Health centre at hotel with sauna, massage and reflexologist.

Vila Vita Parc

PO Box 196
8365 Armaçao de Pêra
Algarve
Portugal

✈ Faro Int. 45km

tel +351 82 315 310
fax +351 82 315 333

vilavita@specialhotels.com
www.specialhotels.com
vilavitapark@mail.telepac.pt
www.vilavita.com

126 Tour operators:
UK Elegant Resorts,
Cadogan Holidays

Member of:
Leading Hotels of the World

On the rugged and beautiful Algarve coast, set amidst 20 hectares of undulating parkland, is the deluxe hotel and resort complex Vila Vita Parc.

The spacious green terraces of the countryside are neatly dotted with hotels and villas, offering tranquillity and privacy for couples who want to spend time alone. Rooms and suites are furnished in Portuguese and Moorish styles, using gentle natural colours and materials. All have satellite television, minibar and views across the vast gardens to the Atlantic Ocean.

The resort is also a haven for sports fanatics, with access to two large, private sandy beaches, a comprehensive range of watersports, volleyball and tennis courts, deep-sea fishing, boat trips and championship golf. There are also two pools and

 ESC21,800-84,650 (103)

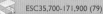 ESC35,700-171,900 (79)

 ESC3,600-12,000

 included

Honeymoon specials
Champagne, mineral water, fresh fruit, bowl of grapes or strawberries and flowers in room on arrival. Room upgrade subject to availability.

a supervised adventure playground for children.

The hotel's Vital Centre provides the perfect retreat for couples wanting to relax and unwind following the hectic events of the wedding day. All treatments are carried out under medical supervision and based on holistic diagnosis.

There are six restaurants serving a selection of light snacks, international specialities and local cuisine. Evening entertainment is offered in the clubhouse and discotheque, and in the many bars dotted throughout the park.

Wedding receptions for up to 350 guests are catered for in the ballroom.

Vila Vita Parc is also an ideal base for exploring the surrounding countryside, caves and grottos, natural springs and quaint villages characteristic of the Portuguese culture and traditions.

Sightseeing

Romantic walks, coastal excursions in the hotel's private yacht, Jeep safaris into the mountains.

Leisure facilities

Tennis, squash, swimming pools, health club with steambath, Jacuzzi, sauna, gym and massage. All watersports, including sailing and deep-sea fishing throughout the summer, mountain biking. Golfing facilities including pitch and putt, driving range and putting green. The Vital Centre, a medically supervised retreat, offers natural treatments.

Spain

flying time
To: Seville, Malaga
London: 2¹/₂ hrs
NY: 7¹/₂ hrs

**climate/
when to go**
Carnival in Feb is
celebrated with
gusto, followed in
spring by elaborate
Easter Week parades
and the first bullfights
of the season.
Summers are dry,
hot and crowded but
great for fiestas.
Autumns are mellow
and warm.

currency
Spanish peseta.

language
Spanish, although it is
easy to get by with
English on the coasts
and in tourist areas.

getting around
By air to all the main
cities. There is an
efficient, reasonably
priced network of
public transport,
from city buses to
underground
services. Taxis, too,
are everywhere.

Romance and Spain have gone hand in hand since the Middle Ages, when Moorish poets introduced the concept of Romantic love and chivalry to Europe.

Spain easily lends herself to dreamy ideals: her land and cities are sweepingly grand and poetic, from the high drama of the Pyrenees and Old Castile down to the charasmatic horse parades, sunbaked hills and beaches of Andalucía. The ancestral mix of Latin temperament and Moorish imagination shows itself vividly in the fanciful architecture, and in the driving rhythms of the famed *flamenco* dance.

For anyone on a honeymoon, it would be hard to beat a romantic stroll through the royal pavilions and rambling gardens of the Alhambra Palace in Granada; and in summer you can do it by moonlight. Or try Córdoba with its spectacular Great Mosque. But for fun, the most famous of all *plazas de toros* are in Ronda and Seville, where you can pick oranges off the trees in the centre of the city.

Speaking of fun, the country is also one of the hippest to be found in Europe. Barcelona, the Catalan capital, has drive and energy, as do Andalucía's cosmopolitan resorts which bristle with designer boutiques and beautiful people lolling under parasols on the sun-drenched beaches

At night, after the requisite *siesta*, the Spaniards really get going. Nothing starts before 10pm, but then, two days can be crammed into one in the fabulous, thumping nightclubs and bars across the country. Like the *tapas*, Spain is a wonderful mix. It blends old and new, glamour and rustic charm, hot days and cool nights, with all the exuberance and delicacy of an uncorked bottle of chilled *Cava*.

Hotel Puente Romano

PO Box 204
Marbella
Spain

✈ Malaga Int. 55km

tel +34 95 282 0900
fax +34 95 277 5766

puente@specialhotels.com
www.specialhotels.com
hotel@puenteromano.com
www.puenteromano.com

130

Member of:
Leading Hotels of the World

Marbella is probably the most elegant and exclusive resort on the Costa del Sol. Located in the heart of the Golden Mile, between Marbella and Puerto Banus, the Hotel Puente Romano nestles along the Mediterranean coast, at the foot of the Sierra Blanca mountains.

The hotel comprises a series of low-rise horizontal buildings constructed in traditional Andalucían style and offering secluded and spacious demi-suite rooms with terraces or balconies overlooking waterfalls and acres of lush subtropical gardens. The hotel staff strike the balance between privacy and impeccable service.

The hotel's three restaurants – El Puente, Roberto Italian and the Beach Club – each different in style, offer a wealth of gastronomic delights. You can select from spectacular buffets and a range of authentic dishes featuring local fish and seafood. When the lights go down, you can boogie at the disco and during the summer months there are themed nights to enjoy. If you decide to venture out for an evening, Marbella and Puerto Banus offer much in the way of fun.

Weddings can also be celebrated in the hotel with receptions for up to 240 guests catered for in one of its top restaurants.

 PTS34,800-42,800

 included

 included

Honeymoon specials
Cava on arrival, full breakfast Puente Romano, room upgrade subject to availability, free entrance to the Casino Torrequebrada. The package costs from PTS23,200-33,500 per double room per night. Optional limousine transfers from Malaga airport at cost of PTS30,000.

Sightseeing and leisure
Visits to local markets and boutiques in the old town, rides in a horse-drawn carriage. Festivals and flamenco shows. Romantic strolls along Puerto Banus harbour and Marbella promenade. Puente Romano Tennis & Fitness Centre, sauna and massage. All watersports plus activities such as polo, horseriding and golf.

Vistamar de Valldemossa

Ctra. Valldemossa
Andratx, Km 2
07170 Valldemossa
Mallorca

✈ Palma 18km

tel +34 971 612 300
fax +34 971 612 583

vistamar@specialhotels.com
www.specialhotels.com
www.vistamarhotel.es

Open February-end October

Tour operators:
UK Simply Spain
Castaways

Situated above a small fishing port, two kilometres from the quaint town of Valldemossa, this elegant hotel offers an enviable mix of charm and comfort. Its 19 double rooms are decorated in an unusual but charming style that fuses antique Mallorcan furnishing with contemporary luxury. Many rooms boast romantic canopy beds and all contain air-conditioning and a minibar.

Dining on site is in the Vistamar restaurant famed for both its authentic Mediterranean cooking and its extensive wine cellar. Should the mood take, a short walk through the olive and pine trees that envelop the hotel brings you to the beachside Marina de Vistamar which offers more casual seafront dining.

Days at the hotel are relaxed. The pool provides exquisite views of the lush green hillside in which the property is hidden and the pleasant beach is just a short walk away. Sightseers will enjoy a gentle stroll into the nearby fishing villages with their bright coloured boats, or visit Valldemossa, renowned for its monasteries, particularly the Carthusian where Chopin wrote 'Mazurca in Mi Minor'. A short drive takes you to the busy hub of Palma. A trip to the world famous cathedral and a stroll along the seafront should not be missed.

131

 PTS26,000-27,000* (7)

 PTS31,000-32,000* (12)

 PTS2,000 per person

Honeymoon specials

Champagne and flowers on arrival. For honeymooners staying one week, the hotel will offer a free car for three days, excluding the cost of petrol and insurance.

* Price for two people plus 7% VAT.

Sightseeing and leisure

Valldemossa is an awe-inspiring historical and artistic centre of Mallorca. The Carthusian Monastery, where Chopin wrote some important pieces, every August organises a classical concert with many famous artists performing. The countryside around the hotel also boasts lovely views and offers good hiking terrain.

Hyatt Regency La Manga

Los Belones
30385
Cartagena
Murcia
Spain

✈ Murcia 25km

Contact:
tel +44 (0) 181 397 4411
fax +44 (0) 181 974 1442

manga@specialhotels.com
www.specialhotels.com
www.barwell.co.uk

132

Tour operators:
UK Barwell Leisure

The beautiful Murcia region in south-eastern Spain is one of the country's best kept secrets. Yet in its midst is one of the world's leading vacation spots, the sprawling La Manga Club Resort – home of the Hyatt Regency.

Offering five-star service, the 192 rooms are spacious and elegantly furnished. All have marble bathrooms, mini bar, satellite TV, and individually controlled air-conditioning. Large picture windows open on to balconies, most affording uninterrupted views across the golf courses or pool. Everything is designed with your comfort in mind.

The resort's many restaurants offer cuisine for all tastes – including a chance to savour some of the delicious seafood which is a speciality of the region.

While the nearby towns of Murcia and Cartegena offer sights for the visitor, La Manga is a resort that's hard to leave. The facilities here are unparalleled. Three 18-hole golf courses, shaded by palm trees and landscaped around beautiful lakes, offer something to challenge players of all levels. There are also 18 tennis courts, miles of equestrian trails and a fitness centre. When temperatures rise, the waters of the Mar Menor nearby are a haven for watersports enthusiasts. Or simply relax and sip a cocktail by the pool – the choice is yours.

🛏 £108-124 (192)

🛏 £200 (7)

🍽 £23

☕ included

Honeymoon specials

Champagne and flowers in room on arrival. Chauffeur collection from airport. Exclusive boat charter. Flight upgrades depending on availability.

Sightseeing and leisure

This hotel is a haven for those who enjoy sport. There are three championship golf courses, tennis, squash, horseriding, among other leisure pursuits. Nearby are the ruins of historical Cartagena and the seaside at La Manga.

Kempinksi Resort
Hotel Estepona

Playa El Padron
Carretera de Cadiz
s/n Km 159
29680 Estepona, Malaga
Spain

✈ Malaga 75km
Gibraltar 45km

tel +34 95 280 9500
fax +34 95 280 9550

estepona@specialhotels.com
www.specialhotels.com
www.costadelsol.spa.es/hotel\
kempinski

The beaches between Marbella and Estepona offer some of the most fashionable surroundings in Europe. Now, with the opening of the Kempinski Resort Hotel at the beginning of 1999, the area welcomes ones of its most exclusive resorts yet.

Framed by subtropical gardens, this five-star Moorish-influenced hotel offers many levels of luxurious accommodation. But no matter whether you choose one of the comfortable deluxe rooms or a palatial private suite you'll be rewarded with a view of the azure Mediterranean Sea just a short walk through the palms away.

Two on site restaurants regale your senses with the tastes and smells of Mediterranean or International cuisine, while two beach bars provide snacks and drinks for informal dining. For the perfect romantic evening choose one of the hotel's special candlelit dinners for two in the privacy of your room or terrace.

When day breaks again, take the short stroll onto the golden sands; swim in the hotel's vast freeform pools; workout in the gym or spoil yourself with a visit to the on site sauna, Turkish baths or beauty parlour. Further afield, visits to many of the area's superb golf courses can easily be arranged at reception.

133

 PTS27,500-47,500

 PTS52,500-300,500

 from US$40

 from US$17-22

Honeymoon specials
Champagne and flowers on arrival. Upgrades to honeymoon suites depending on availability.

Sightseeing and leisure
Freeform swimming pools; on site sauna, gym, watersports centre, Turkish bath and beauty facilities. Also, the area is renowned for its selection of superb golf courses; tee times can be arranged at reception.

Las Dunas
Beach Hotel & Spa

La Boladilla Baja
Ctra. Cadiz Km 163.5
Estepona 29689
Malaga
Spain

✈ Malaga 80km

tel +34 95 279 4345
fax +34 95 279 4825

lasdunas@specialhotels.com
www.speciahotels.com

134

Tour operator:
UK Elegant Resorts

Member of:
Leading Hotels of the World

The Las Dunas Beach Hotel & Spa, a five star, Grand Luxe property, is situated directly on the beach in the heart of the Andalucian coastline, between Marbella and its neighbouring village, Estepona. It is one of the most romantic and luxurious hotels at the 'Costa de Marbella'.

The 73-room, flamingo-coloured beach hotel has been constructed in an Andalucian style with a Moorish influence, to compliment the traditional buildings in the region and to reflect the area's cultural heritage. The property is surrounded by lush, sub-tropical, landscaped gardens and fountains,

creating the feel of a Spanish *hacienda*, offering magnificent views over the Mediterranean Sea to Gibraltar and North Africa.

The hotel offers luxurious accommodation and excellent personal service. The Michelin-starred Maitre Cuisiner, Heinz Winkler, was awarded with the 'Grand Prix de l'Art de la Cuisine 1997' by the Academie Internationale de la Gastronomie and supervises the cuisine at Lido Restaurant. At the new lifestyle venue, Piano Bar & Bistro Felix, Euro-Asiatic flavours prevail, whilst the Beach Club features Andalusian delights.

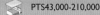 PTS26,000-47,000

PTS43,000-210,000

🍽 PTS8,000

☕ PTS2,700

Honeymoon specials

Buffet breakfast for two, candlelit dinner, champagne and chocolate-dipped strawberries on arrival, two bathrobes personalised with your name, entrance to Spa, including sauna and Jacuzzi. Package costs PTS50,000 (not including room rates).

Sightseeing and leisure

Regena Sol Kur Clinic offers traditional and alternative medicine, Spa including 'Dr Schulte's World of Beauty', 40 golf courses along the coast. Pueblos Blancos, inland hilltop villages with ancient moorish fortresses and white-washed cottages. Mabella flea market and Puerto Banus, luxury boat anchorage, art galleries.

Marbella Club

Bulevar Principe Alfonso
von Hohenlohe
s/n - 29600
Marbella
Spain

✈ Malaga Int. 62km

tel +34 5 282 2211
fax +34 5 282 9884

marbella@specialhotels.com
www.specialhotels.com
www.marbellaclub.com

Tour operators:
UK Elegant Resorts

Member of:
Leading Hotels of the World

135

Formerly the residence of Prince Alfonso von Hohenlohe, an Austrian aristocrat, and now an exclusive club resort and hideaway of the rich and famous, the Marbella Club occupies a prime location along the Golden Mile – Spain's fashionable south coast resort.

A luxurious complex of rooms, suites and bungalows built in Andalucían style, it is surrounded by well-tended, subtropical gardens. There is a wide range of sports facilities, both on site and in the vicinity, including tennis at the nearby Puente Romano Tennis & Fitness Club, swimming and golf.

The hotel's restaurant serves a range of international dishes featuring seafood and local fish. In summer, hundreds of candles, placed in the trees, light up the terrace to create the perfect scenario for romantic, al fresco dining. A rich buffet lunch is served in the Beach Club beside the sea.

In the evenings, guests can relax to the sounds of live piano music in the bar or venture into Puerto Banus and Marbella town to sample the nightlife in the many bars and casinos.

The exclusive Beach Club is a popular venue for wedding receptions of up to 250 as guests can enjoy cocktails against a backdrop of incredibly romantic sunsets and breathtaking scenery.

US$236-500 (84)
US$315-2,127 (45)
US$51-80
US$17

Honeymoon specials
Champagne and flowers in room on arrival. Room upgrade subject to availability.

Leisure facilities
Sauna and two swimming pools on site. Massage by appointment. Tennis, golf, horseriding, clay pigeon shooting and all watersports nearby.

Sightseeing
Visits to Spanish markets and quaint Andalucían villages. Traditional bull fights in season. A short walk to Marbella's old town and the famous yacht harbour with its cafes, restaurants and boutiques. Day trips to Granada and the fabulous, graceful Moorish palace of Alhambra.

Dazzling white, icing-sugar snow, a fresh cold wind, the scent of pine trees. Only the whoosh, whoosh, whoosh of skis breaks the silence...

flying time
To: Geneva or Zurich
London: 1¹/4 hrs
NY: 8-9 hrs

climate
Winters are cold, with a lot of snow at high altitude. Summers are warm; the Ticino area has a Mediterranean climate.

136

when to go
July-Aug is high season. Prices are highest and pistes busiest at Christmas and New Year, half-term and Easter.

currency
Swiss franc.

language
German in some areas, French in others, Italian in Ticino. Most people speak some English.

getting around
The Swiss railway system is efficient and the stunning views on the mountain lines are an added delight.

Dramatic and beautiful, this small country, only a sixth the size of Britain, boasts mountain peaks that rise 15,000 feet and serene, glassy lakes that plunge to unfathomable depths.

Switzerland's loveliest cities hug the lakesides, among them sophisticated and elegant Geneva on the shore of Lac Leman. In winter, the old town's cosy wood-panelled restaurants serve up *kirsch*-laced cheese fondues. In summer, tables are moved into the streets, and windsurfers and sleek yachts take to the water. Steamers carry visitors out of the harbour, past lakeshore villages, to Lausanne and Montreux.

Geneva is a gateway to both the French and the Swiss Alps, and within two or three hours' drive are dozens of mountain resorts offering sports and walking holidays in summer, and some of Europe's best skiing in winter. In fact, Switzerland has more than its fair share of glamorous ski resorts, not least chic, traffic-free Zermatt and Gstaad, a favourite of Europe's wealthiest families and film stars. In summer, celebrities who prefer fresh mountain air to the congested beaches of the French Riviera flock to Gstaad's luxury chalets and hotels.

On the Italian border you find a real gem – the Ticino region. The resorts here could be mistaken for holiday spots on the Mediterranean, by virtue of their sunny weather and long summer season, palm trees and purple bougainvillaea. Only the blue water here is Lakes Maggiore and Lugano, not the sea. Life goes on simply in the rugged mountains but on the manicured lakefront promenades of Lugano, Locarno and Ascona, the scene is rich, upmarket and positively glitzy.

Badrutt's Palace Hotel

Badrutt's Palace Hotel
CH-7500
St Moritz
Switzerland

✈ Samedan 7km

tel +41 81 837 1000
fax +41 81 837 2999

badrutts@specialhotels.com
www.specialhotels.com
www.palace-st-moritz.ch

138 Member of:
Leading Hotels of the World

Perched like a fairy castle, high in the snow-capped peaks of the Swiss Alps, Badrutt's Palace Hotel is a resort born out of tradition which was begun in 1896 by Caspar Badrutt, the grandfather of the present owners.

The tradition and excellent service are as much a hallmark of this hotel now as they were then and can be seen in the discreet charm and elegance of the halls and lobbies as well as the rooms and suites where the solid furniture and rich fabrics create a cosy atmosphere to contrast with the breathtaking scenery of the Swiss Alps outside.

The restaurants, bars and lounge areas continue the theme of good-natured cosmopolitan opulence while a choice of nightclubs, an arcade of shops and boutiques and a sculpted indoor swimming pool add a dash of glamour. As part of the complex, a farmhouse, the Chesa Veglia, dating from 1658 now houses three restaurants, two bars and The Club.

When the snow falls, winter sports – all types of skiing particularly – are a must. Come summer, there are alpine flowers blooming everywhere, sailing, horseriding hot air balloon trips to take and mountain walks to enjoy.

In fact, whether it snows, rains or shines, Badrutt's Palace Hotel never loses its charm.

 SFr280-1,720 (220)

 SFr1,000-4,000 (20)

 included

 included

Honeymoon specials
Includes room upgrade if available, a breakfast buffet at a specially decorated table, VIP treatment, welcome cocktail and bottle of champagne. Honeymooners get free use of pool, Jacuzzi, gym and a massage, the natural ice rink as well as a free Rolls-Royce transfer from St Moritz railway station.

Sightseeing and leisure
Mountain scenery is all around, much of it best enjoyed on one of the many mountain railways. Championship skiing and polo (seasonal), concerts, shopping and museums. The hotel offers indoor golf, Jacuzzi, fitness centre and beauty parlour. Balloon rides and sailing can also be arranged.

Castello del Sole Ascona

Via Muraccio 142
CH-6612 Ascona
Switzerland

✈ Lugano-Agno 40km

tel +41 91 791 0202
fax +41 91 792 1118

castello@specialhotels.com
www.specialhotels.com
castellosole@bluewin.ch
www.integra.fr/relais/
chateaux/castellosole

Closed 1 Nov-15 Mar

Member of:
Relais & Chateaux

The hotel Castello del Sole Ascona, created from the ruins of an old Patrician tavern built in 1532, enjoys an idyllic setting on the shores of Lake Maggiore. In keeping with local tradition, the hotel has been reconstructed using granite, bricks and chestnut wood to retain both charm and style.

Double rooms are located both in the main building and in the newly-built pavilion with garden and inner colonnade, reminiscent of a cloister, which also houses luxurious suites. All rooms have air conditioning, loggia and wonderful views of the landscaped gardens.

The elegant Tre Stagioni restaurant provides a range of culinary creations prepared with natural products from the estate, including their own Merlot wine.

As one may expect, the service in the restaurant is both attentive and discreet.

For the more active-minded honeymooners, you can choose from a variety of sports activities. The hotel boasts a fitness centre, running track and pool among other pursuits, and afterwards, you can visit the beauty parlour. Or perhaps you'd rather while away the time in the peace and tranquillity of the gardens. There is access to private beaches with small boats, and a private bus service to nearby Ascona.

139

SFr480-690 (67)

SFr840-1,320 (18)

SFr50-90

included

Honeymoon specials

Honeymoon packages of two and three nights cost SFr1,210-2,640 including champagne breakfast with caviar and smoked salmon, candlelit dinner, lunch *al fresco*, a free beauty treatment for ladies and a free massage for gentlemen.

Sightseeing and leisure

Cycling, hiking and boat trips. Excursions into Italy, or a short stroll around the old town of Ascona. Free use of the hotel's running track, swimming pool, fitness centre with sauna, thermarium and solarium. Tennis, windsurfing, massage and 18-hole golf course at extra charge.

Information & Reservations
UK 0870 606 1296
INT. +44 870 606 1296

Bahnhofstrasse
3920 Zermatt
Switzerland

✈ Geneva 90 mins

tel +41 27 966 6600
fax +41 27 966 6699

zermatterhof@specialhotels.com
www.specialhotels.com
www.zermatt.ch/zermatterhof

Closed Oct-Nov

Tour operators:
UK Elegant Resorts
Cadogan Holidays

Member of:
Preferred Hotels

140

Dwarfed by the towering slopes of the mighty Matterhorn, lies Zermatt, home to the five-star Grand Hotel Zermatterhof.

The hotel was opened in 1879, yet recent renovations have seen this historical building updated with the ultimate in modern convenience. Eighty-six rooms are available including those with canopied beds or beamed ceilings. Two-thirds of the rooms offer majestic mountain views and all offer the elegance and charm that has thrilled hundreds of guests including kings, princes, heads of state and celebrities alike.

The comfort of the hotel is hard to leave but with three excellent restaurants, excursions aren't really necessary. Every taste and dining occasion is catered for.

If you do venture outside, you certainly won't be disappointed. The resort is known for its year-round ski season, yet in summer the area around the hotel is lush and green. Nightlife and shopping are also excellent in the region, which has become a luxury playground for guests from around the world. Whether it's outside exploits or indoor luxury you're after, the Zermatterhof can oblige.

SFr420-770
SFr640-1,790
SFr45-95
SFr25

Honeymoon specials

Flowers, fruit, Swiss chocolates and champagne in room on arrival. Horse carriage transfer, deluxe dinner, free room service, room upgrade to a suite when possible. Also breakfast buffet and free use of sports facilities. Package price from SFr1,320-3,400.

Sightseeing and leisure

Semi-Olympic indoor pool, golf: putting and chipping green plus driving net, fitness room, sauna, whirlpool, massage and steambath. Excursions to Matterhorn, various mountain railways, museums, and of course skiing almost all year-round.

Le Montreux Palace

Grand Rue 100
1820 Montreux
Switzerland

✈ Geneva 90km

tel +41 21 962 12 12
fax +41 21 962 17 17

montreux@specialhotels.com
www.specialhotels.com
sales@swissmtx.mail.att.net
www.montreux-palace.com

Tour operators:
UK Kuoni, Gullivers

Situated on the idyllic shores of Lake Geneva and with breathtaking views of the French Alps, Le Montreux Palace was built at the start of the century. Connected by richly decorated ballrooms, this wondrous hotel has become know as a beautiful piece of *Belle Epoque* architecture in one of the most popular cities in the world.

The 235 bedrooms feature all the mod cons, including individual air-conditioning, amid modern yet sophisticated decoration. These sumptuous rooms offer both comfort and style, a perfect combination for relaxation and romance.

Within the hotel itself are a selection of restaurants offering a variety of food. Whether you would like a light snack or a sumptuous three-course romantic candlelit meal, all tastes are catered for. For that after-dinner drink in the perfect setting, try Harry's New York Bar or Bar Rose d'Or. For the truly adventurous, the nightclub Backstage is worth a visit.

For relaxation there is a fitness room, Shiatsu massage, outdoor swimming pool and tennis courts. In the city of Montreux, golf, skiing, boat cruises and hot air ballooning are within easy reach.

141

SFr450-650 (180)
SFr850-3,500 (53)
from SFr70
from SFr28

Honeymoon specials

Suite offered if wedding dinner is held in Montreux Palace or Chateau d'Oron. Package: Deluxe lakeview room for two nights, breakfast buffet, one five-course candlelit dinner in the hotel's gourmet restaurant, champagne, chocolate, fruits and flowers in room, welcome drink, use of fitness facilities. Price: SFr1,180-1,593 per couple.

Sightseeing and leisure

Several boutiques, hairdresser, manicurist, Shiatsu massage, outdoor swimming pool and tennis court. Excursions to Gstaad and Zermatt. Also, in Montreux there is golf, waterskiing, windsurfing, skiing, hang-gliding, boat cruises, rafting, hiking, hot air ballooning, horseriding and mountain biking nearby.

Palace Hotel Gstaad

3780 Gstaad
Switzerland

✈ Geneva Int. 160km

tel +41 33 748 5000
fax +41 33 748 5001

palace@specialhotels.com
www.specialhotels.com
www.palace.ch

Closed April-May; Oct-18 Dec

Tour operators:
UK Elegant Resorts

142

Member of:
Leading Hotels of the World

This deluxe hotel, surrounded by pine trees and adorned with castle turrets and towers, is perched atop a hill above the village of Gstaad in the Bernese Alps. Owned and managed by the same family for two generations, the Palace Hotel exudes a friendly and welcoming atmosphere.

The rooms and suites are decorated with soft floral prints, large wooden beams and traditionally carved furniture. Most have private balconies with views extending across snow-capped peaks.

Le Restaurant is a perfect setting in which to enjoy a variety of international cuisine. For more informal dining, there is La Fromagerie, which boasts delicious traditional dishes such as *fondue* and *raclette*, or the canopied terrace set against the backdrop of a superb Alpine panorama.

After dinner, guests can dance the night away to the live band, or try out the GreenGo disco, one of Gstaad's most popular night spots.

Or, there is the opportunity to be pampered at the hotel's Beautymed Centre, offering a wide variety of treatments provided by 'Clinique of the Prairie' of Switzerland. You can also shape up at the gym in the health and fitness centre or take to the

ski slopes. Hot air ballooning, horseriding and even heli-skiing are all available nearby for alternative ways to explore the area.

The hotel is happy to make arrangements for weddings, and will organise everything from flowers and orchestras to a Rolls Royce or horse-drawn carriage to convey the bride and groom.

 US$215-860 (76)

 US$692-1,650 (35)

🍽 from US$50

☕ US$20

Honeymoon specials
Flowers, fruit and champagne on arrival. Welcome gift. Free access to pools, gym, sauna and the GreenGo nightclub. Special deals available, please enquire. Hire the whole hotel for Sfr1,000 per person (min. 100 people) including two nights accommodation, breakfast, wedding reception and dinner. When possible, honeymooners will receive a room upgrade.

Sightseeing and leisure
The Beautymed Centre offers a wide variety of beauty treatments provided by the famous 'Clinique of the Prairie' of Switzerland. Swimming pools, tennis, squash, gym, fitness centre with sauna, steam bath and massage. Horseriding, year-round skiing. Trips to Church of Saanen and the Lauenen Lake nearby. There are also several festivals throughout the year.

Suvretta House

Via Chasellas 1
7500 St Moritz
Switzerland

✈ Zurich 220km
Milano 175km

tel +41 81 832 11 32
fax +41 81 833 85 24

suvretta@specialhotels.com
www.specialhotels.com
suvrettahouse@compunet.ch
www.engadin.ch/suvrettahouse

Tour operators:
UK Elegant Resorts

Located in the famous town of St Moritz, this hotel has all the glamour and glitz you would expect to find in one of Europe's top resorts. Set in an inspired location, ringed by tall, fragrant pine trees and larch and with a stunning view of the mountains and lakes of the Upper Engadine, this grand hotel, which was constructed in 1911, is still just a stone's throw from the centre of town.

And with a private ski lift and a chair lift it is also one of the best places from which to explore the excellent ski slopes in winter or the greenery, flower blossoms and colourful mountain scenery in summer.

Personal service is the key to the success of this elegant hotel. The staff create a restful, relaxed atmosphere and carry on the local tradition of warm hospitality and a desire to make sure every visitor will always dream of returning.

Mouth-watering cuisine awaits you at Suvretta House. What could be better than indulging in one of the chef's carefully planned local specialities after a day on the slopes? Along with brightly burning log fires to warm you, hot baths to soothe weary limbs and hugely comfortable rooms with beautiful mountain views, the personal care will astound you and make you feel right at home. Summer or winter, this is a place where sport and relaxation go hand in hand and where everyone is made to feel that extra bit special.

143

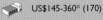 US$145-360* (170)
 US$645-1,015** (40)
 US$36-65
 included

Honeymoon specials
Complimentary flowers, fruit basket and local wine on arrival.

* Prices per person per day on half-board basis inc. taxes.
** Prices per room per day on half-board basis inc. taxes.

Sightseeing and leisure
Engadine mountains, horseracing events, polo, dog races, cricket on frozen lake, skating marathons; in summer hiking, biking, golf and the British Classic Car Meeting. Beauty treatments, massage, solarium, gym, indoor pool. Ice skating rink, curling, tennis, golf driving range and putting green.

Turkey

flying time
To: Istanbul, Antalya
London: 3-4½ hrs
NY: 10½ hrs

climate/ when to go
Warm throughout the year, Turkey is a popular winter sun destination, especially along the coast.. Istanbul is a good destination to visit any time of year.

currency
Turkish lire.

language
Turkish but English is widely spoken.

getting around
Internal flights operate regularly between the major cities. There are also good bus and train connections. In Istanbul, explore on foot or travel by taxi. Also use the boats – ferries, water taxis and sea buses.

The place where east meets west, where the familiarity of Europe blends easily with the spice of the Orient. A heady mix which is best explored in the ancient, and beautiful, city of Istanbul. Lying on the banks of the Bosphorus, 2000 years of history permeates the air, from the sumptuous Topkapi Palace to the six slender minarets of the famous Blue Mosque and the frenetic alleys of the Bazaar Quarter.

A city dominated by the swath of water that cuts through its heart, exploring the intricacies of the waterway and the city beyond is all part of the mystery and beauty of ancient Istanbul.

Beyond the city lies 5,000 miles of stunning coastline from the beautiful bay of Izmir, encircled by tall mountains, to Patara with its 11 miles of sandy beach. The vast waters of the Black Sea in the north gives way to the Bosphorus, the Marmara Sea, the Aegean in the west and the Mediterranean in the east.

But Turkey is a destination full of surprises. Amazingly, tulips were first grown in Turkey many, many years ago and St Nicholas (or Father Christmas as he his known today) was born here. Turkish food, also, is exotic and divine and rates among Europe's top cuisines.

The other lasting memory is the warmth of the people of this land. They are kind and giving and believe that a visitor is a 'guest from God' and should be welcomed accordingly.

Information & Reservations
UK 0870 606 1296
INT. +44 870 606 1296

Ciragan Caddesi 84
Besiktas 80700
Istanbul
Turkey

✈ Istanbul 25km

tel +90 212 258 3377
fax +90 212 259 6687

ciragan@specialhotels.com
www.specialhotels.com
www.ciraganpalace.com

In the city where east meets west, this palace is the perfect place to blend the spice and mystique of the east with the glamour and modern-day comfort of the west.

Home of the last Ottoman Sultans, the Ciragan Palace is the only hotel in Istanbul located directly on the shores of the striking and mysterious Bosphorus. The property is surrounded by beautifully manicured gardens, terraces and promenades that skirt the shoreline.

Choose between sumptuous suites in the rambling 19th-century marble palace itself, or rooms and suites in the grand hotel in the grounds. Whichever you decide on, you can rest assured your surroundings will be quite stunning and the service excellent.

Of course no visit to Istanbul would be complete without a Turkish massage which can be arranged at the hotel. There are experts on hand to work out any knots you may have developed during your pre-wedding day rush. And for the more active, there is also an indoor and outdoor swimming pool, a sauna and fitness centre, as well as a 9-hole putting green and a solarium at your disposal.

Beyond the magic of this fine hotel, explore the mixing of the cultures and the history of three great civilizations from the Romans and Byzantines to the Ottoman Empire before returning to the calm oasis that is the Ciragan Palace.

145

 US$260-550 (282)

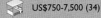 US$750-7,500 (34)

🍽 US$42-89

☕ US$26

Honeymoon specials
Local champagne, fruits and sweets on arrival. Continental breakfast and dinner included in some packages.

Leisure facilities
Full range of leisure and sporting activities, such as pools, sauna and fitness centre. There is also a putting green.

Sightseeing
Istanbul is the cultural and artistic centre of Turkey with galleries, architecture and historical sights on the hotel's doorstep. The hotel itself is a 19th century historical palace. Situated on the shores of the Bosphorus, the views are spectacular and the hotel and palace are surrounded by beautiful gardens and rambling terraces.

flying time
To: London,
Manchester,
Glasgow, Edinburgh
NY: 7 hrs
LA: 12-13 hrs

climate
Famously wet. Cold
but not necessarily
icy in winter, warm
but not necessarily
sunny in summer.
You should not rely
on the weather.

when to go
Apr-May for green
landscapes lit by
starbursts of
wildflowers. June
kicks off the tourist
season. Sept-Oct
for gentle warmth,
mellow light with
fewer tourists.

currency
Pound sterling. In
Southern Ireland the
Irish pound or punt.

language
English.

getting around
Internal flights to
main cities rarely
take as much as one
hour. Public transport
is efficient – both rail
and buses.

The United Kingdom is an island nation, made up of two main islands and more than 5,000 smaller ones, with a sea which is always near. Whether at the tight coves and jagged cliffs of Cornwall, the wild Atlantic coastline of Connemarra in the west of Ireland, or the gently sloping, pebbly shores of the English Channel. This is most certainly a place of variety and surprises.

The English countryside is crowded with natural wonders including caves, ancient woods, wild waterfalls, fertile meadows and bleak moorland. It also has many glorious man-made features – stately homes with follies and manicured parks; Neolithic standing stones, ruined castles and abbeys. And few cities can match for culture and elegance the sophisticated cosmopolitan capital of London.

Scotland is famous for its unspoilt and rugged countryside yet offers metropolitan delights in equal measure in places like Edinburgh and Glasgow. Alternatively, to get away from it all, there are the stunning islands of the Hebrides, rich in history and wildlife, the glories of the snow-capped Highlands and the grandeur and melodic charm of the great lochs.

Haunting melodies are in plentiful supply in Ireland. So is a wealth of culture and beautiful scenery. A scraping fiddle in a Dublin pub, or a beer by a peat fire in County Mayo – everywhere you go the people are easy to meet and invariably courteous and friendly. Here it is possible to stay in tranquil country houses where the proportions and the furnishings of the rooms are redolent of a more gracious age.

Whether you honeymoon in England, Scotland or Ireland, you will find yourself amidst the culture, style and convenience of modern-day Europe and lose yourself in wilderness and beauty.

Chewton Glen

New Milton
Hampshire BH25 6QS
England

✈ Heathrow 85 miles
Southampton 22 miles

tel +44 (0) 1425 275 341
fax +44 (0) 1425 272 310

chewton@specialhotels.com
www.specialhotels.com
sales@chewtonglen.com
www.chewtonglen.com

Member of:
Relais & Chateaux

Located in 70 acres of wooded and landscaped parkland, in the quiet of the English rolling countryside, Chewton Glen Hotel contains over 250 years of rich heritage.

Its simple 18th-century manor house exterior gives no hint of the luxury within. Each of the beautiful guest rooms is furnished to the highest standards and touches like overstuffed sofas, roaring log fires and the decanter of fine sherry in the rooms explain why this hotel has been cherished by its many regular guests – including the late Cary Grant.

Many guests come to luxuriate in the facilities and treatments available from the modernised health spa. Others enjoy the natural beauty of the grounds and proximity to sites such as Stonehenge and the New Forest. Yet all who stay enjoy the chance to dine in the hotel's Marryat restaurant, which currently holds a coveted Michelin Star.

It is no wonder, therefore, that Chewton Glen has a reputation as the primary UK country house hotel. In the last eight years it has won no less than 23 awards. It's currently the only privately owned Five Red Star Hotel in Britain and was recently proclaimed Best Resort Hotel in Britain by the UK's Condé Nast *Traveller* magazine.

147

🛏 £230-355 (53)

🛋 £355-530 (16)

🍽 from £50

☕ £12.50-16

Honeymoon specials
Chewton Glen offers special packages; information available upon request.

Sightseeing
Lymington, Ringwood, Christchurch, Salisbury Markets, Stonehenge, Salisbury and Winchester Cathedrals, various National Trust houses.

Leisure facilities
Health club offers over 30 treatments using the finest natural products. There is a 9-hole, par-3 golf course on site, two indoor tennis courts, two outdoor courts, croquet lawn, gym, pool, sauna, steamroom and hair salon. Resident tennis professional.

Fawsley Hall

Fawsley
nr Daventry
Northamptonshire
NN11 3BA
England

✈ Birmingham 72km

tel +44 (0) 1327 89 2000
fax +44 (0) 1327 89 2001

fawsley@specialhotels.com
www.specialhotels.com

148 Member of:
Grand Heritage Hotels

Fawsley Hall is a real-life country house hotel, lovingly restored over the last 20 years. With parts of the building dating back to the 15th century, the hotel is steeped in history. The gardens and lakes were designed by none other than the renowned landscape gardener Capability Brown, while the restaurant occupies what was once the Elizabethan kitchen and upstairs is a room where the great lady herself, Elizabeth I, actually slept in 1575.

Antiques abound, from the vaulted grand entrance through to the comfortable rooms. Stone fireplaces, grand sofas, ancient wooden doors and Tudor-plastered, cream-fresh walls all provide the comfort and solidity that one would expect of an English country house. The bedrooms are spacious, with wide, well-sprung beds, crisp linen and sumptuous pillows.

The Hall's restaurant is something else again. With a three-star Michelin chef acting as consultant, you are in for a real treat. Dishes on the menu include such mouth-watering delights as red mullet gazpacho or roast pigeon and braised Savoy cabbage with *foie gras* and lentil sauce. No trouble is too much to create the perfect recipe: the mushrooms for the risotto are flown in specially from France.

🛏 £160-260 (27)

🛏 £415-710 (3)

🍽 £16-50

☕ included

♿ 🍾 🚁

Honeymoon specials
Champagne and flowers in room on arrival.

Leisure facilities
The hotel offers tennis court, golf nearby and beautiful walks around the property and surrounding countryside.

Sightseeing
Nearby are historic places to visit such as Warwick Castle and Shakespeare's home of Stratford-upon-Avon. Althorpe is also close by, and many rambling Capability Brown gardens for walks.

Halcyon Hotel

81 Holland Park
London W11 3RZ
England

✈ Heathrow 20km

tel +44 (0) 171 727 7288
fax +44 (0) 171 229 8516

halcyon@specialhotels.com
www.specialhotels.com
www.halcyon-
hotel@compuserv.com

Member of:
Johansens
Best Loved Hotels

Discreetly occupying two imposing and superbly restored *Belle Epoque* townhouses in this beautiful residential area, the Halcyon is a short taxi ride from Harrods, Piccadilly and Oxford Street; the shops, theatres, museums and nightlife of London.

Described by the *Los Angeles Times* as "London's most elegant little hotel, the city's best-kept secret", your welcome in the impressive reception with its antique grandfather clock and roaring fire will set the tone for your stay. The hotel won the 1998 AA Hotel Guide Courtesy & Care Award.

All the individually designed rooms, some with four poster beds, have marble bathrooms, and are furnished with striking antiques and fabrics. French windows and covered balconies feature in many rooms. A stroll down the broad avenue will bring you to the historic park itself, 54 acres of woodlands and gardens where peacocks roam.

The hotel's restaurant, The Room, is famous in its own right and serves distinctive international cuisine accompanied by a well-chosen wine list. The Cocktail Bar also offers an elegant and relaxing haven.

Guests benefit from membership of the nearby exclusive Vanderbilt Tennis Club and Lambton Place Health Club with indoor tennis courts, swimming pool, Jacuzzi, sauna and steamroom.

149

🛏 £225-650 (24)
🛋 £305-650 (18)
🍽 £18-40
☕ £15

Honeymoon specials
Junior suite, champagne breakfast, chauffeur driven car from the airport, flowers in room on arrival, newspapers.

Sightseeing and leisure
All the sights and attractions of a central London hotel: Kensington Palace, Portobello Antiques market, Albert Hall, Knightsbridge, Harrods, theatres and cafes. Holland Park is nearby for running/walking. Health club, 'About Face' local beauty salon. Make-up artists supplied on request.

The Lodge and Spa at
Inchydoney Island

Clonakilty
West Cork
Ireland

✈ Cork 30 miles

tel +353 23 33143
fax +353 23 35229

inchydoney@specialhotels.com
www.specialhotels.com
www.inchydoneyisland.com

Tour operators:
UK Erna Low, Thermalia
Quest of the Classics

150

The lovely island of Inchydoney in West Cork, Ireland, is a haven of peace and tranquillity. Here, the sky is endless, the scenery breathtaking, the very air pervaded with a delightful calm that Ireland is so famous for. The warm gulf stream waters caress the shores and rocky promontories and the traditional Irish hospitality ensures that all guests receive a real 'County Cork welcome' at the Lodge and Spa.

The residents' lounge and library are warm and cosy with comfy armchairs clustered round an open fire and a piano waiting for an evening sing song. All the rooms are large but very warmly decorated in attractive hues of orange and yellow. Original artworks and pieces grace the walls throughout and from the front windows you have an interrupted sweeping panorama of the vast landscape and ocean beyond.

The Gulfstream Restaurant, with its huge sea-

 US$290-418 (4)

 US$218-290 (67)

 US$30-50

 US$16.50-20

Honeymoon specials
Complimentary champagne and flowers in room on arrival.
Transfers from airport to the Lodge.

facing windows, is a bright and cheery room and serves a fine selection of international cuisine as well as traditional Irish specialities. Its impeccable surroundings and decor are inviting and you'll feel not only welcome, but treated with wonderful hospitality and service.

   While here, you will want to make the most of the luxury Thalasso spa with its Jacuzzi's, huge freeform swimming pool and vast range of treatments. There are 18 in total, and there are experts on hand to advise should you be undecided which to go for first. There is also reflexology, hydrotherapy and various aerobics programmes for the fitness buffs. Outside, other healthy activities may tempt you, including cycling the lanes of West Cork, golf, sailing and horseriding. For romance, stroll along the famous Inchydoney beaches at sunset before a late night pick-me-up at the Dunes Pub.

Sightseeing

Michael Collins Memorial, Cork English Market, racing at Kinsale, Glendore, Castle Townsend.

Leisure facilities

Thalasso spa with 18 treatments using warmed sea water plus beauty salon which uses Edelle products.

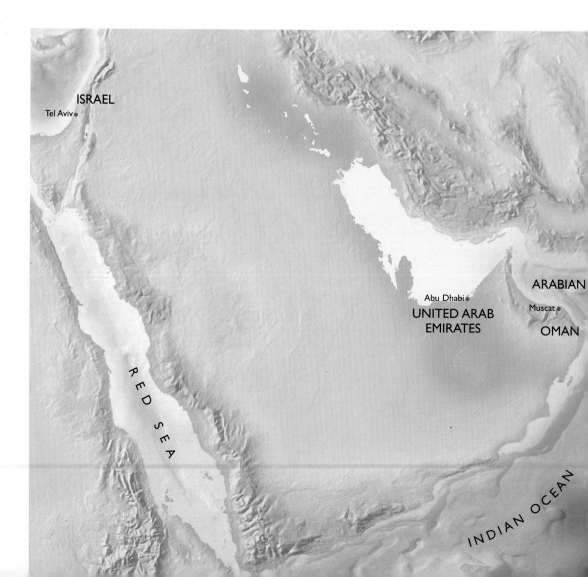

ISRAEL

Tel Aviv

ARABIAN

Abu Dhabi

Muscat

UNITED ARAB
EMIRATES

OMAN

RED SEA

INDIAN OCEAN

T ravel to most parts of the Middle East is left far behind. This is the land of 'The Thousand and One Nights'; a mixed bag of colour and magic, wonderful hospitality, spectacular archeological sites and history, adventure and surprise.

Romantic Crusader castles perch spectacularly on mountain ranges in the deserts of Syria while in Yemen's Old City mosque minarets rise high above the ancient houses. Jordan's one-time capital Petra, built in the 3rd century BC, was forgotten for a thousand years and only rediscovered in the 19th century.

Israel can offer the eerie, but awe-inspiring, Dead Sea, diving pleasures in the Red Sea, and the historical Jerusalem, perhaps the most fascinating city in the world.

As well as the sights, there are beautiful beaches aplenty, snake charmers, lively coffee houses, belly dancers, bazaars bursting with carpets, Bedouin rugs, spices and pearls and a whole range of activities from skiing to desert safaris.

For those with a taste for the strange and exotic, the Middle Eastern countries can certainly prove to be a very richly rewarding honeymoon destination.

Israel

154

flying time
To: Tel Aviv
London: 5 hrs
LA: 16-17 hrs
NY: 12 hrs

climate
Summers (Apr-Oct) are hot and dry. Winters are mild with some rain, though it can be chilly in Jerusalem, for example. The warmer south can be uncomfortably hot in mid-summer.

currency
Shekles but US dollars are readily accepted in hotels, bars and markets.

language
Arabic, Hebrew and English.

when to go
Summer is the main season on the Mediterranean coast while autumn, winter and spring are the most popular seasons to visit Eilat and the desert. Spring is a good time for birdwatching.

The State of Israel is young, celebrating its 50th anniversary in 1998, but the history of the land is palpable.

The landscapes of fertile plains and arid desert seem little changed from descriptions in the Bible.

Its surprisingly small area contains a rich variety of scenery, and ancient and religious sites. In winter you can ski on the snow-capped slopes of Mt Hermon in the north or take a jeep safari into the southern desert. In summer you can wonder at Roman monuments in the morning and swim in the Mediterranean after lunch. You will never be far from a beach. Along the Mediterranean coast Tel Aviv, Herzliya and Netanya have long stretches of sand, abundant watersports, and a huge choice of eating places and nightlife, while at the Red Sea resort of Eilat you can enjoy year-round sunshine and world-class Scuba diving.

Jerusalem must be right at the top of any visitor's sightseeing agenda. The stones of this fascinating city breathe history, and it is as sacred to Muslims and Christians as to Jews. While Jews offer prayers at the Western, or Wailing Wall, along the Via Dolorosa pilgrims follow the alleyways where Jesus is said to have carried the cross to his crucifixion.

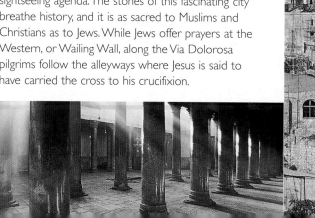

The American Colony Hotel

PO Box 19215
Jerusalem 97200
Israel

✈ Ben Guirion 45 mins

tel +972 2 6279777
fax +972 2 6279779

american@specialhotels.com
www.specialhotels.com
www.americancolony.com

Member of:
Relais & Chateaux

Tour operators:
UK & US Utell Int.

The American Colony Hotel has been catering for travellers to the Holy City for over 100 years. A major draw is its central location. It can be hard to believe, as you stroll in the lush gardens of the hotel, that just a few minutes away are such evocative sites as the Western Wall, the Garden of Gethsemane and the Damascus Gate.

The hotel is a former Pasha's Palace, meaning the 84 rooms and suites are all opulently designed and equipped with all amenities. On site are several restaurants, a bistro-type for small meals and snacks at the Poolside, and the Arabesque dining room with its high class menu and beautiful setting in the courtyard for memorable evenings.

After dining retire to one of the hotel's bars and lounges. Ibrahim's Summer Bar is in the middle of the gardens, while the Cellar Bar has the biggest single malt selection in the country and takes you into the world of Humphrey Bogart's *Casablanca*.

Modern Jerusalem is a mix of ancient history and contemporary culture and as such caters for the most sophisticated tourist tastes.

Days can be spent exploring Jerusalem, with its immense religious and archaeological interests. In the evening choose from dance, theatre and film, all which are just minutes from 'home'.

155

 US$190-345 (76)

 US$360-410

 included

Honeymoon specials

Package based on a four-night stay. This includes a Pasha-style room with an upgrade to the best available room, a bottle of sparkling wine, flowers, fruit basket and sweets on arrival, honeymoon cake, guided half-day tour of the Old City, gift from the hotel, and champagne breakfast served in the room. Cost: US$1,500.

Sightseeing and leisure

Within 10 minutes are the holy sites of Jerusalem's Old City, including the Western Wall, Dome of the Rock, Garden of Gethsemane, Holy Sepulchre and the Via Dolorosa.

Dan Eilat

Hotel Area
North Beach
Eilat 88101
Israel

✈ Eilat 2km

tel +972 7 636 2222
fax +972 7 636 2333

daneilat@specialhotels.com
www.specialhotels.com
www.danhotelses.com

156

Located on the sweeping coast of the glorious Red Sea, Eilat is a vacationer's dream. White sands, blue seas and an abundance of marine life lie to the south, while desert and astonishing valleys span the north.

Set on its own stretch of beach within this paradise you'll find the gleaming white walls of the Dan Eilat hotel. With its 378 comfortably furnished rooms it offers every convenience the traveller needs. The restaurants and bars in the property are too numerous to list but all offer high standards of cuisine and attentive service. It's easy to work up an appetite in the hotel's two pools, the extensive fitness gym and on the squash courts.

Outside there is much to explore. The unspoilt desert beckons visitors to its stillness and the nearby Great Rift Valley is one of the world's leading natural phenomena. Diving and snorkelling in the area are excellent and of course, no trip to Eilat would be complete without a trip to the world famous dolphin reef where these beautiful mammals let you enter their world just for a while, but create an experience you will never forget.

 US$224-582 (382)

 US$350-1,550 (47)

 US$30-50

 US$7-15

Honeymoon specials
Room upgrade, champagne and flowers on arrival.

Sightseeing and leisure
All manner of sports including squash and tennis. The hotel also has its own gym, Turkish Bath, sauna, spa and Jacuzzi. Rich tropical marine life to be explored, coral reefs, underwater observatories and wildlife nature reserve nearby.

Eilat Princess Hotel

Taba Beach
PO Box 2323
Eilat 88000

srael

✈ Eilat Airport 10km

el +972 7 636 5500
ax +972 7 637 6333

princess@specialhotels.com
www.specialhotels.com
nisrael.com/princess

Tour operators:
UK All main operators

Poised between the granite rockface of the desert and the immense blue expanse of the Red Sea, the Eilat Princess sits among extensive landscaped gardens on the southernmost tip of Israel.

The rooms are dressed in cool cotton prints, with king-size beds and balconies that provide sweeping views across the bay to Jordan and Saudi Arabia. Each floor also offers suites with an exotic theme ranging from Thai to Russian, Indian to Chinese. All are romantic and secluded.

Authentic Creole, traditional French, delicate Szechwan, and exotic Japanese are among the several varieties of cuisine that are prepared by award-winning chefs in a variety of venues.

The countless pools and sundecks around the landscaped gardens are connected by a series of bridges with a Venetian inspiration. Whirlpools, waterfalls, waterchutes and underwater grottos are among the park's attractions, and a variety of watersports are also available. The semi-private bathing beach offers unparalleled diving and snorkelling, and guests can be pampered at the hotel's spa complex with 12 treatment rooms, beauty parlour and health bar.

157

For those wishing to hold their reception here, the hotel has extensive experience in organising receptions and can provide in-house designers and florists to assist with all preparations.

US$257–541 (356)

US$430–1300 (64)

from US$37

from US$20

Honeymoon specials

Champagne, flowers and cake on arrival. Room upgrade subject to availability. Free shuttle service to/from hotel. Honeymooners can enjoy a champagne breakfast in their room. Free entrance to the Sansara Spa and Fitness Centre. Plus 10% discount on à la carte restaurants at the hotel.

Sightseeing and leisure

Trips to underwater observatory, dolphin reef, ostrich farm. Outdoor Jacuzzi, waterslides, tennis courts and Sansara Spa and Fitness Centre with Finnish sauna, gym, private massage and treatment rooms. Scuba diving, parasailing, windsurfing, snorkelling and waterskiing are available nearby.

Jerusalem Hotel

4 Antara Ben Shaddad St
PO box 19130
Jerusalem
Israel

✈ Ben Gurion 40km

tel +972 2 628 3282
fax +972 2 628 3282

Toll free reservations:
UK 0800 3282393
US +800 657 9401

158

jerusalem@specialhotels.com
www.specialhotels.com
www.jrshotel.com

Originally built by a feudal lord in the heart of the ancient city of Jerusalem, the Jerusalem Hotel, which is family-owned, has been lavishly refurbished in recent years. The authentic Arab architecture of the last century has been retained and accentuated in the high ceilings, arched windows, cool stone flagging and secluded vine garden. The thick stone walls, cut from creamy Jerusalem stone, have been exposed and pointed with a traditional Arabic plaster.

Each of the 14 rooms is individually and timelessly decorated with antiques and has a beautiful oriental inspiration. Private balconies overlook the twisting narrow streets and clamorous markets of Jerusalem's Old City, and the ancient peaceful slopes of The Mount of Olives.

The Eastern influence is continued in the excellent Palestinian cuisine, served to guests at The Vine Restaurant, in the privacy of the pretty garden. Flavourful Bedouin dishes and other local ethnic foods are also a must to try.

From the hotel's enviable location in the heart of Jerusalem – only 100 metres from the famous Damascus Gate – it's easy to wander among a number of historical and religious sites, stroll along the city ramparts at sunset, browse bustling markets, or trek into the nearby Judaen Desert.

 US$85-115 (14)

 from US$15

 included

Honeymoon specials
Flowers and champagne on arrival. Complimentary night tour to the Windmill Garden, with magnificent views of Jerusalem's Old City walls.

Sightseeing and leisure
Visits to the main markets of the Old City, the Holy Sepulchre, Wailing Wall and Garden Tomb. Hiking trails nearby. Musical and cultural events throughout the year. Beauty salons and health spas available in the area.

Royal Beach Hotel

Eilat
Israel

✈ Eilat Central 2km

Contact:
Central Reservation Office
North Beach, Eilat 88000

tel +972 7 636 8888
fax +972 7 636 8811

royalbeach@specialhotels.com
www.specialhotels.com
royal-beach@isrotel.co.il

Part of: The Isrotel Hotel Chain

The Royal Beach Hotel sits at the southern tip of Israel. Here, shimmering desert and red-hued mountain ranges meet the coral-filled waters of the Red Sea. The resort boasts three swimming pools with cascading waterfalls and wide expanses of lawns dotted with sunbeds and shaded by date palms which overlook the hotel's beach.

All 366 rooms and suites boast south-facing balconies which command sweeping views across the bay. Works of art, rich furnishings and wooden furniture lend a regal feel, while bright floral arrangements add a welcoming touch.

American, Italian, Chinese and Jewish cuisine, all prepared with the freshest ingredients, are served with elegance and style in a variety of speciality and ethnic restaurants.

Eilat is characterised by the Red Sea and offers every possible experience in, on, under and around the water. The Coral Beach nature reserve is one of the richest displays of marine life and corals in the world – to be observed by diving, snorkelling, glass-bottom-boat excursions or at the underwater observatory. Visitors to the Dolphin Reef can view and even swim with these amazing mammals.

159

 £709 (315)

 £1,269 (18)

 US$50-150

 US$13

Honeymoon specials
Complimentary dinner for two, special VIP treatment, surprise gifts in the room, two t-shirts from the hotel, room upgrade subject to availability, plus photo album.

Leisure facilities
Health club, gymnasium, sauna, Jacuzzi, Synagogue, all watersports. Deep-sea fishing.

Sightseeing
Safaris, swimming with dolphins, underwater observatory, desert exploration by camel, mountain bike, air-conditioned car or all-terrain vehicle. Trips to Timna Valley National Park featuring King Solomon's pillars, Red Canyon, biblical wildlife reserve and bird-watching park.

The Gulf States

This area of the Middle East has long been a hot-bed of political activity. It is also rich in history, oil and archaeological interests. To travel to the Gulf States is to experience a culture unlike any other.

flying time
Oman: 7 1/2 hrs
UAE: 7 hrs

**climate/
when to go**
The best time to visit
is Nov-Mar when it is
mild during the day
(25-35°C) and cooler
at night (17-19°C).
April-Oct can get up
to 49°C with 90%
humidity. The Gulf
States are Muslim so
dress appropriately.

160

currency
Oman: Omani Rial
UAE: UAE Dirham

language
Arabic but English
is widely spoken in
tourist areas.

getting around
Taxis or courtesy
buses from hotels.
International driving
permits are needed
for car hire and
women are not
allowed to drive
alone.

visas
Those with Israeli or
South African stamps
in their passports are
forbidden entry to
Oman.

Oman

Occupying the south-eastern tip of the Arabian Peninsula, boasting 1,700 kilometres of coastline, Oman is a country of contradictions. The north of the country sees rugged mountains framing swathes of desert, yet the south is lush and green. Picturesque old buildings sit shoulder to shoulder with modern architecture and at the coast, working coconut groves brush alongside white sand beaches that frame the cool blue sea.

Oman has much to offer the active visitor including diving, rock climbing, sand-skiing and golf. There is a rich archaeological history to explore and exquisite silver and woven bargains to be had in the labyrinthine *souk* in Muscat. And remember, getting lost is half the fun.

United Arab Emirates

Established in 1971, the United Arab Emirates consists of seven separate Emirates, or states. Bordered by Oman to the east and Saudi Arabia to the south, it's the north-eastern tip of the country that draws most visitors to its miles of untouched beaches framed by the calm seas of the Arabian Gulf.

For many visitors the beaches vie for attention with the cosmopolitan towns of either Dubai or Abu Dhabi. Here hotel accommodation is first class and the duty free bargains unrivalled. Yet outside of the major towns there is much to do as well. Caves, sand dunes, archaeological explorations and natural hot springs offer a myriad of experiences to fill every day.

Al Bustan
Palace Hotel

PO Box 1998
Muttrah
Sultanate of Oman

✈ Seeb Int. 35km

tel +968 799 666
fax +968 799 600

albustan@specialhotels.com
www.specialhotels.com

Tour operators:
UK Elegant Resorts
Kuoni

Enjoy the grand and exotic and stay at what is reputed to be one of the finest hotels in the world.

The Al Bustan Palace is set in 200 acres of lush gardens, surrounded by a dramatic mountain backdrop, sea and beach. Originally built to host the 1985 Gulf Cooperation Council Summit in Muscat and used to host heads of state, prime ministers and other government ministers, the hotel is now a sumptuous retreat for leisure travellers.

A five-star hotel, it boasts some 250 rooms, including a selection of junior and grand deluxe suites. All have modern day amenities from telephone with voice mail to video cassette recorders, 24-hour room service and valet service.

Indulge in the finest Middle Eastern cuisine and the best gourmet dining in Muscat at the Al Marjan Restaurant or enjoy live Arabic entertainment at the Al Hamra Supper Club. The choice is wide but more local culture is available at the Seblat al Bustan where an authentic Omani dinner with traditional music is hosted once a week.

Make the most of the superb leisure facilities, from the four floodlit clay tennis courts and full time instructor to the state-of-the-art, fully equipped gym and beauty salon, variety of watersports and deep-sea fishing trips or coastal cruises launched from the resort's marina.

161

🛏 US$297-365 (200)
🛎 US$368-1,215 (50)
🍽 US$32
☕ US$17
♿ 🍷 🚁 Ⓢ

Honeymoon specials
Upgrade to a superior room depending on availabilty, complimentary bottle of sparkling wine, flowers and fruit basket on arrival.

Sightseeing and leisure
Bait Al Zubair Museum, featuring antique Omani artefacts and jewellery. Muttrah Souq for gold jewellery, silver and pottery. Al Alam Palace, Jalali and Mirini forts.

Ajman Kempinski
Hotel & Resort

PO Box 3025
Ajman
United Arab
Emirates

✈ Dubai 26km
Sharjah 20km

tel +971 6 451 555
fax +971 6 451 222

ajman.kempinski@kemp-aj.com
ajman@specialhotels.com
www.specialhotels.com

162

Characterised by its miles of pure white sand, Ajman is one of the seven Emirates that make up the UAE. Relatively unknown to tourism, it offers a quiet alternative to the nearby hustle and bustle of Dubai or Abu Dhabi.

Set directly on a private stretch of this perfect, powdery sand, the ultra-modern Ajman Kempinski offers every visitor an irresistible combination of kind hospitality and rich tradition.

No matter what your preference the hotel has a room to suit your needs. Select from top-class deluxe seafront rooms, private cabanas or the ultimately luxurious royal suite. Whichever you

choose you are never far away from the hotel's unparalleled facilities.

Gourmands will relish evenings spent sampling Arabic, Szechwan, Indian and Mediterranean cuisine in the six on site restaurants. Meanwhile, sports-lovers will revel in the vast fitness and watersports opportunities. Try bowling, tennis, putting or book excursions to the spectacular ship wrecks through the PADI dive centre. Shoppers can take the free shuttle to nearby Dubai where the shopping is second to none, or visit the small town of Ajman with its traditional boat building and markets.

🛏 US$205-288* (189)

🛋 US$411-1,370* (12)

🍽 from US$28

☕ US$13

Honeymoon specials
The hotel's package includes flowers, dates, champagne in the room and a traditional gift from the region, from Dhs 708 staying in a double room. Supplement for junior suite of Dhs 500 per night*.

Prices subject to 15% service charge.

Sightseeing and leisure
Excursions around the typical fishing village of Ajman. The Dhow building dock and museum are main attractions. Guests may use the hotel's shuttle bus for shopping in nearby Dubai. Also, there is tennis, watersports, diving, gym, massage, reflexology, aromatherapy, golf putting green, squash courts nearby.

Hilton Beach Club

PO Box 26878
Dubai
United Arab
Emirates

✈ Dubai Int. 15km

tel +971 4 445 333
fax +971 4 446 222

beachclub@specialhotels.com
www.specialhotels.com

Tour operators:
UK Abercrombie & Kent
US Hilton Reservations
Worldwide +800 445 8667

Jumeirah is Dubai's most exclusive resort area and here, on a stretch of fine white sand, you'll find the private bungalow style rooms that make up the Hilton Beach Club.

There are 50 suites in all dotted around the tropical gardens and freshwater streams that surround the resort. Each room boosts a spacious lounge, music system, TV, video, Jacuzzi and large balcony or terrace. Whether you look over the gardens, the large pool or the private beach that surrounds the resort your view will be sublime.

Airy terraces or chic lounges characterise dining in the resort and many cuisines are catered for in the three restaurants and two bars just a short walk from your room. If you can't move from your sunbed, delivery can also be arranged. Also on the premises you'll find a superb health and fitness club, squash and tennis courts, two pools and many watersports.

Yet, the list of things to do doesn't end at the hotel's gate. Desert safaris, birdwatching, *souk* visits, or trips merely to explore the natural beauty of the area can easily be arranged for you – or why not hire a car and set out on your own?

163

 US$590-2,330 (50)

 US$30

US$17

Honeymoon specials
Complimentary sparkling wine and flowers on arrival.

Sightseeing and leisure
Choose from tennis, volleyball, squash and all watersports. There is also a health club in the hotel with state-of-the-art equipment. The beach is right on your doorstep, as are tropical gardens and lush surroundings to meander through. Also nearby are championship golf courses.

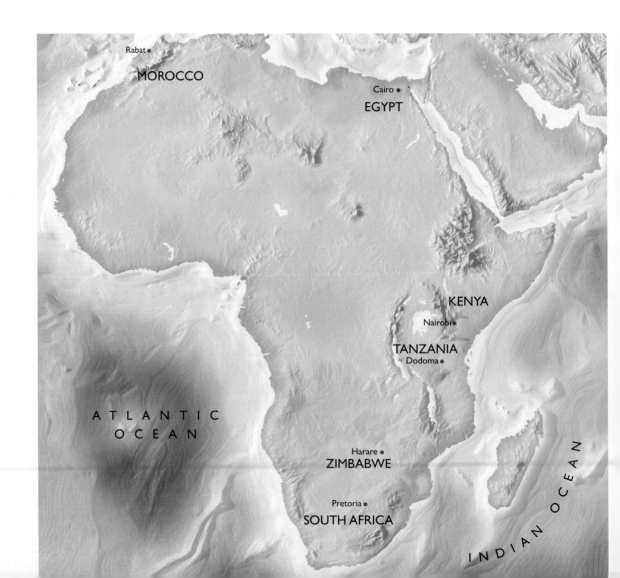

Rabat •
MOROCCO

Cairo •
EGYPT

KENYA
Nairobi •
TANZANIA
Dodoma •

ATLANTIC
OCEAN

Harare •
ZIMBABWE

Pretoria •
SOUTH AFRICA

INDIAN OCEAN

Africa

Africa...next to Asia, the largest continent in the world and a heady mixture of peoples, languages, climates and landscapes.

If camping out under a star-filled sky while a herd of elephants slowly make their way across the grassy plains is appealing then Africa is the place to be. Likewise, if living it up with the jet-set in Marrakech or strolling in the footprints of caliphs in Cairo is more tempting, Africa can provide that too.

In fact, there are many Africas from which to choose – North and South. From the stark beauty of the Sahara Desert to the snow-capped peaks of Kilimanjaro, from the mud huts of a Masai village in Kenya to the ancient stone pyramids at Giza in Egypt, from the rapacious cries of street-hawkers in Tangiers to the ravenous roar of prairie lions in one of the wildlife-packed national parks – no other land on earth provides such contrasts. Those seeking romance, excitement, even a little danger, can do no better.

There are endless ways to create a memorable honeymoon in this vast and historic land. Each country offers diverse experiences. The East African Swahili countries of Kenya and Tanzania make easy 'beach and bush' locations, combining safari drives through such famous African national parks as The Masai Mara, Serengeti and Ngorongoro Crater, with lazy days spent soaking up the sun on their Indian Ocean coastlines and exotic islands.

Zambia, often described as 'real Africa', offers exciting safaris in the wild and remote parks of Kafue and the South Luangwa, and relaxation on the golden sands of Lake Malawi.

Zimbabwe is defined by the path of the Zambezi River, which cascades over the mighty Victoria Falls. Visitors often take a raft or canoe

her tempestuous rapids, and explore the many tiny riverine islands which are set in the magnificence of the powerful landscape. In Botswana, the islands and clear water channels of the Okavango Delta, 'Jewel of the Kalahari', are best explored by dug-out canoe, or even from the back of a huge African elephant.

The desolate landscapes of Namibia are intensely dramatic; many who visit the richly coloured desert dunes of Soussesvlei and the elemental Skeleton Coast find breathtaking beauty. The waterholes of Etosha attract large numbers of southern African wildlife.

South Africa is a land of extremes. From the cosmopolitan cities of Johannesburg and Cape Town to the safari experience of Kruger National Park, the beautiful Garden Route and its many fabulous beaches, it has something to offer every visitor.

Egypt

Herodotus, the ancient Green historian and traveller, once described Egypt as 'the gift of the Nile'. Indeed, for thousands of years it has been the grand playground of emperors and kings.

The Pharaohs, Greeks, Romans, Arabs, Turks and British have all ruled here and modern Egypt is a delightful mixture of traditions.

In the colourful, bustling city of Cairo, always thronged with people, the medieval and contemporary Western world come together – townsfolk in long, flowing robes mingle happily with the Reebok and blue jean-clad and city traffic competes with ancient donkey-drawn carts.

History lovers will find plenty to savour. Visit the overwhelming Pyramids at Giza and Luxor, built on the site of the famous ancient city of Thebes, with its truly magnificent and awe-inspiring architecture.

For true relaxation take a camel caravan through the vast desert, a lazy cruise down the Nile or a dream dive in the crystal-clear waters of the Red Sea. Here, beautiful white sand beaches abound and the underwater wonders of vibrant corals and exotic fish provide among the best Scuba diving in the world.

flying time
To: Cairo
London: 5 1/2 hrs
NY: 12 hrs

when to go
The best time to visit is in the cool season from Nov-Mar, though the coastal area is nice year-round. Oct is a good off-season month when tourist crowds are low.

currency
Egyptian pound.

language
Arabic.

getting around
There is a good system of public transport. If you have lots of money and little time, air travel is the way to go. Buses service virtually every town and 5,000km of rail connects just about every town in the country. You can hire service taxis which carry car loads of people between towns.

167

Cairo Nile Hilton

Tahrir Square
Cairo
Egypt

✈ Cairo 24 km

tel +20 25 78 04 44
fax +20 25 78 04 75

Reservations
tel +202 575 8000
fax +202 579 9817

nile@specialhotels.com
www.specialhotels.com

168

From your spacious balcony at the Nile Hilton astounding views reveal why the hotel's central location makes it a perfect base for travellers to Cairo. Adjacent to the Egyptian museum and overlooking the bustle of town and the tranquillity of the Nile, it's just a short walk from all the major attractions and shopping areas.

Four hundred and thirty-one rooms are on offer and all are comfortably furnished in modern style. The hotel's Junior and Presidential suites contain kitchen facilities for the ultimate in convenience.

A huge list of restaurants and bars cater to every need offering everything from snacks to gourmet meals. Will you choose to dine in the rooftop restaurant or will the spin of the roulette wheel in the casino tempt you to tables of a different kind?

However you spend the evening use the day to explore the magic that encompasses this mysterious city – the pyramids rising majestically from the sand, a sunset cruise past the lush palms of the Nile and the hustle and bustle of the souks. Shopping in Cairo should not be missed and best buys include jewellery, cotton and antiques in the Kasr el Nil region 10 minutes from the hotel.

 US$150*

 included

included

Honeymoon specials

Champagne and flowers in room on arrival. Transfer from airport to hotel.

* Prices quoted are special honeymoon rates and are per room per night, with a minimum three-night stay.

Sightseeing and leisure

Shopping in Cairo for leather products, jewellry, antiques, carpets. The great pyramids of Egypt are nearby for sightseeing excursions. Also Jackie's Joint, a popular disco. The hotel features a swimming pool, tennis and squash facilities plus gym and health club.

Conrad International
Sharm El Sheikh

PO Box 102
Ras Nosrani
Sharm El Sheikh
Egypt

✈ Sharm El Sheikh 5km

tel +20 62 670585
fax +20 62 670580

conrad@specialhotels.com
www.specialhotels.com
www.hilton.com

169

Situated on Ras Nosrani Bay, in 37 acres of lush, landscaped gardens fronting a stretch of more than 1,600 feet of beautiful beaches, this Conrad hotel provides the perfect coastal destination.

Located across from the Tiran Island, considered to be one of the best diving spots in the world, guests can enjoy other watersports as well, like windsurfing, waterskiing and deep-sea fishing.

And in the hotel, there are extensive sports and recreational features, including a fully-equipped health club, fresh water outdoor swimming pool, tennis courts plus an aqua centre.

There are a choice of eight different ways to eat at the resort with specialities including Italian, Oriental and seafood, as well as a poolside bar and cafe, not to mention 24-hour room service.

 US$120-150 (245)

 US$350-650 (6)

 US$20

 US$10

Honeymoon specials
Honeymooners are treated as VIPs with room upgrade and a basket of fruit in room.

Leisure facilities
All manner of watersports available from Scuba diving to deep-sea fishing. Tennis and basketball courts, health club, freshwater pool and Jacuzzi.

Sightseeing
The Red Sea's coral reefs, Ras Mohamed National Park and the Monastery of St Catherine are all well worth exploring.

Information
UK 0870 606 1296
INT. +44 870 606 1296

The Hilton Dahab &
Red Sea Cruise

c/o Nile Hilton
Annex Office No. 6-8
Cairo
Egypt

✈ Sharm 12km

tel +20 62 640 310
fax +20 62 640 424

Reservations
tel +202 575 8000
fax +202 579 9817

dahab@specialhotels.com
redsea@specialhotels.com
www.specialhotels.com

170

Few countries can rival Egypt for the sheer magnificence of its history and monuments. Whether guests choose to stay at the Hilton's luxurious Dahab resort, surrounded by stunning views of the Sinai mountains, or to step aboard the Hilton M.V. Gaia for a week-long cruise, all Egypt's wonders are there to be explored and enjoyed.

The exciting cruise takes in, among other sites, the Valley of the Kings and the temple at Luxor. As well as these, there is a visit to Petra city on Bedouin guided horses and a day-long excursion to Jerusalem or Eilat with an evening return to Sharm El Sheikh. While aboard, it is easy to have fun in the panoramic restaurant or the three lively bars.

At the Dahab resort, with its bungalow complex overlooking a lagoon, fun is no problem either. Located 100kms from Sharm El Sheikh, it is close to the major Sinai attractions of St Catherine and the Coloured Canyon. With three restaurants and the rooftop Windjammer disco and bar, eating and drinking options are tempting. The private beach and the watersports (especially windsurfing), diving and tennis mean there is always something to do.

Whether by boat or on land, the Hilton aims to make the most of Egypt and provide a welcoming base from which to explore this magical country.

US$150*

 included

 included

Honeymoon specials

Flowers and champagne on arrival. A free Scuba diving lesson and a romantic dinner at the Dahab. Based on a four-night stay at Hilton Dahab, or a seven-night stay on the Cruise for US$420 per room per night.

Prices quoted are special honeymoon rates and are per room per night, with a minimum four-night stay.

Sightseeing and leisure

Excursions to Luxor, Petra, Wadi Rum, Jerusalem, St Catherine, Ras Mohamed. Tours of Eilat, and Safaga. There is also a diving centre, waterskis, jetskis, health spa with sauna and steam room, Jacuzzi, boutique and hairdresser.

Hotel Sofitel Alexandria Cecil

Saad Zaghloul Sq
Alexandria
Egypt

✈ Alexandria 10 mins

tel +203 483 7173
fax +203 483 6401/484 0368

alexandria@specialhotels.com
www.specialhotels.com

171

Experience the buzz of one of the most historical cities in the world at the Alexandria Cecil. In the heart of the business, shopping and entertainment centre of the city, the hotel has been welcoming guests since 1929 and has been recently refurbished. As well as its impressive heritage, you can enjoy panoramic views of the Eastern harbour.

Sip cocktails to live music at Monty's Bar, named after Field Marshall Montgomery, who resided at the hotel during World War II. In the summer months, visit the Roof Garden for wonderful views, or Cafe Trottoire for snacks and drinks on the seafront terrace.

All rooms come with air conditioning, satellite TV, minifridge and a private balcony. Other facilities include a fitness room, sauna and hairdresser.

When darkness falls, the wide variety of nightlife will ensure you are kept amused. the Casino offers the chance to try out your luck at American roulette, Black Jack or on the slot machines. The lively Orientheque is a disco set in an oriental atmosphere, or you could visit Caesar's Palace, Alexandria's prime night club which features live performances and folkloric shows.

 US$134-166 (83)

 US$174-220 (3)

 US$13

 US$8

Honeymoon specials
Mineral water, flowers, tart and fruit basket in room on arrival. Free local newspaper, upgrade to suite upon availability. There is a 20% discount on normal room rate for honeymooners.

Sightseeing and leisure
Antiques market, Coptic church, Bompy's Pillar, Gerco Roman museum, plus cinemas and theatres. The hotel also offers a fitness room and hairdressing salon.

The Mena House Oberoi
Hotel and Casino

Pyramid's Road
Giza
Cairo
Egypt

✈ Cairo Int. 35km

tel +20 23 83 32 22
fax +20 23 83 77 77

mena@specialhotels.com
www.specialhotels.com
obmhosm@oberoi.com.eg

172

The former hunting lodge of Khedive Ismail, King of Egypt, the Mena House Oberoi is set in 40 acres of palm and jasmine-scented gardens. More like an amazing palace than a hotel, in Ottoman style with Arabesque arches, antiques and chandeliers creating Eastern ambience reminiscent of the era when Pharaohs ruled the land. As a lasting reminder, rising above the hotel as a stunning backdrop are the Pyramids of Giza.

The Mena has always attracted its fair share of stars and VIPs. Everyone from the likes of Sir Winston Churchill, Field Marshal Montgomery, Charlie Chaplin and 'ole blue eyes' Frank Sinatra have stayed here when they've visited the country. The late King Gustav of Sweden even spent his honeymoon at this grand hotel.

Perhaps they came for all the stunning scenery and culture that this delightful city and country has to offer. Or perhaps they came for the wonderful welcome and hospitality of the Mena House Hotel, with its champagne breakfasts, quality dining and truly excellent service.

Apart from sightseeing (which is a must in Egypt) there is plenty to do in or nearby the hotel. Luxuriate in the magnificent pool, enjoy a game of golf, go for a scenic horseride: above all, have fun.

 US$175-250 (486)

 US$660-1,450 (13)

🍽 US$22-31

☕ US$13

🅂 🤸 🍾 (incl)

Honeymoon specials
Fruit basket and wine on arrival, complimentary candlelight dinner and invitation to The Sound & Light Show, transfers from airport, plus one free night for every six consecutive nights booked. Cost from Garden rate of US$170 per night to Palace rate US$200.

Sightseeing
Great pyramids of Giza, ancient ruins, markets and bazaars of Cairo, camel rides.

Leisure facilities
Tennis courts, golf, swimming pool. Barbers and beauty salon.

Sofitel Old Cataract

Abtal el Tahrir Street
Aswân

Egypt

✈ Aswân Int. 15 mins

tel +20 97 31 60 00
fax +20 97 31 60 11

Accor Reservations Service UK
tel +44 (0) 181 283 4500

www.accor.com
www.sofitel.com

Tour operators:
UK Kuoni, Jules Vernes
US Abercrombie & Kent

Built on a pink granite outcrop, overlooking the Nile River, the Sofitel Old Cataract has a long and distinguished history. Built in 1899, celebrities and royalty alike have passed through its doors. Made famous in the film, *Death on the Nile*, this is a dramatic and striking hotel.

The exterior reflects the Victorian era in which it was built, while the interior retains its original influences of oriental and Moorish designs. Walking into the old-fashioned lobby, with polished marble floor and high red and white Islamic arches, visitors can see for themselves the beauty and character of the hotel as soon as they arrive.

The 136 bedrooms all have a different shape and decor. Special touches include Persian carpets, antique and hand carved furniture. Some rooms feature a spectacular view of the Nile from their balconies. In addition to the bedrooms, there are eight theme suites – Agatha Christie, Sir Winston Churchill and Presidential are examples – which all offer panoramic views of Elephantine Island.

The Old Cataract offers three restaurants. The 1902 Restaurant is a showcase of elegance; The Terrace is one of the most popular places, offering snacks and afternoon tea; and for a more relaxed setting, guests can dine in the pool-side restaurant.

173

 US$110-240* (123)

 US$350-900* (8)

 from US$30

 US$16

Honeymoon specials
Flowers in room on arrival and complimentary afternoon tea. Room upgrade subject to availability.

Leisure facilities
The hotel has an outdoor swimming pool, tennis courts and designated reading and games room.
* Prices quoted do not include service and tax.

Sightseeing
Aswân, Egypt's southern-most city, is superbly located along the Nile. Places to visit include the Philae Temple, Abu Simble Temple and Botanical Gardens and trips to Elephantine Island. There is also a camel market on Tuesdays, Felucca cruises on the Nile and *souks*.

Sofitel Winter Palace

Cornish El Nile Street
Luxor
Egypt

✈ Luxor Int. 10km

tel +20 95 380 422/25
fax +20 95 374 087

winter@specialhotels.com
www.specialhotels.com
www.exvitt.it

Tour operators:
UK Abercrombie & Kent

174

Built on the 4,000-year-old site of ancient Thebes, the grand and monumental city of Luxor in Egypt has seen Pharaohs come and go. The temples and pyramids remain, as do the relics of Greek, Roman, Arabic and Turkish civilisations. This is a place of legends where every building, every stone even, has a story to tell. Here, on the banks of the mighty Nile, can be found the Winter Palace Hotel – a luxurious and serene mixture of Victorian style and Eastern elegance.

Built at the end of the last century in a tropical garden, the former palace with its majestic entrance hall, domed restaurant and richly decorated rooms and suites, has preserved its authenticity while at the same time bringing itself up to date. Modern comforts blend in effortlessly with the soft tones of wood panelling, crystal chandeliers and fine furnishings to make this a hotel fit, literally, for royalty.

Kings and Queens, Tsars and Tsarinas, princes and princesses, stars and starlets, writers, explorers and politicians: all have passed through the Winter Palace's doors or moored their yachts on the quayside opposite. It is not necessary however, to actually be royalty to visit the palace – all guest are given the red carpet treatment.

 US$95-250 (96)

 US$400-900 (6)

🍴 à la carte

 US$17

Honeymoon specials
Fruits, flowers and welcome drink on arrival. Romantic, sunset Felucca with afternoon tea. Free transport to and from airport. Room upgrade when available.

Sightseeing and leisure
Facilities include tennis, squash, swimming pool. Excursions include visits to Luxor temple and museum, Karnak temple, Mumiphication museum, Sound and Light show. West Bank with the Valley of Kings, Valley of Queens, Colosses of Memnon and Medinet Habu.

Taba Hilton Resort

Taba
South Sinai
Egypt

✈ Sharm 260km
Eilat City 10km

tel +20 62 53 01 40
fax +20 25 78 70 44

Reservations
tel +202 575 8000
fax +202 579 9817

taba@specialhotels.com
www.specialhotels.com

The Taba Hilton is in Egypt's beautiful Sinai Peninsula coastal region, close to the border of Israel. Set on its own private beach in the Gulf of Aqaba on the Red Sea, it offers the perfect blend of activities and relaxation.

The spacious resort contains 326 rooms spread over 10 floors. Each has a balcony that overlooks the sea. Rooms are large and neatly furnished with satellite television and air-conditioning.

The Palm Court is the main hotel restaurant which offers excellent buffet dining. For a more intimate evening, try the delicious Moroccan cuisine at the Marahaba restaurant or even enjoy a taste of Italy at the superb Casa Taba.

On site facilities are varied. The hotel offers two swimming pools and a Jacuzzi. There are also five floodlit tennis courts and a fully equipped watersports and diving centre. Finally, evenings can be spent in the hotel's gambling casino and any winnings can be easily spent in the hotel's shopping mall or the beachfront Bedouin Market.

Car rental is easily arranged at the hotel and makes it easy to visit some of the amazing sights nearby. Don't miss the history and incredible natural beauty of Mt Sinai and the total silence of the extraordinary Coloured Canyon.

175

US$170* (326)

included

included

Honeymoon specials
Champagne and flowers in room on arrival. One free watersport activity complimentary, Scuba diving hour, plus a romantic dinner at the Casa Taba Restaurant.

* Prices quoted are special honeymoon rates and are per room per night, with a minimum four-night stay.

Sightseeing and leisure
Excursions to Sinai Peninsula, diving around the world famous coral reefs of the Red Sea. The hotel boasts swimming pools, floodlit tennis courts, aquasport centre, diving centre and Jacuzzi. Camel rides can be arranged.

Kenya

To: Nairobi
London: 9 hrs
NY: 17 hrs

Apr-May sees the
long rains, Jun-Oct is
hot and dry. Nov
sees the short rains
and Dec-Mar is very
hot and humid.

The Kenyan shilling,
but US dollars are
widely accepted.

The official language
is Swahili, though
English is widely
spoken.

Air Kenya and many
private airlines
connect the national
parks and towns.
There is a daily
railway service from
Nairobi to
Mombasa.

The colourful diversity of wildlife, scenery and people
of Kenya, its coastline lapped by the Indian Ocean, has
long carried the influence of Arabian traders who found
their way to these shores nearly ten thousand years ago.

In recent years much of Kenya is perceived to have
become over-developed by mass tourism, but there
remain many wonderfully unspoilt locations.

The Masai Mara is characterised by huge expanses of
rolling savannah grassland and flat-topped Acacias, and
its open plains make for good game viewing. As the
name suggests, it is the homeland of the nomadic
Masai tribe who continue to herd their cattle
across this land and northern Tanzania, still living in
accordance with their age-old traditions and
distinguished by their proud nature, and a distinctive
red cloth that they wear. In August the Mara provides
fresh pasture for the millions of wildebeest that also
follow the seasonal change across the border. The
spectacle of the wildebeest migration across the Sand
River can be viewed in spectacular fashion from the
elevation of a hot air balloon, a trip which can be
arranged from most of the surrounding lodges.

The confluence of the Arab, Portuguese, Indian and
African cultures add a hint of spice to any time taken
on Kenya's coast, or on its offshore reefs and islands so
rich with aquatic life. This exotic coastline provides the
ideal finale to any Kenyan honeymoon.

Borana Lodge

PO Box 24397
Nairobi
Kenya

✈ Borana airstrip 3km

tel +254 2 574 689
fax +254 2 564 945/577 851

borana@specialhotels.com
www.specialhotels.com
mellifera@swiftkenya.com

In a valley which meanders out of Laikipia Plateau onto the plains of northern Kenya is the deluxe hideaway retreat of Borana Lodge. The lodge appears to be cut off from the outside world and yet is within easy reach of Kenya's famous national parks and reserves.

Six cottages made of stone, cedar and thatch are gathered around a main house in the shadow of Mount Kenya blending into the natural surroundings. Each cottage is different in design and layout and has its own bathroom and verandah. All have a fireplace and some have large four-poster beds. The interiors echo the spirit of Africa with furniture made of rough hewn cedar, leather and hand-woven and hand-painted fabrics and fine East African art.

The main house has a morning room where guests can relax and take in the awe-inspiring easterly views over the river gorge and beyond before enjoying a meal 'estate-style' around the large rosewood table. Good, homemade traditional and exotic fare is served, with the emphasis on fresh produce obtained every day from the ranch.

For a truly memorable experience, trips to Borana can be combined with luxury tented safaris led by professional guides deep into the heart of Kenya.

177

 US$360* (6 cottages)

 included

 included

Honeymoon specials

In the honeymoon cottage, guests receive complimentary wine, sundowners, activities on the ranch, guided walks and game drives. The honeymoon cottage package costs US$360* per person per night.

Plus wilderness area conservation fee of US$30 per person per day.

Sightseeing and leisure

Game walks and drives with professional guides. Day trips to Samburu National Reserve and Aberdare National Park, a forest with incredible scenery and wildlife. Flights to Lake Turkana to visit archaeological sites. Cultural visits to local Samburu community highlighting aspects of their life, from spear making to traditional song and dance. Also, there is horseriding, swimming and massage available on request.

Desert Rose

PO Box 24397
Nairobi
Kenya

✈ Private airstrip 40 mins

tel +254 2 577374
fax +254 2 564945

desert@specialhotels.com
www.specialhotels.com
mellifera@swiftkenya.com

178

Hidden by the towering slopes of Kenya's Mount Nyiru, this tiny lodge hotel offers the chance to experience all the beauty nature has to offer.

Each of the five houses which characterise the accommodation is carved out of local rocks and timber and contains a beautiful four-poster bed and other luxurious facilities. A particular highlight of this unique resort is the open-air, en suite bathrooms that offer heart-stopping views.

The dining room is handcrafted in locally quarried slate and is finely finished in cedar and olive woods, yet the care taken on the decor is surpassed by that taken on the food which is first-class and offers the perfect end to your days of exploration at Desert Rose.

For this is not a resort that suits the idle. With some of the most incredible scenery you'll ever experience on your doorstep, this is an area that demands and deserves to be explored. Rugged mountainscapes, lush greenery and, of course, animals. Wild boar, baboon, aardvark and leopard are close by to entertain walkers. And at the end of the day cool off in the fresh waterfalls that tumble close to the resort.

US$325* (5 cottages)

🍽 included

☕ included

🍾

Honeymoon specials

Bottle of wine in room on arrival, plus room decorated with indigenous plants.

* Prices quoted are per person per night.

Sightseeing and leisure

Riverine forest, 200 species of birds, dramatic landscape, local villages and Samburu people, camel treks, fishing on Lake Turkana, archaeological interests at Koobi Fora.

Galdessa Camp

PO Box 24397
Nairobi
Kenya

✈ Local airstrip 10km

tel +254 2 574 689
fax +254 2 577851

galdessa@specialhotels.com
www.specialhotels.com
mellifera@swiftkenya.com
www.galdessa.com

Tour operators:
UK Cazenove & Lloyd
US Frontiers Travel

179

Set in the middle of Kenya's largest national park, Tsavo East, the elephant park, Galdessa is one of the country's newest and most private hideaways.

The camp, which caters to a maximum of 16 guests, is located on the southern bank of the Galana river, the sole source of permanent water in the area and home to some of Tsavo's best wildlife. Elephant, rhino, buffalo and antelope come to drink, while predators lurk in the shade.

The Honeymoon Suite enjoys a charming private location well away from the rest of the camp, faces the river, and has its own adjoining seating area with a water wallow and elevated viewing platform.

Inside, through the use of natural woods, stone and canvas, an authentic contact is maintained with the world outside – manifest in the stone sink and tables, timber floors and enormous beds made out of wood from the park. It is truly an eco-tourism camp, as electricity here is solar generated and all wastes, including water, are recycled or treated.

The cuisine is known to be the best in East Africa and 22 experienced staff will attend to your needs round the clock. Enjoy dining in the comfort of one of the two lodges in the middle of the untamed wilderness, or, for that more intimate experience, privately in the suite.

 US$650* (6)

 US$750 (2)

 included

 included

  (incl)

Honeymoon specials

Honeymooners can enjoy meals in the privacy of their suite with dedicated waiter service. Romantic dinners are served al fresco in the bush. Price quoted is per room and includes all meals, activities and drinks, except champagne. Room upgrade is subject to availability.

* Plus park fees of US$23 per person per day.

Sightseeing and leisure

Safaris in Kenya's largest national park, Tsavo East. Game drives during the day and at night, walking safaris with professional guide, meals in the bush, sundowners, fishing along the river.

Information & Reservations
UK 0870 606 1296
INT. +44 870 606 1296

PO Box 90352
Mombasa
Kenya

✈ Moi Int. 20km

tel +254 11 485721/4
fax +254 11 485453

serena@specialhotels.com
www.specialhotels.com

Tour operators:
UK British Airways Holidays
Kuoni

Member of:
Leading Hotels of the World

180

Mombasa
Serena Beach Hotel

Situated close to Shanzu Beach just a few miles north of Mombasa, Kenya's 'Second City', the Mombasa Serena Beach is the only hotel on the Kenyan coast to be offered membership of the Leading Hotels of the World.

Inspired by the legendary 13th-century Swahili town of Lamu, the resort's 166 rooms and suites lie in flat-roofed Arabesque houses dotted around shady courtyards. Once inside, ethnic designs give a feel for this warm and beautiful country, while in the suites, the muslin canopied beds add a distinctive air of romance.

Traditional African fare as well as international cuisine are available to tempt you at the resort. Choose from the elegant Fountain restaurant with its outside terrace and gourmet cuisine or visit one of the informal Swahili evenings to capture a true taste of the vibrant local life.

The large swimming pool offers the chance to cool off from the heat of the day or step onto the beautiful sugary beach to enjoy the huge variety of watersports on offer. Outside the resort, you shouldn't miss trips to visit the hippos at nearby Bamburi Nature Trail, to buy jewellery at Bombolulu, or to spend a day on safari at the Shimba Hills National Reserve further inland.

 US$120-220* (166)

 US$320-420*

iOi US$18

☕ US$11

Honeymoon specials
Fruit and flowers in room on arrival. Complimentary canapes and sparkling wine every evening. Room upgrade subject to availability.

* Prices subject to 28% taxes and are on halfboard basis.

Sightseeing and leisure
Facilities include hairdressing salon on site, massage and beauty centre nearby. Historical sites of Fort Jesus, Gede Ruins Malindi. Bombolulu workshops and cultural centre. Bamburi nature trail. Mamba village and crocodile farm.

Ol Donyo Wuas

Chyulu Hills
Kenya

✈ Own airstrip 50 mins from Nairobi

tel +254 2 88 2521/4475
fax +254 2 88 2728

donya@specialhotels.com
www.specialhotels.com
Bonham.Luke@swiftkenya.com

Closed in May

Tour operators:
KENYA Richard Bonham Safaris

Stunningly situated among the rugged Chyulu Hills and overlooking the snow-capped peaks of Mount Kilimanjaro, the private lodge Ol Donyo Wuas has exclusive access to one of the few remaining wilderness areas of East Africa.

Each of the seven charming, thatched cottages has a cosy open fireplace and verandah with panoramic views across the vast unspoilt plains toward distant mountain peaks. The beautifully crafted furniture is locally made and establishes an intimate and comfortable atmosphere.

A typical day at the lodge might well begin when dawn is still reflected in the snow of Mount Kilimanjaro's summit. Early morning and late evening are the best times for game viewing. Trekking into the bush on foot, horseback, or in a specially converted open-top Landrover, guests can watch oryx, gerenuk, zebra, eland, giraffe and wildebeest roam the plains, always on the lookout for cheetah and lion. The early evening is the perfect time for observing predators in action, and as the heat of the sun dies down, guests are taken to a suitable spot for a 'sundowner' cocktail. Back at the lodge, an invigorating hot shower and then a romantic candlelit three-course dinner under the stars round off a perfect day.

181

 US$350* (7 cottages)

 included

 included

 (incl)

Honeymoon specials
Wine in room on arrival. All drinks are included. A stay at Ol Donyo Wuas can be combined with days at other safari lodges. A full itinerary, including international flights, can be arranged.

* Prices quoted are per person per night.

Sightseeing and leisure
Tailor-made riding and walking safaris with support crew and mobile tented camp are available at an extra cost of US$50-100 per person per day. Bird shooting can be arranged during the season July to October. Trips to local Maasai village and Amboseli National Park.

Morocco

182

If exotic is what you're looking for, Morocco is the place for you. This spectacularly diverse land of majestic mountains, green valleys, medieval cities, fertile plains, vast deserts and unspoiled beaches is bursting with a myriad of colours, tastes and scents. Its vibrancy and allure provide an intense and unforgettable experience, an everlasting inspiration for the senses.

Morocco is unique in that it is the African country closest to Europe in geographical and cultural terms, though it seems very far from Europe with its deeply Islamic culture. Many of the cultural influences come from the French-dominated colonial days while the artistic and architectural influence are closer to geographically-nearby Spain.

The beautiful city of Marrakech, low and pink before a great shaft of mountains, is an entrancing place to be. Famed for its markets and festivals, its beating heart is the huge square in the old city – Djemaa El Fna.

Rows of food stalls fill the air with mouth-watering aromas and at night it turns into a magical realm where stories are told, fire swallowed and poison snakes played with. The *souks*, or markets, here are among the best in the country. They are piled high with rugs, woodwork, jewellery, crafts and Moroccan leather, which is said to be the softest in the world.

Hyatt Regency Marinasmir

Route de Ceuta Via
Tetouan 93200
Morocco

✈ Tangier Int. 80km

tel +212 9 971 234
fax +212 9 971 235

marinasmir@specialhotels.com
www.specialhotels.com
www.hyatt.com

183

When guests open their doors at Marinasmir they encounter an enchanted land of markets and bazaars, mysterious ancient cities, plenty of bustling crowds and quiet back streets: a land, in short, a place called Morocco.

The all-suite hotel offers the refined luxury of a palace. The spacious rooms all have individual balconies and afford breathtaking views of the pool, gardens and sea beyond. Indoors, the decorations are Moorish in inspiration with tiled flooring and ornate fabrics.

The Neptune restaurant serves up spicy dishes of Moroccan and Spanish origin while the poolside Cascade caters for light snacks, fresh salads and grilled dishes. There is also a piano bar with live entertainment and just down the road guests will find the Marina which has a variety of lively discos and restaurants open during the summer months.

To work off the calories there is Club Olympus, a state-of-the-art gym offering, among other things, massage, aerobics and tennis. For golf fanatics, there is an 18-hole course 15 minutes away. But it's not all sport here. The region is rich in culture and history and there are many places to visit including ancient fortifications at Teouan and the tiny white and blue city of Chaouen, hidden in the mountains.

🛏 US$92-245 (51)

🛋 US$195-888 (8)

🍽 US$18-27

☕ US$7-12

Honeymoon specials
Wine and fruit on arrival. Upgrade to suite depending on availability.

Leisure facilities
Marina, beach, aqua park, golf course nearby, tennis, fitness centre, sauna and gym, horseriding.

Sightseeing
Tetouan Medina and markets. Excursions to Chaouen, a quaint Moroccan village in the mountains.

Hotel La Gazelle d'Or

BP 60
Taroudant
Morocco

✈ Agadir 48 miles

tel +212 8 85 2039
fax +212 8 85 2737

gazelle@specialhotels.com
www.specialhotels.com

Tour operators:
UK Elegant Resorts

184

Set just outside the walls of the tiny medieval village of Taroudannt, in southern Morocco, Hotel La Gazelle d'Or is a perfect, luxurious hideaway.

The 30 stone-walled cottages that make up the resort lie in 25 acres of tropical gardens. Each cottage is furnished in Arabian style with mosaic and tiling creating a cool environment in which to sleep or sit. Sumptuous touches such as fresh flowers and thick towelling robes fill every room.

Morocco is famous for its highly flavoured cuisine and at the tented dining room within the property you'll be able to enjoy dishes such as *tagine* or richly scented *cous-cous*.

During the day, two swimming pools, riding stables, croquet and a massage and beauty centre fill time in the resort and outside there is much to explore. Historic Taroudannt offers a taste of the true Morocco with its bustling spice market and ancient fort. Nearby visit the towering Atlas Mountains or the splendid Amagour waterfalls.

If you'd prefer to spend the day at the beach, the hotel will be happy to arrange excursions to the white sands of Imouzer. Just one example of the impeccable service that has given La Gazelle d'Or its international reputation as a stunning and outstanding place to stay.

 US$265 (28)

 US$375-785 (2)

 US$35-55

 US$25

🍾

Honeymoon specials
Complimentary wine, flowers, hamman (steambath) for two on arrival.

Sightseeing and leisure
The ancient walled town of Taroudannt is two kilometres away, with colourful markets everyday. Many natural sights of interest in the area, such as the Amagour waterfalls.

La Mamounia

Avenue Bab Jdid
Marrakech
Morocco

✈ Marrakech 10 mins

tel +212 4 44 44 09
fax +212 4 44 46 60

mamounia@specialhotels.com
www.specialhotels.com
www.mamounia.com

Tour operators:
UK Elegant Resorts
US Abercrombie & Kent

La Mamounia, in the heart of Marrakech, stands in a 200-year-old park that was the wedding gift of a Sultan to his son. No ordinary hotel would look at home in such prestigious grounds but then La Mamounia is no ordinary hotel.

Designed in 1922, the hotel is a fascinating mixture of Moroccan architectural tradition and modernist Art Deco. In the entrance lobby a chandelier illuminates a gold, vaulted ceiling. At ground level, marquetry-panelled arm chairs and Moroccan rugs rest on geometric marble floors. The happy alchemy is continued throughout the public areas, restaurants and bars, even to the grand casino, through to the suites and rooms where 1920s blends effortlessly with such details as fine Moroccan tiling and lusty fabrics.

The hotel has attracted a galaxy of VIPs from the world of stage, screen, fashion, politics and royalty. Winston Churchill painted a picture of the gardens from his hotel window during World War II. More recently Nicole Kidman and Tom Cruise came here for a bit of rest and privacy.

The hotel has a palm-lined pool, tennis, squash, gym, and a new golf driving range on site. There is also horseriding nearby. Outside is the multi-faced, contradictory and beautiful city of Marrakech.

185

 MAD1,700-4,600 (171)

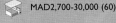 MAD2,700-30,000 (60)

|O| MAD450

 MAD190

Ⓢ ♿ 🍾

Honeymoon specials
Four-night, three-day package including Moroccan/American buffet breakfast daily, one dinner (food only) in one of the hotel's restaurants, a bottle of champagne, flowers and fruit on arrival, one horse-driven carriage ride, transfers to/from the airport, costs from MAD8,680 per couple in low season in a room overlooking the gardens.

Sightseeing
Djema Al F'Naa square, Saadian Tombs, Bahia Palace, plus Marrakech's bustling souks.

Leisure facilities
On site are a pool, Jacuzzi, squash, golf driving range, beauty salon, Hamman sauna, massage. Horseriding and golf nearby.

In this most cosmopolitan and sophisticated country, reminders of a fascinating history abound, and its sheer size and diversity means that there is something here for every visitor, including a range of accommodation, from beach-front bungalows to characterful tented lodges in the bush.

flying time
To: Johannesburg or Cape Town
London: 11 hrs
NY: 15 hrs

climate/ when to go
Cape Town is best visited Sept-Apr. The rest of the country experiences rain in the summer Oct-Mar.

currency
South African Rand.

language
A wide variety including English, Afrikaans, Zulu, Xhosa and South Sotho.

getting around
South African Airways' efficient network of internal flights connects most of the major towns, the national parks and other attractions.

In addition to safaris to its national parks, South Africa offers activities that tend not to be found on the rest of the continent such as hiking, walking, riding, cycling, wine tasting and scenic train journeys. For wildlife enthusiasts, the Kruger National Park and its surrounding private reserves offer extremely good game viewing and luxuriously appointed lodges. Open-sided vehicles and well trained guides, who are adept at spotting the 'big five', ensure that your safari is as memorable and exciting as possible.

The famously lovely Garden Route from Port Elizabeth to Cape Town follows the coastline. The secluded bays and beaches, waterfalls and forests make this one of the most dramatic drives in the world, and its destination is one of the most romantically situated cities in the world.

Table Mountain provides a magnificent backdrop to many fine beaches, and acres of vineyards and gardens, and the waterfront is an ideal spot to relax and sample the fine cuisine that is on offer.

There is so much more to experience in South Africa. Perhaps the verdant hills and valleys of the Waterberg, the stark landscapes of the Kalahari Desert, or the Indian Ocean coastline around Durban. For those who wish to end their trip in a tropical paradise, Benguerra Island, off the coast of Mozambique, is a short flight from Johannesburg, and can provide a marvellous finale to your African honeymoon.

The Bay

Victoria Road
Camps Bay
Cape Town
South Africa

✈ Cape Town Int. 25 min.

tel +27 21 438 4444
fax +27 21 438 4455

bay@specialhotels.com
www.specialhotels.com
res@thebay.co.za
www.slh.com/slh/

188 Tour operators:
UK Carrier Int.
US African Travel

Member of:
Small Luxury Hotels

The Cape Town area was described by Sir Frances Drake as 'the fairest cape in the whole circumference of the earth'. And The Bay provides the perfect base to explore these awesome wonders. Just 10 minutes from Cape Town's centre, it overlooks the stunning Camps Bay beach and prides itself on first-rate personal service and a great international reputation.

The superb beachfront location gives visitors the perfect chance to soak up the sun on the sand or take in the atmosphere of this vibrant area at 'Sandy B', the new beach-style bar. Every room offers a spectacular view either of the shimmering Atlantic Ocean, majestic Table Mountain, or the craggy Twelve Apostles. All have their own private entrance lobby and en suite bathroom.

The top-class restaurant, Tides, which is attached to the hotel, gives you that incredible view of the entire sweep of Camps Bay beach and serves outstanding fresh fish and the chance to sample the impressive array of South African wines on offer. The poolside Espresso Bar is great for a casual lunch while soaking up the rays.

The Bay is situated within easy reach of the Cape's most celebrated scenic attractions; including lush golf courses, beaches, the winelands, Victoria & Alfred Waterfront, Table Mountain and Kirstenbosch Botanical Gardens.

🛏 US$85-207 (71)
🛏 US$242-450 (6)
🍽 US$5-17
☕ US$7.50
♿ 🍷 ⊚

Honeymoon specials
If wedding is held in The Bay's Rotunda banqueting centre then first night is complimentary. Strawberries on arrival in summer months. Room upgrade subject to availability.

Sightseeing and leisure
Excursions to Table Mountain, Cape Point, Camps Bay Beach, Kirstenbosch Botanical Gardens, Robben Island. Also, Stellenbosch and Franschoek Winelands and local craft markets. Leisure facilities on site.

Belvidere Manor

PO Box 1195
Kynsna 6750
South Africa

✈ George 75 km

tel +27 44 387 1055
fax +27 44 387 1059

belvidere@specialhotels.com
www.specialhotels.com
www.belvidere.co.za

Tour operators:
UK Carrier Tours

Belvidere Manor forms part of the historical South African village of Belvidere in the Western Cape. Nestling amid ancient oaks and flourishing hibiscus, on the banks of Knysna's Lagoon, the house is a national monument as well as wonderful place to relax and explore the wonders of the surrounding countryside.

The accommodation comprises 34 sumptuous cottages scattered around the estate and rolling gardens. Each is a home-away-from-home. Plump and comfortable sofas, soft lighting and artworks make staying in an easy and pleasant option. From the windows and wide verandah, however, magnificent views of the lagoon or gardens make venturing out into the warm African sunshine a tempting proposition as well.

For the perfect private dinner, guests can make use of the cottages' self-catering facilities. For something special, there is a selection of excellent restaurants in the area – including the Manor House's own.

At the heart of South Africa's Garden Route, Knysna offers plenty of opportunity for adventure and is the ideal centre from which to explore. Nearby are hiking trails, forest and cliff walks, boating aplenty and, of course, a good selection of beautiful beaches.

189

🛏 US$85-130 (17)

🛎 US$73-110 (17)

🍽 US$15

☕ US$6.50

♿ 🍾 👤

Honeymoon specials
Complimentary champagne on arrival.

Leisure facilities
On site there is a swimming pool, kayak hire, boat trips plus bird sanctuary. Nearby is a golf club, beauty salon, fishing, sailing, Scuba diving.

Sightseeing
Locally are magnificent beaches, indigenous forest, Art Festival (24 Sept-3 Oct 1999) annually, oyster festival (July) annually. Theatre in Krysna, daily markets and shopping centre.

Kedar Country Lodge

Private Bag 1
Muldersdrift 1747
Johannesburg
South Africa

✈ Sun City 20km

tel +27 11 957 2099
fax +27 11 957 3212

kedar@specialhotels.com
www.specialhotels.com
kedar.retreat@pixiew.co.za
recaflin@global.co.za

190

In the foothills of the Pilanesberg, on the historic farm of President Paul Kruger, Kedar Country Lodge offers the perfect getaway. The Lodge and the Paul Kruger historic house, a national monument, are an hour and a half's drive from Johannesburg and Pretoria, and just 15 minutes from Sun City and the Pilanesburg Game Reserve.

This attractive stone-built complex gently blends rustic charm with the natural beauty of the bushveld surroundings that brings an aura of peace and tranquillity. The suites and deluxe rooms, all en suite, have been decorated in vibrant hand-painted ethnic-print fabrics and tasteful African artworks. The prolific birdlife and private herds of impala and blesbok will delight guests as they stroll around the bushveld paths in this haven for nature lovers.

An attractive pool terrace with bar, dining room and outdoor barbecue area provide the perfect setting in which to relax and indulge in the unique African pastime of 'sundowners' as the sun sets. A visit to the Paul Kruger House Museum, situated at Kedar, provides a fascinating insight into a bygone era in South Africa's history.

 US$40-48 (12)

 US$98-196 (3)

 US$5-13

 US$5

 (incl)

Honeymoon specials

Champagne and fruit in the room on arrival. Arrangements can be made to sleep in the historic house of Pieter Kruger, adjacent to the Paul Kruger House Museum.

Sightseeing and leisure

Walks along bush paths with views of private gameherds. Swimming and birdwatching. Pilanesberg Game Reserve nearby, safaris can be arranged; 15 minutes drive to Sun City, arts and crafts studios and fishing.

Misty Hills Country Hotel

Private Bag 1
Muldersdrift 1747
South Africa

✈ Lanseria 10km
Johannesburg Int. 70km

tel +27 11 957 2099/3040
fax +27 11 957 3212

misty@specialhotels.com
www.specialhotels.com
recaflin@global.co.za

Member of:
Warwick Int. Hotels
Toll free numbers:
UK 0500 556 555
US/Canada 1 800 203 3232
S Africa 0800 600 892

At the foothills of the majestic Swartkop Mountains, deep in the heart of the Kromdraai Valley, lies the Misty Hills Country Hotel.

An ex-monastery, this is a charming stone-built complex with 40 rooms. All are decorated with bright local fabrics and handmade furnishings and topped off with quaint thatched roofs, and offer an atmosphere rich in local charm but high in Western comfort.

In the grounds lies the Carnivore restaurant, aptly named as it's renowned for its famous, extensive barbecue. A roaring open fire roasts the meat in front of you and the joints of beef, lamb and even crocodile are skewered on ornate Masai swords. It's a unique experience and a meal you'll never forget – although 'herbivores' can of course choose from a delectable menu of fresh, local vegetarian dishes.

Days can be spent cooling off in the shimmering pool, in the quiet confines of the on-site pub or taking advantage of the Japanese reflexology garden. Or why not venture out on safari or visit the mysterious Wonder Caves nearby. Don't miss the chance to take a romantic hot air balloon ride over the plains. Who knows what sights you'll spot from the sky?

191

 US$220*

 included

 included

Honeymoon specials
Champagne and fruit in the room on arrival.

Sightseeing
Lion and rhino game park, Sterkfontein and Wonder Caves, cultural village, arts and craft studios, botanical gardens, casino.
*This is a fully-inclusive rate.

Leisure facilities
Two swimming pools, fitness centre, games room, lounge/library and outdoor chess. Pub and restaurant on site. Golf, hot air ballooning, trout fishing, as well as shopping malls and cinemas nearby.

Tanzania

flying time
To: Tabora
London: 11 hrs
NY: 17 hrs

when to go
April and May are
the months of the
long rains, June-Oct
is hot and dry, Nov
brings the short
rains, and Dec-Mar
is very hot and
humid.

currency
The Tanzanian
shilling, though US
dollars is widely
accepted.

language
The official language
is Swahili, though
English is widely
spoken.

getting around
Specialist transfer
operators and
internal airlines
connect major
towns, national
parks and airports.

From the snows of Mount Kilimanjaro, across the endless plains of the Serengeti, and to the crystal clear waters of its Indian Ocean islands, Tanzania is one of the most beautiful countries to visit in Africa.

With some of the most unspoilt beaches in Africa it is ideally suited to a honeymoon. On top of that, there is the opportunity to safari in the national parks, as well as freshwater lagoons and verdant forests that reach to the white coral sands and azure waters of the Indian Ocean. On the mainland there are idyllic resorts, and offshore islands such as Zanzibar, Mafia and Mnemba offering some of the best diving, watersports and big-game fishing in the Indian Ocean.

Few things can compare with the joys of watching the spectacles of nature unfurl before you – the migration of the wildebeest, a solitary leopard languidly sleeping in the branches of an Acacia, or a cheetah racing across the sun-bleached savannah. You can start your day in this country with a dawn balloon ride over the plains, and end watching the sun set while taking cocktails on your verandah. Whether you choose to stay in a beautifully appointed hotel or to sleep under canvas, the sounds of the African night will envelop you.

The southern parks of Selous and Ruaha offer an insight into the Africa of old. Vast and remote, these parks remain the preserve of some of the most discerning safari operators, who offer game walks for guests seeking a chaperone into the heart of the bush. Take boat rides along the waterways where colourful birdlife flourishes alongside hippo and crocodile.

Kinasi, Mafia Island

Mafia Island
Tanzania

✈ Dar es Salaam 130km

Contacts:
PO Box 18033
Dar es Salaam, Tanzania
tel +255 51 843 501
fax +255 51 843 495

Africa Archipelago
tel +44 (0) 181 780 5838
fax +44 (0) 181 780 9482

kinasi@specialhotels.com
www.specialhotels.com
kinasi@intafrica.com
www.mafiaisland.com

Closed Apr-May

193

Mafia Island, with its studded islets, sandbanks and beaches lapped by crystal clear waters, lies a short distance off the great Rufji Delta and was once a regular stop for Arab and Persian dhows plying the coastal waters from Mozambique.

Kinasi, a small, luxury lodge which was once a private home, is in an idyllic spot to the south of the island in the beautiful Chole Bay. Now there are 12 luxury palm-topped bungalows spread throughout acres of coconut plantation. Each room is decorated with traditional, brightly coloured African fabrics, with furniture designed by Kinasi's own carpenters, hand-blown glassware and works of art to create a stylish but personal feel. They also have large verandahs and en suite bathrooms.

Staff in traditional dress are very friendly and serve top-notch local dishes featuring fresh seafood, tropical fruit and vegetables. If you can tear yourself away from the table, activities centre on the sea. The diving here is among the best in the world. Isolated islets and coves provide great places to swim and picnic in private.

The terrace overlooking the Bay is a prime spot for wedding ceremonies with a romantic feel, and receptions for up to 30 guests can be arranged in the grounds or on the island atolls.

 US$130-150* (12)

 included

 included

(incl)

Prices are per person.

Honeymoon specials
Champagne and flowers in the room on arrival. Private dinners and personal valet. Entertainment by the local choir and drummers. Laundry included.

Leisure facilities
Diving, snorkelling, sailing, fishing, excursions by road and sea, volleyball, badminton, tennis and swimming pool.

Sightseeing
Visits to local villages can be arranged, also to Persian ruins and other archaeological sites, coastal forest and traditional boat-building yards. Guided tours to coconut plantations. Birdwatching on the tidal flats and mangroves. Romantic picnics in coves and channels around the island.

Kirurumu Tented Lodge

Lake Manyara
PO Box 2047
India St, Arusha
Tanzania

✈ Kiliminjaro Int. 130km

Contact:
tel +44 (0) 181 428 8221
fax +44 (0) 181 421 1396

kirurumu@specialhotels.com
www.specialhotels.com
hoopoeuk@aol.com
www.hoopoe.com

194

Tour operators:
UK Hoopoe Adventure Tours
US Explorers World Travel

Experience the excitement of the heartland of Africa with a touch of style at Kirurumu Tented Lodge. Overlooking Lake Manyara with stunning views across miles of untouched Africa, this is the gateway to the Ngorongoro Crater and the spectacular Serengeti. A place of true tranquillity where the chorus of birdsong and cicadas will awake you each morning and you can look forward to close encounters with the game of Africa in its natural surroundings.

Accommodation is in spacious tents sheltered by thatched roofs, with beautifully carved Arab-style four poster beds. All have bathrooms en suite.

The restaurant, which is open on one side, provides a magnificent sweeping outlook across the bush and an informal, relaxed atmosphere. Lunch and evening meals change daily and are produced using only the freshest fruit, vegetables and herbs, some from the lodge's own organic garden. And, like a true African watering hole, the bar is always open.

Guided nature walks and game drives are on offer to Ngorongoro Crater, Lake Manyara, Tarangire and Serengeti National Parks, or guests can simply experience the sights and sounds of Africa from the comfort of their tents.

 US$160 (20 tents)

 US$160 (1)

 included

 included

Honeymoon specials
Champagne and flowers in tent on arrival. Price for honeymooners is per person per night including all meals and drinks.

Sightseeing
Nature walks with Maasai guide are complimentary. Safari game drives to Lake Manyara, Tarangire, Ngorongoro Crater and Serengeti National Parks can also be arranged and will be quoted on an individual basis..

Ras Kutani

Dar es Salaam
Tanzania

✈ Private airstrip 2km

Contact:
Selous Safari Co Ltd
PO Box 1192
Dar es Salaam

tel +255 51 34 802
fax +255 51 112 794

kutani@specialhotels.com
www.specialhotels.com
selous@twiga.com

Closed mid-April to end May

Tour operator:
UK TTI Ltd

Hidden in tropical forest and flanked on one side by a freshwater lagoon, Ras Kutani lies beside the Indian Ocean on a crescent of deserted beach, white sands and gentle surf, cooled by trade winds.

Traditional bamboo and thatch cottages perfectly harmonise with this serene and idyllic setting. Located on a hill overlooking the ocean, alongside the lagoon or directly facing the beach, each cottage offers complete privacy. All have king-size beds, and spacious verandahs with hammocks for those lazy afternoons.

A selection of fine wines from around the world complements exotic menus which often feature the area's abundant seafood.

Hotel staff are happy to organise wedding receptions for up to 40 people in the hotel or the surrounding area. A stay at Ras Kutani can also be combined with a visit to the Selous Game Reserve, the largest in Africa where guests can enjoy the truly authentic experience of sleeping under canvas. The Selous Safari Camp offers first-class accommodation 'in the bush'.

  US$360 (18)

 US$720 (1)

 included

 included

Honeymoon specials
Sparkling wine with the first dinner. Room upgrade subject to availability. Daily bouquet of flowers in the room. Airport transfers and laundry are included.

Leisure facilities
Full range of watersports including laser sailing, surfing, windsurfing, fishing and snorkelling.

Sightseeing
Safaris to Selous Game Reserve. Game drives, boat and walking safaris led by professional guides. The capital of Tanzania, Dar es Salaam, a journey of just 10 minutes by light aircraft.

Sopa Lodges

PO Box 1823
Arusha
Tanzania

✈ Serengeti Seronera airstrip 40km
✈ Ngorongoro airstrip 40km
✈ Tarangire airstrip 30km

tel +255 57 6896
fax +255 57 8245

sopa@specialhotels.com
www.specialhotels.com

For those who like to view their wildlife in comfort, the Sopa group of lodges in Tanzania's finest game parks may well be ideal. Luxurious bedrooms, swimming pools, shopping boutiques and well-stocked bars mean that guests are far from roughing it, even though they are in the vast and untamed African wilderness with its abundant game and stunning scenery.

There are three Sopa Lodges from which to choose, all in Tanzania. In Serengeti, guests can wake up every morning to seemingly endless views across the plains, rich in wildebeest and other indigenous animals. At Ngorongoro, breakfast can be enjoyed in a rondavel-style dining room with breathtaking views of the crater floor below. In Tarangire, an evening dip

Serengeti Lodge

US$280 (79)

included

included

Ngorongoro Lodge

US$280 (92)

included

included

Tarangire Lodge

US$280 (75)

included

included

in the vast open-air swimming pool could well come as a refresher before a luxury Bar-B-Que buffet under the stars.

Any one of the three eco-friendly Lodges offers the wonders of local wildlife, birdlife and natural flora to be found in these fabled landscapes. Memorable game viewing and adventure are as much on the menu as the sumptuous meals to be enjoyed in the Sopa restaurants.

Honeymoon specials

Complimentary sparkling wine, fruit basket and flowers on arrival. Make sure to phone ahead and give the resorts plenty of notice.

Sightseeing and leisure

Outdoor swimming pool, two boutiques, satellite television and wildlife films at all properties. Walking trips, visits to Masai villages and spectacular game drives in the Crater at Ngorongoro. Annual wildebeest migration and hot air balloon safaris at Serengeti. Birdwatching at Tarangire is a spectacle not to be missed.

Zimbabwe

Zimbabwe is thought to have been the site of King Solomon's mines, because it is so rich in mineral wealth and good farmland. With its beautiful and varied scenery, it is surely one of Africa's most loved countries.

The country is also home to the spectacular Victoria Falls, one of the natural wonders of the world. Its many national parks are considered some of the best on the continent, with the greatest variety of means to take an adventurous safari – day or night drives, walking safaris, boat game drives, white-water rafting, canoeing, kayaking, or floating on a houseboat.

You will find a massive variety of game, all in beautiful, unspoilt surroundings, which is an ideal introduction to the many wonders of Africa. The Zambezi River that marks the boundary with Zambia is a must on any visit to Zimbabwe; especially at the Victoria Falls. Here,

many thousands of tons of water cascade down the escarpment sending spray up to 500 metres in the air, giving the falls the name 'the smoke that thunders'.

The adventurous may raft through the rapids or bungee-jump from the bridge at the top. There are also some excellent canoe trips on the Upper Zambezi involving fly-camping on its riverine forest islands. Hwange National Park, the largest reserve in Zimbabwe, is famous for its huge population of over 25,000 elephant. Also home to all the major African predators and plains game, including black rhino and wild dog, Hwange is a superb park in which to be

captivated by the magic of life in the bush.

Lake Kariba is one of the world's largest man-made lakes; guests can watch the wildlife that comes to the water's edge from luxurious lodges on the shoreline, from islands on the lake, or even from a houseboat. Lake Kariba and the bordering Matusadona National Park have prolific birdlife and compelling scenery. Here you can experience the best sunsets in the world as the sinking orb transforms the lake into a pool of molten copper and gold while taking in the haunting cry of the fish eagle as it gracefully circles its prey.

The Matopos National Park, just south of Bulawayo, is the last resting place of Cecil Rhodes. Huge balancing boulders, piled like strange natural totems, are the most intriguing feature of this area, as they seem to defy gravity. This is the site chosen by the San bushmen for their intriguing rock paintings, still miraculously preserved in well-camouflaged caves.

Africa Archipelago

CONTACT:

Africa Archipelago
6 Redgrave Road
London SW15 1PX
England

tel +44 (0) 181 780 5838
fax +44 (0) 181 780 9482
worldarc@compuserve.com
www.tanzania-
web.com/worldarc

200

Through many years of experience we know that choosing the right honeymoon requires meticulous planning and detailed, up-to-date knowledge. We specialise in tailor-making honeymoons to East and Southern Africa, as well as to some of the more exotic islands in the Indian Ocean.

We have taken care to select some of the most untouched and romantic destinations in Africa. Most of the accommodation we recommend is in small, exclusive camps, lodges and island hideaways, all of which offer the best in personalised service.

The African dream is one of the most evocative. Just imagine waking to the sound of the Indian Ocean lapping the coral sands of your private island, or gazing down on migrating wildebeest on your verandah as the African sun sets over the Zambezi.

This vast continent has a huge range of landscapes, wildlife and activities, as well as a beautiful coastline and islands, and it is very important to us that we arrange exactly the right honeymoon for our clients.

Please contact us in London, where we can arrange a personal presentation, or over the internet where we have many pages devoted to honeymoon ideas, and let us arrange the Africa honeymoon of your dreams.

Information & Reservations
UK 0870 606 1296
INT. +44 870 606 1296

27/29 James Martin Drive
PO Box ST 274
Southerton
Harare
Zimbabwe

✈ Hwange 55km

tel +263 4 660 554
fax +263 4 621 216

hide@specialhotels.com
www.specialhotels.com

Tour operators:
UK Grenadier, Art of Travel
US Fun Safaris

Zimbabwe's largest national park, Hwange, comprises 14,650 square kilometres of untamed wilderness inhabited by some of the most prolific game herds in Africa. Containing over 100 species of animals and 400 species of birds, it is also one of the few remaining sanctuaries in Africa where herds of elephant may be seen roaming the plains. The Hide Safari Camp offers the perfect way to experience the wonders of this African treasure.

Specially constructed hides, near the waterholes, are a photographer's paradise as herds of elephant, buffalo, giraffe and wildebeest are just some of the animals to be seen. Game viewing excursions, by foot or in comfortable overland vehicles, are also available. Whether guests go in search of big game or just want to trek up the 'fossil rivers' of Kennedy Plans, safaris can be tailor made to suit individual requirements.

Accommodation is in East African style canvas tents, comfortably furnished with en suite shower and other facilities. Each has a large porch area where guests can relax and view the game at their leisure. Although The Hide is right in the heart of the African bush, the candlelit dinners are served with a great deal of elegance and style around a huge dining table.

201

US$250-US$295 (10)
included
included

Honeymoon specials
Honeymoon tent with complimentary champagne.

Sightseeing and leisure
Game drives or walks with professional guides. A variety of species can be seen, including elephant, buffalo, wildebeest, zebra, giraffe and baboon, lion, leopard and cheetah. Guests can also view game from the underground Hide.

Katete Safari Lodge

PO Box 41
Kariba
Zimbabwe

✈ Landing strip 15 mins

tel +263 61 2807
fax +263 61 2892

katete@specialhotels.com
www.specialhotels.com

Tour operators:
UK Elegant Resorts
Zimbabwe Sun

This luxurious thatched lodge in the heart of the African Bush, downstream from the legendary Victoria Falls, has been built to blend into the banks of the spectacular Lake Kariba – a huge man-made inland sea, home to buffalo, elephants, lion and waterbuck.

The rooms are very spacious with large en suite bathrooms and Victorian furnishings in the style of *Out of Africa*. All have a private balcony, from where guests can watch elephants move graciously along the lakeshore or witness the famous African sunsets cast red and orange hues across the water.

Safaris, on foot, by boat or vehicle are an ideal way to explore the vast bush landscape and national parks teeming with game and birdlife. All are led by professional guides and leave twice daily at dawn and sunset.

Guests dine in romantic fashion – *al fresco* by candlelight – in great style with silver service, full five-course meals and an excellent range of wines.

 US$355-456 (16)

 US$969 (1)

|O| included

☕ included

(incl)

Honeymoon specials
Fruit and wine on arrival. All meals, drinks and safaris are covered by the all-inclusive rates, which start at US$355 per person per night.

Sightseeing and leisure
Visits to craft markets nearby. Safaris. Swimming pool, fishing and birdwatching.

Information & Reservations
UK 0870 606 1296
INT. +44 870 606 1296

Musango Safari Camp

Private Bag 2019
Kariba
Zimbabwe

✈ Kariba 20 min

tel +263 61 2391/3241
fax +263 61 3242

musango@pci.co.zw
www.specialhotels.com
www.classicsafaricamps.com

Situated on its own island, just off the shoreline of the Matusadona National Park, Musango Safari Camp provides the opportunity to get close to an abundance of wildlife from buffalo and elephants to the rare and elusive black rhino.

The thatched covered safari tents are large and luxurious featuring en suite bathrooms built out of natural stone and verandahs offering panoramic views across the bay of the Matusadona National Park and mountains. There is also a swimming pool and a bar-cum-lounge (the bar is one of the best places from which to view game).

Musango has the highest guides to guests ratio on Lake Kariba and specialises in walking safaris into the National Park and the nearby Wildlife Sanctuary. Game viewing is also conducted from one of the camp's many available boating cruises. Guests can also enjoy the serene and peaceful canoe trips up one of the adjacent creeks where the bird and wildlife is both prolific and enchanting with the scenery breathtaking.

For added romance during your visit, staff can organise moonlit dinners on a pontoon floating out on the calm waters of the lake. Romance, however, is in the very air at Musango, from the moment the dawn breaks to the campfire stories after sunset.

203

US$220-260 (6)

US$220-260 (2)

🍽 included

☕ included

Honeymoon specials
Champagne in room on arrival, candlelit dinner arranged on a pontoon on the lake, private meal at honeymoon suite also arranged on request. The two honeymoon suites have their own private plunge pool on the front verandah.

Sightseeing
Visits to local village, game viewing, walking, cruising by boat along the shorelines, canoeing, fishing, trips to the Rhino Orphanage Programme, plus specialised birdwatching trips on request.

Information & Reservations
UK 0870 606 1296
INT. +44 870 606 1296

124 Josiah
Chinamano St.
PO Box 1718
Harare
Zimbabwe

✈ Kariba 20km

tel +263 4 722233
fax +263 4 720360

sanyati@specialhotels.com
www.specialhotels.com
sanyati@icon.co.zw
ldf@mail.pci.co.zw

Tour operators:
UK On safari

204

Sanyati Lodge

Situated alongside the spectacular Sanyati Gorge, Sanyati Lodge nestles against the steep rugged hills of the Matusadona mountain range overlooking the gleaming waters of Lake Kariba. Natural stone walls, rough plaster, indigenous timber and thatch make this lodge merge quietly into the landscape in harmony with the surrounding environment.

Eleven luxury rooms are scattered throughout the extensive gardens. An elegant blend of natural fabrics in light neutral colours, layers of cream muslin, wrought iron and local basket weave have created a stunning interior. You can experience magnificent views of the lake while bathing in the glass-fronted bathroom or watch the stars above while taking an open-air shower.

For a romantic dining experience, the Lodge offers a five-course candlelit dinner, silver service-style, with local dishes such as Kariba Bream and Inyanga Trout on the menu.

The nearby Matusadona Game Park is home to a variety of wildlife, including the rare black rhino. You can view the game from Landrovers, take a cruise, or follow their tracks of big game. There's also fishing and canoeing down the Sanyati Gorge.

Weddings can be arranged at the local Kanba chapel or in the romantic grounds of the lodge.

 US$190-270 (9)

 US$230-450 (2)

 included

included

Honeymoon specials
Flowers, fruit and champagne in room on arrival.
Upgrade to the honeymoon suite subject to availability.

Sightseeing and leisure
Game viewing cruises, fishing, walking in the nearby Matusadona game park and game drives.

Information & Reservations
UK 0870 606 1296
INT. +44 870 606 1296

PO Box 10
Victoria Falls
Zimbabwe

✈ Victoria Falls Int. 22km

tel +263 13 4751
fax +263 13 4586

victoria@specialhotels.com
www.specialhotels.com

Tour operators:
UK Elegant Resorts
Zimbabwe Sun

An opulent building in the grandest of colonial styles, the Victoria Falls Hotel occupies a prime site in front of one of the most spectacular natural wonders of the world. The hotel was built back in 1904 and has been recently restored to bring back the full glory of the original Edwardian features, creating an atmosphere of elegance and grandeur. Some bedrooms have awe-inspiring views of the world's largest sheet of falling water.

The award-winning Livingstone Restaurant offers silver service, *á la carte* and *table d'hote* menus. The Pavilion Brasserie serves light snacks and buffets, while Jungle Junction is an informal restaurant for barbecues. Traditional afternoon tea is served on the verandah affording views of the gorge of the Falls and bridge linking Zimbabwe to Zambia. Activities include helicopter rides, game drives and sunset cruises along the Zambezi. A private path leads from the hotel directly to the Falls.

Hotel staff are delighted to arrange wedding ceremonies in the chapel, in front of the Falls Bridge or in the beautiful extensive grounds of the hotel. And wedding receptions are fully catered for.

Team the romantic Victoria Falls Hotel with the exclusive Katete Safari Lodge for a unique safari experience in the heart of Zimbabwe.

205

 US$335-414 (168)
 US$567-756 (14)
 from US$20
 included

Honeymoon specials
Flowers and sparkling wine on arrival. Room upgrade depending on availability.

Leisure facilities
Swimming pool, tennis courts. Touring desks and assistants for booking activities at the hotel. White-water rafting on the rapids of the Zambezi, bungee jumping.

Sightseeing
Visits to the spectacular Victoria Falls, crocodile farm and nature sanctuary and two national parks. Sundowners on the Zambezi, sipping champagne. The Flight of Angels helicopter tour providing a fabulous vista of the river. Visits to craft markets, local villages, and African Spectacular, a traditional African dance show.

Indian Ocean Islands

Athousand miles from anywhere, scattered on the waters between the coasts of India and Africa, dozens of Indian Ocean islands fringed delicately by long stretches of dazzling white beaches make perfect, secluded honeymoon retreats.

Their very remoteness is part of their charm. The Seychelles, the Maldives, the Comores and the larger island-nations of Mauritius and Sri Lanka share the magic of being well and truly away from it all. On any of these isles you find yourself adapting very quickly to a slower pace and tuning into nature.

In the Seychelles you can wonder at giant tortoises, and in the markets of the Comores or Perfume Isles breathe in the heady scents of ylang ylang, jasmine and patchouli.

Yet more natural wonders lie beneath the ocean. For Scuba divers this is a magical part of the world and non-divers can explore the underwater marvels with a snorkel, mask and flippers.

When on Mauritius you can walk among the brilliantly-coloured corals on the sea bed wearing a special helmet, and from Mahé in the Seychelles you can stay dry, but still get some glorious close-ups of the reef from an innovative sub-sea viewer.

ARABIAN SEA

SRI LANKA

MALDIVES

SEYCHELLES

INDIAN OCEAN

MAURITIUS

Benguerra Lodge

✈ Vilanculo 25km across sea

Contact:
PO Box 87416
Houghton 2041

tel +27 11 483 2734
fax +27 11 728 3767

benguerra@specialhotels.com
www.specialhotels.com

Member of:
Classic Camps of Africa

Situated off the coast of Mozambique and accessed by air, the luxurious Benguerra Lodge offers unsurpassed exclusivity in a tranquil and remote setting. The island is encircled by silver beaches, turquoise seas and coral reefs supporting a vast array of jewel-like fish.

The luxury thatched lodge is flanked by secluded chalets merged into a natural milkwood forest bordering Benguerra Bay. Each chalet, built on stilts with reed walls and thatched roofs, has a double room with en suite bathroom and a private balcony with views overlooking the ocean.

A mosaic of forest, savannah and wetland ecosystems sustain a diverse abundance of flora and fauna in this idyllic island getaway, which is now a designated nature reserve.

Fresh seafood and exotic Portuguese dishes are served at the lodge where service is attentive and discreet. A comprehensively stocked bar offers a wide range of wines and imported liqueurs.

This is a haven of peace and tranquillity and an ideal base to try out activities such as snorkelling, diving and sailing on a dhow. You can drive to a remote part of the island and picnic and sunbathe in seclusion, explore the birdlife or simply comb deserted beaches in solitude and serenity.

207

 US$235

 included

☕ included

Honeymoon specials

Complimentary champagne in room on arrival. All meals and accommodation, teas and coffees, daily laundry, snorkel trip with lunch, Landrover trip, island tour and sunset cruise in a *dhow*. 3-, 4-, 5- and 7-night packages cost from US$1,086.

Sightseeing and leisure

Visits to mainland markets and local church services. Sailing to see flamingos. Talks with local witchdoctor. Romantic walks along secluded beaches. Birdwatching. Sunset cruises on *dhow* or yacht. Deep-sea, fly fishing and snorkelling. Fully-equipped diving facility. Sailing on catamaran.

Maldives

There is a place on this earth where you go to do nothing but chill out – the Maldives. These 1,190 dots of land in the Indian Ocean are the closest you can get to being castaways.

flying time
London: 13-14 hrs
NY: 19-20 hrs

**climate/
when to go**
Tropical. Always hot at 25-30°C. High season is Nov-April when the weather is dry and hot. May-Oct it is wetter with high humidity and the possibility of heavy monsoon showers.

currency
The Rufiyaa, but prices at resort hotels are usually in US dollars.

language
Dhivehi. Many people speak some English.

getting around
By *dhoni*, speed boat, sea plane or helicopter.

208

If it is peace, quiet and your own private palm tree that you want, look no further. Hotels here do not have their own garden, they have their own island, with dazzling white-coral sand beaches and temptingly tepid azure sea. About 80 of the tiny, scattered islands have been developed for tourism, with just one resort hotel apiece. These are car-free zones you can walk around in a matter of minutes. Some are of the 'no news, no shoes' variety, with few facilities and no hot water, which is what some folks like. Others have mod cons such as air conditioning, a swimming pool, tennis courts, spa and a choice of restaurants – essential ingredients in other peoples' idea of honeymoon heaven.

The time-honoured and fun way of getting about this country – 99% of it being sea – is by *dhoni*, a wooden-hulled water-taxi, though nowadays there are speed boats and helicopters for long distances.

The islands are grouped in 26 atolls, each atoll surrounded by coral reef teeming with fish; no wonder more than half the visitors to the Maldives go Scuba diving. This is one of the world's very best dive sites and a superb place to take up the sport. Certified divers should be sure to take their log book and certificates and to take out insurance.

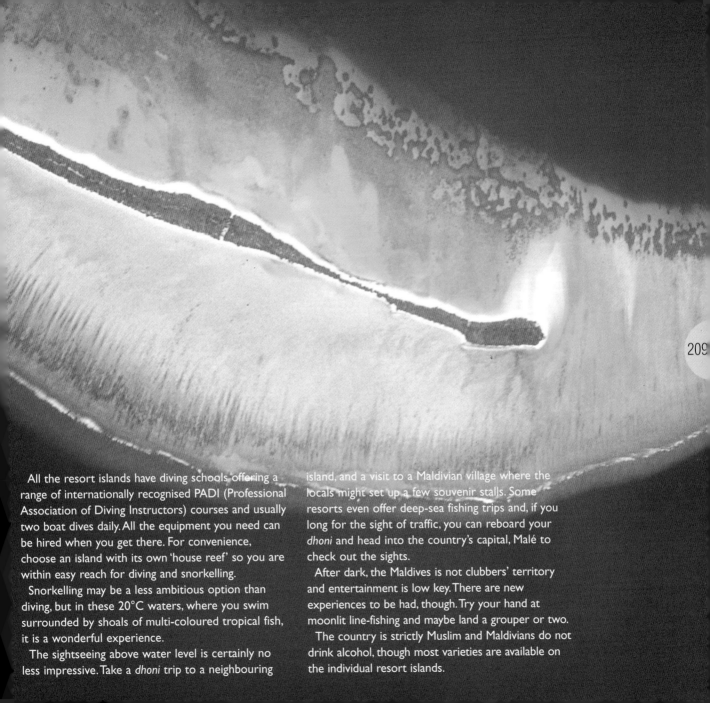

All the resort islands have diving schools offering a range of internationally recognised PADI (Professional Association of Diving Instructors) courses and usually two boat dives daily. All the equipment you need can be hired when you get there. For convenience, choose an island with its own 'house reef' so you are within easy reach for diving and snorkelling.

Snorkelling may be a less ambitious option than diving, but in these 20°C waters, where you swim surrounded by shoals of multi-coloured tropical fish, it is a wonderful experience.

The sightseeing above water level is certainly no less impressive. Take a *dhoni* trip to a neighbouring island, and a visit to a Maldivian village where the locals might set up a few souvenir stalls. Some resorts even offer deep-sea fishing trips and, if you long for the sight of traffic, you can reboard your *dhoni* and head into the country's capital, Malé to check out the sights.

After dark, the Maldives is not clubbers' territory and entertainment is low key. There are new experiences to be had, though. Try your hand at moonlit line-fishing and maybe land a grouper or two.

The country is strictly Muslim and Maldivians do not drink alcohol, though most varieties are available on the individual resort islands.

Baros Holiday Resort

c/o 39 Orchid Magu
20-02 Malé
Maldives

✈ Malé 16km

tel +960 323 080
fax +960 322 678

baros@specialhotels.com
www.specialhotels.com

Tour operators:
UK Kuoni

210

Situated in the North Malé Atoll, the private island that houses Baros Holiday Resort is as close to perfection as you'll get. Lush ferns and foliage offer shade from the bright sun that lights the resort and around the island stretch white sand beaches and calm blue seas.

Tucked discreetly among the island's thick lush vegetation are 32 standard rooms and 31 deluxe bungalows, all with thatched roof, and a terrace providing the perfect venue to watch the day drift away. Close to these lie the highlight of the resort, 12 wooden cottages built on stilts in the sea.

Succulent steaks and seafood served with an Asian twist are the specialities of the hotel's four restaurants. After dining relax in the Captain's Bar with its unique nautical design.

The diving and snorkelling here are superb. But you may also like to try windsurfing or catamaran sailing, as both are easily arranged. Also unmissable are excursions to the local islands – many of which are uninhabited. Pack a picnic and enjoy your own desert island for the day. As the sun goes down, you'll be collected and taken back to the luxury of Baros where another perfect evening awaits.

 US$170-180* (32)

 US$170-200* (31)

🍴 included

☕ included

Honeymoon specials
Fruit basket and a bottle of wine in room on arrival.

* Prices quoted are on a full-board basis.

Sightseeing and leisure
Daily entertainment programme. Also, most watersports are available including boating, fishing, diving, windsurfing, catamaran sailing, skiing and canoeing. You can also go island-hopping and take excursions to the capital of Malé.

Full Moon Beach Resort

c/o 39 Orchid Magu
20-02 Malé
Maldives

✈ Malé 6km

tel +960 323 080
fax +960 322 678

fullmoon@specialhotels.com
www.specialhotels.com

Tour operators:
UK Kuoni

As your speedboat skims across the crystal clear waters that surround the North Malé Atoll, Full Moon Beach shines like a jewel in the distance, offering a taste of luxury in this beautifully deserted island paradise.

With 52 water bungalows and 104 two-storey guesthouses to choose from, the resort is one of the larger in these islands. However, each room is spacious and all offer amazing, uninterrupted sea views. Furnishings are simple to reflect local style but this traditional look is combined with modern comforts, as all rooms are air-conditioned and contain telephones and mini bars.

Dining takes place under the stars at one of the hotel's many restaurants and bars. Choose from many: elegant dining on steak and seafood or relax in the casual atmosphere of the on site pizzeria. None of the restaurants will disappoint.

There's also much to fill your days at the resort. Diving and watersports are obviously on offer but you can also workout in the gym, work on your backhand in the tennis courts or work on your tan as you relax by the swimming pool. All you have to decide is whether to choose a pina colada or fresh coconut water drunk straight from the shell. The choice is all yours.

211

 US$170-180* (52)

 US$170-200* (104)

⦿ included

included

Honeymoon specials
Fruit basket and a bottle of wine in room on arrival.

* Prices quoted are on a full-board basis.

Sightseeing and leisure
Booking of sightseeing trips and excursions to other islands can be arranged at the hotel. There is also a swimming pool, children's pool, shopping arcade, gym and tennis courts.

Laguna Beach

c/o 39 Orchid Magu
20-02 Malé
Maldives

✈ Malé 12km

tel +960 445 903
fax +960 443 041

laguna@specialhotels.com
www.specialhotels.com

Tour operators:
UK Kuoni

Located on the northern tip of the South Malé Atoll, this first-class resort is set in lush green gardens and surrounded by abundant coral reefs both just waiting to be explored.

The hotel offers 115 deluxe rooms housed in two-storey bungalows or, choose to stay in one of the 17 stunning, over-the-water suites that stretch out across the colourful reefs. Here your closest neighbours are the fish and stingrays that dance playfully underneath your overseas verandah.

Italian, Chinese and continental cuisine are on offer in the five hotel restaurants. But for those quiet evenings, you can order room service to allow yourselves the privacy you may well be needing. Either way, the food is outstanding and the service top-notch.

Of course, no trip to the Maldives would be complete without experiencing life under the water. Diving and snorkelling can be arranged by the hotel – as can sailing, windsurfing and fishing. If you'd prefer not to get your feet wet, the hotel is also happy to arrange excursion island-hopping or to the nearby town of Malé. Or why not just stay on site and enjoy all the facilities they have to offer. After all, at the Laguna Beach, Heaven really is a place on earth.

 US$170-180* (115)

 US$170-200* (17)

 included

 included

Honeymoon specials
Fruit basket and a bottle of wine in room on arrival.

* Prices quoted are on a full-board basis.

Sightseeing and leisure
Boating and fishing, diving, windsurfing and catamaran sailing. Health club, gym, sauna, tennis courts, table tennis and billiards. You can also go island-hopping and take excursions to the capital of Malé.

Information & Reservations
UK 0870 606 1296
INT. +44 870 606 1296

c/o 39 Orchid Magu
20-02 Malé
Maldives

✈ Malé 24km

tel +960 443 847
fax +960 442 665

nakatcha@specialhotels.com
www.specialhotels.com

Tour operators:
UK Kuoni

Situated on the western side of the North Malé Atoll, Nakatchafushi houses 51 round, thatched bungalows set in lush tropical grounds festooned with flowers and shrubs.

Each of these idyllic self-contained units faces the beach and comes equipped with air conditioning, mini bar and tea and coffee making facilities. Inside, pastel coloured decor and white marble floors create an air of cooling calm that aids in your quest for relaxation and tranquillity.

The hotel has four restaurants and dining is available late into the evening for the night owls among you – and there is much to do in the evening. Choose to go night fishing, to dance till the early hours in the disco, or simply to sit back with a cocktail in the over-water bar and watch the fish play the night away in the tropical waters of the lagoon. Staying up late is never a problem at Nakatchafushi as tomorrow you can spend the day relaxing on the miles of sugary white sand that line the resort.

If you'd prefer to keep busy there's a whole world of experiences to explore both underwater and on land, including sightseeing, diving and sailing. Opportunities and delights never end in this secluded private island hideaway.

213

US$170-200* (51)

🍽 included

☕ included

Honeymoon specials
Fruit basket and a bottle of wine in room on arrival.

* Prices quoted are on a full-board basis.

Sightseeing and leisure
Booking of sightseeing trips and excursions to other islands can be arranged at the hotel. There is also a swimming pool and guest gift shop.

Soneva Fushi

Kunfunadhoo Island
Baa Atoll
Maldives

✈ Male Int. 115km

tel +960 230 304/5
fax +960 230 374

soneva@specialhotels.com
www.specialhotels.com
www.soneva-pavilion.com

Contact:
Soneva Pavilion Hotels
tel +44 (0)1296 660800

214

Tour operators:
UK Elegant Resorts

Member of:
Small Luxury Hotels

Blessed on all sides by a private shallow lagoon encircled by a coral reef, the tiny island of Kunfunadhoo is a Robinson Crusoe-style hideaway in the middle of the Indian Ocean. At the edge of the lapping, clear waters, just a few steps up on the beach, are the villas of the Soneva Fushi resort.

All the rooms are naturally styled with thick wooden frames and cane blinds in soft, light colours to reflect the vibrance and warm ambience of the island. Some have four-poster beds. Modern furnishings are tastefully concealed inside natural objects – such as a coconut desk, or rattan – maintaining modern living standards right in the midst of nature.

By day, guests can lunch under a canopy of trees by the beach, or enjoy a simple, romantic, desert island picnic on one of the many surrounding islands of The Maldives. At night the restaurant serves a range of delightful dishes, including Western, Asian and New World cuisine. For romantic dining, guests can choose to dine al fresco on a private beach by lantern light.

Experienced beauty and body therapists are on hand to ease the mind and soul with a soothing massage.

Weddings receptions can be arranged for up to 124 guests in the restaurant or on the beach.

 US$150–825 (55)

 US$430–1,115 (7)

🍽 US$45

🍵 US$15

Honeymoon specials
Champagne on arrival and candlelit romantic dinner (all year round). From April to July 1999, honeymooners receive champagne on arrival, candlelit dinner, desert island picnic, plus one free beauty treatment for each partner. Standard rates apply.

Sightseeing and leisure
Local fishing village, excursions to the islands of Mahlos and Eydhafushi. Maldivian band *Bodubeeru* every Friday. Spectacular coral reef and underwater life. A wide variety of watersports including snorkelling, windsurfing, diving and game fishing.

Taj Maldives

Maldives

✈ Malé 50 mins by boat

Taj Coral Reef Resort:
Post Bag No. 53, North Malé Atoll
tel +960 44 1948/1903
fax +960 44 3884

Taj Lagoon Resort:
Post Bag No. 53, South Malé Atoll
tel +960 440037
fax +960 445925

Taj toll free reservations:
UK 0800 282 699
US/Canada 800 458 8825

coral@specialhotels.com
www.specialhotels.com
coralreef.maldives@tajhotels.com
lagoon.maldives@tajhotels.com

Member of
The Taj Group of Hotels

South-west of Sri Lanka about 128km lie the secluded islands of the Maldives and here, set in lush green vegetation, on acres of tropical paradise, you'll find two stunning resorts: Taj Coral Reef Resort and Taj Lagoon Resort; each resort being an island by itself.

At the new Taj Coral Reef, there are two types of accommodation available. The Garden Villas are set in the tropical grounds of the hotel and each contains comfortable furnishings, garden hammocks and an exotic open-air shower. Marine lovers will relish the chance to stay in one of the water bungalows with their glass walls offering panoramic views of the calm turquoise waters.

The Taj Lagoon Resort, meanwhile, is built on stilts with palm-thatched roofs. All have private balconies and sun decks. They stand at the water's edge and when the tide is in guests can sit out on the porch imagining they are in a boat at sea.

Both hotels offer fine international cuisine as well as local Maldivian favourites. And no matter which type of food you choose at either resort, the surroundings are just as sensational as the food.

By day, wander round these idyllic islands, explore the sugary beaches and colourful marine life that characterise the Maldivian islands.

215

 US$155-325*

 US$26

 included

Honeymoon specials
Special package deals, room upgrade subject to availability, champagne and flowers on arrival. Candlelit dinner on the beach with a complimentary bottle of wine.

* Prices are subject to change.

Other Taj hotels
The Taj Group of Hotels has an extensive selection of fine hotels across south Asia. You can choose to stay in one of their 'gateway' hotels: The Taj Palace Hotel or Taj Mahal Hotel, New Delhi; Taj Mahal Hotel, Bombay; or Taj Coromandel, Madras; all members of Leading Hotels of the World, en route to your chosen Taj honeymoon spot.

Mauritius

flying time
London: 11-12 hrs
NY 17-18 hrs

climate
Any time but do not expect tropical weather from May-Oct. Hindu festivals, Cavadee (Jan-Feb) and Divali (Oct) are spectacular.

currency
The Mauritian Rupee.

language
The official language is English. French, Creole, Hindi and Chinese are also spoken.

getting around
Local bus, taxi or car hire.

This is one of the largest Indian Ocean islands. Its 720 square miles pack in an amazing variety of landscapes, from the soaring mountain peaks of extinct volcanoes to gushing waterfalls and field after field of wind-rippled sugar cane.

Around the coastline there is an almost unbroken circle of coral reef. The gentle north coast gives way to wildly rugged southern scenery, and an east coast of sugary-white beaches and shallow lagoons with warm, waist-high waters.

The one million people who live here are a harmonious mix of races and cultures. African, Indian, Chinese and European settlers have given the island its different faces, traditions and religions. In even the smallest village you will find a mosque, a Hindu temple and perhaps a Christian church. Everyone joins in the spectacle and jollity of festivals that seem to happen almost weekly.

The food is a *pot pourri* too, featuring spicy samosas and 'gateaux piments', Chinese sweet-and-sour dishes, and the delicate but aromatic home-grown flavours of smoked marlin and the palm heart that has been nicknamed 'millionaire's salad'.

Millionaires and celebrities feel at home on Mauritius, which has some of the region's most sophisticated hotels. The island's infrastructure is well developed and things work pretty efficiently. In the capital, Port Louis, tower blocks are starting to dwarf the old colonial buildings, though it only takes a walk through the Victorian wrought iron gates of the central market to find yourself in a scene that hardly seems to have changed in a century.

Odorous halls are thronged with housewives eyeing up freshly caught sailfish and the goat that goes into a tasty curry. Grains and pulses overflow from huge sacks in the warren of stalls, where you haggle with vendors over the price of gaily printed beach clothes, carvings, vanilla pods and spices to take home as souvenirs.

If you enjoy sports, Mauritius is the island for you, with Scuba diving, yachting, deep-sea fishing for marlin and tuna, and all sorts of watersports with the latest equipment. There is also the opportunity to play golf on a choice of 18-hole courses, and the spectacle of horseracing at the Champ de Mars.

When you want a change from the beach, take a day trip on a catamaran, or join a bus tour round the island. Or jump in your own hired car – an open-top jeep is fun – and seek out the dodo (stuffed) in the Mauritius Institute museum; the 85 varying types of palm trees in the marvellous Botanical Gardens at Pamplemousses; and history-brought-to-life at Domaine des Pailles, the island's nearest equivalent to a theme park, where you can see how sugar cane is made into rum – the islanders' favourite tipple.

Special Honeymoon Hotels
Information

Internet

Visit our website for information on hotels and resorts featured in the 1999 edition of Special Honeymoon Hotels. Access additional details and pictures on some of the hotels located in these pages and find out more of what Special Hotels has in store for you.

www.specialhotels.com

plus...

Information hotline

Call our worldwide telephone hotline for details on hotels featured in the 1999 edition. Our telephone operators will provide information on more than 170 hotels and resorts and will be able to direct your call for reservations, and in many cases make bookings for you.

There are many different ways of booking and getting the best value from the world's great hotels and resorts. It is our job to help you do so.

Within UK 0870 606 1296
Outside UK +44 870 606 1296

Telephone lines will be operational between 10.00am-5.00pm (UK time) Monday-Friday.

All calls from the UK will be charged at national rate; calls made from overseas will be charged at standard international rate. Daytime calls: 6.7p per minute; evening calls: 3.5p per minute; weekends: 2.5p per minute.

Internet www.specialhotels.com

Information hotline 0870 606 1296
+44 870 606 1296

Paradis

Le Morne

Mauritius

✈ Mauritius Int. 70km

For reservations contact:
Beachcomber
tel +44 1483 533008
fax +44 1483 532820

b@bctuk.demon.co.uk
paradis@specialhotels.com
www.specialhotels.com

Lying on a private peninsula at the south-westerly tip of Mauritius, the Paradis resort nestles sweetly between le Morne and the Indian Ocean in beautifully landscaped gardens. Spread out on a seemingly endless strip of golden beach where one can always find a quiet secluded spot to be alone, the Paradis is an idyllic setting for romance.

All the rooms extend along the white beach encompassing the peninsula. The 280 rooms and 13 luxury villas are both elegant and spacious yet traditionally designed to retain Mauritian flavour.

The resort's four restaurants serve a delicious range of national and international dishes in stylish and intimate settings.

Surrounded by some of the island's most amazing natural wonders, you can hike around waterfalls or visit the volcanic lake at Grand Bassin. For golf fanatics the challenging 18-hole championship course is nearby, which blends perfectly into the relief of the peninsula. Free and unlimited land and watersports, tennis, squash and aerobics are also available. Or you may decide to just laze around the swimming pool, rejuvenate yourself in the massage parlour or shape up in the gym.

219

 RS3,375-8,438

 RS7,050-13,838

 included

 included

Honeymoon specials
Flowers, fruit and wine in the room on arrival. Candlelit dinner with wine, souvenir gift from the management. A package costs from £1,536 based on two weeks for the price of one. Another package available throughout the year includes a 40% discount for wives arriving with their newly wed husbands.

Sightseeing and leisure
Rochester and Tamarind Falls, Black River Gorge, Grand Bassin Lake and the Casela bird park nearby. Sauna and massage. Extensive watersports including deep-sea fishing and Scuba diving. Swimming, golf and full use of the gym.

Royal Palm

Grand Baie
Mauritius

✈ Mauritius Int. 75km

For reservations contact:
Beachcomber
tel +44 1483 533008
fax +44 1483 532820

b@bctuk.demon.co.uk
palm@specialhotels.com
www.specialhotels.com

Perfectly positioned on a golden stretch of one of the most exclusive beaches in Mauritius, the Royal Palm blends European comfort with tropical elegance.

The rooms are brightly furnished with silk carpets and Indian artefacts handpicked by the manager. Each one is sea facing. Ground floor rooms open on to private verandahs, with only a small neat lawn separating them from the beach. For pure indulgence, the three-bedroomed Royal Suite has a personal valet service, en suite bathrooms with jet bath, Jacuzzi and steps which take you directly to the beach.

French-trained chefs create a range of culinary delights featuring seafood and local dishes such as *rougaille* made from the hearts of palm trees.

There are a wide range of sports on offer including waterskiing, sailing and windsurfing. Or you can work out in the fitness centre, relax in a Turkish bath or have an invigorating massage to replenish energy levels.

Don't forget to explore the historic streets of the island's capital, Port Louis, and stroll through the renowned Pamplemousses botanical gardens.

 RS5,175-9,038 (57)

 RS11,325-33,713

 approx RS1,200*

 included

Honeymoon specials

Flowers, fruit and wine in the room on arrival. Plus a souvenir gift.

Leisure facilities

Hotel fitness centre with gymnasium, Turkish bath, sauna and massage. Waterskiing, sailing, windsurfing, tennis and squash available.

Sightseeing

Trips to the local fishing village of Grand Baie and the island's capital city, Port Louis with its shops, restaurants, markets and festivals. Visits to Domaine les Pailles, a restored former colonial sugar estate, or Pamplemousses botanical gardens.

* An à la carte menu is also available.

Shandrani

Plaine Magnien
Mauritius

✈ Mauritius Int. 6km

For reservations contact:
Beachcomber
tel +44 1483 533 008
fax +44 1483 532 820

b@bctuk.demon.co.uk
shandrani@specialhotels .com
www.specialhotels.com

Overlooking Blue Bay in the south-east of Mauritius, the Shandrani, (meaning 'Goddess of the Moon' in Hindi), is surrounded by badamiers, flame trees, palm trees, bougainvilleas and many other exotic plants. The resort features finely worked thatch roofs, stone colonnades set with ceramics and delicately sculptured woodwork.

The rooms are spacious and bright, furnished with wood and rattan. You can gaze out across the lagoon from the secluded terraces, or relax in the luxurious bathrooms which provide views of the sea less than 20 metres away.

Excellent restaurants, each one cultivating a different ambience, offer a range of dining options from Chinese and Indian to Creole and local seafood specialities.

The resort is happy to arrange excursions to historic sights and natural wonders on the island. Most notable is the volcanic lake at Grand Bassin. You may prefer to spend your days sailing, playing tennis or pitch and putt golf, or trying out one of the vast range of watersports on offer.

Wedding and honeymoon couples are also invited to attend a blessing of love by a Hindu priest, and the staff are more than happy to provide assistance with wedding arrangements.

221

RS3,225-5,663

RS4,163-11,363

🍽 included

☕ included

Honeymoon specials

Flowers, fruit and wine in room on arrival. Candlelit dinner with wine, souvenir gift. Blessing of love by a Hindu priest. Package costs from £1,500 based on two weeks for the price of one. Another package available all year includes a 50% discount for wives arriving with their newly-wed husbands. Discounts available for wedding guests.

Sightseeing and leisure

Trips to Curepipe, Grand Bassin, Rochester and Tamarind Falls and the naval museum in the historic town of Mahebourg. The resort has a resident band, folkdancing, theme evenings and astronomy evenings. Extensive land and watersports including Scuba diving, sailing, tennis and golf nearby. Sauna and massage available.

The Residence

Coastal Road
Belle Mare
Mauritius

✈ Plaisance 48km

tel +230 401 8888
fax +230 415 5888

residence@specialhotels.com
www.specialhotels.com
residenc@intnet.mu
www.theresidence.com

222

Tour operators:
UK Elegant Resorts
Indian Ocean Connection

Located on one of the most beautiful beaches in Mauritius, guests at The Residence could forgive themselves for thinking they had gone back in time. With its grand, high-vaulted entrance lobby, columned terraces and freeform pools the hotel seems to be part of the Roaring Twenties when times were good and the living was easy.

The rooms and suites, decorated in harmonious blends of beige and white continue the illusion. Fresh flowers sit on glass topped tables, dark-wood four poster beds are made with crisp linen and cool, silver-white sofas look expectant, waiting for someone to recline elegantly on them.

The best of modern international cuisine is on offer in The Dining Room, prepared from native produce. For something a little more spicy, Creole dishes can be enjoyed in the oceanfront setting of The Plantation, enlivened by the sounds of local entertainment. Afternoon tea is a treat with delicate teas and a wide selection of pastries and cakes.

There is also a selection of watersports, including waterskiing and land-based activities such as tennis. If you choose to go deep-sea fishing, take a catamaran cruise or go diving, it can be arranged. If you prefer to be less active, an evening stroll along the beach or a massage in The Sanctuary is just as enticing.

🛏 RS3,800-7,590 (151)

🛋 RS5,770-18,265 (20)

🍽 RS1,200

☕ included

Honeymoon specials

Champagne and flowers in room on arrival. Room upgrade when available.

Sightseeing and leisure

The Sanctuary health and beauty centre in the hotel, swimming pool, children's pool, complimentary Jacuzzi. Waterskiing, windsurfing, snorkelling and tennis. Local attractions include the botanical gardens and capital of Port Louis with its bustling market.

Trou aux Biches

Triolet
Mauritius

✈ Mauritus Int. 70km

For reservations contact:
Beachcomber
tel +44 1483 533008
fax +44 1483 532820

b@bctuk.demon.co.uk
trou@specialhotels.com
www.specialhotels.com

Ideally positioned on the north-west coast of Mauritius, the romantic chalet-style Trou aux Biches sits on the pristine shores of a calm and protected lagoon.

The shingled and thatched chalets typical of the island are discreetly set in extensive tropical gardens. Traditional prints and furnishings are combined with contemporary comforts in the wooden chalets, and each has a private terrace.

The two restaurants are beautifully positioned close to the lagoon with wonderful views of the reef, and are especially romantic in candle light. Themed evenings with traditional dancing and food allow you to taste a little of the local culture.

Land and watersports on offer include sailing, waterskiing, windsurfing and tennis. Excursions can be arranged to the local village or nearby botanical gardens. A beauty centre and massage parlour allow you to unwind in luxury. For golf enthusiasts, there is the splendid 9-hole course with a thatched roof clubhouse.

The beach house, La Bella Vista, is a delightful location for a wedding ceremony and staff here are happy to make the necessary arrangements. Each newly-married couple is offered the chance to plant a palm tree in celebration of their marriage.

223

RS3,525-5,813
RS7,050-11,625
     included
    included

Honeymoon specials

Flowers, fruit and wine in the room on arrival. Candlelit dinner with wine, souvenir gift. This package costs from £1,567 for two weeks for the price of one. Another package is available all year including a 50% discount for wives arriving with their newly-wed husbands. Discounts available for wedding guests.

Sightseeing and leisure

Trips to the local fishing village of Grand Baie and the island's capital city, Port Louis. Shops, restaurants, markets and festivals nearby. Visits to Domaine les Pailles, a restored former colonial sugar estate, or Pamplemousses botanical gardens. Extensive land and watersports including Scuba diving are available at no extra charge. Beauty centre with massage.

Seychelles

flying time
London: 10-12 hrs
NY: 18-19 hrs

climate/
when to go
Tropical. Hot and humid Nov-Feb although slightly cooler and drier Mar-Oct. The temperature stays at a constant 20-30°C all year.

currency
The Seychelles Rupee.

language
Creole although English and French are widely spoken.

getting around
By ferry, plane or helicopter between the islands. By bus, taxi or hire car on Mahé and Praslin.

You cannot return from the Seychelles without having acquired a new skill — sega dancing.

The sexy, hip-wiggling dance is the traditional accompaniment to folk tunes that express 200 years of history on these beautiful, far-flung islands.

The Seychelles archipelago is made up of 115 islands, spread over such a vast area that getting between them often involves flights rather than boat trips. An amazing fact is that only a handful are inhabited and 90% of the population live on Mahé. This is where international flights land and most visitors stay.

It is here that you find the country's tiny capital, Victoria, with its echoes of former British rule. The island's main beach, and by far the busiest on the Seychelles, is a long curve of pale sand known as Beau Vallon Bay. This is excellent for watersports and for people-watching, but if you want a beach all to yourself, hire a car for a day and explore the coastline.

A worthwhile day trip takes you on a glass-bottom boat or a submarine to see the coral reef of the Marine National Park, then to Moyenne Island, where you can meet the giant tortoises and bask in the blissfully warm waters of a shallow lagoon.

Mahé and the other main island, Praslin, are both rocky and have huge granite boulders littering their powdery white sands. Both are lush and hilly, with jungly tropical scenery and splashes of pink, purple and scarlet flora highlighted against the emerald green. A walk in Praslin's mysterious Valley de Mai brings you under the shadow of rare and exotic plants, like the coco de mer palm, which can only be found in this part of the world.

From Mahé you can take day trips to other islands, but as they differ so much in scenery and style, the very best way to experience the Seychelles is to island-hop. Frequent flights make it easy to combine islands. On La Digue, where there are no cars, you do your sightseeing from an ox-drawn cart or a bicycle, and become part of a way of life that seems stuck in a time-warp.

Cousin, Aride and Bird islands are breeding grounds for millions of seabirds but you do not need to be a keen birdwatcher to marvel at the colourful parrots, weaver birds, magpie robins and fairy terns.

Watersports, diving, snorkelling and game fishing are on offer at most of the island resorts and on Mahé and Praslin you find some nightlife. Be prepared to attempt the latest variation on the sega, even if it's only at the local disco.

Do try and venture beyond the sometimes bland 'international' food on the hotel menus and sample some typical Seychellois cooking. Local produce, like tuna, octopus and crab, chicken, breadfruit and yams, is jazzed up to delicious effect, with coconut milk and generous dashes of spice.

Fisherman's Cove

PO Box 35
Mahé
Seychelles

✈ Seychelles Int. 15km

tel +248 247 247
fax +248 247 742

fisherman@specialhotels.com
www.specialhotels.com

Tour operators:
UK Kuoni

The Seychelles archipelago is a jewel set in the transparent lagoons of the Indian Ocean. On the island of Mahé, home to rare and exotic birds and lush flora and fauna, Le Méridien Fisherman's Cove is a little paradise in its own right. Situated at the tip of the beautiful beach of Beauvallon, the local architecture of simple stone and slate blends well with the tropical gardens which surround it.

The rooms and cottages all have their own terrace affording ocean views. The cottages have small private gardens where couples can relax in serenity and seclusion. The decor is bright and comfortable with wood panelled walls, colourful rugs and bedspreads, cane furniture and pottery lamps. And for the totally tropical touch, all rooms have direct access to the beach.

The hotel has two restaurants. On the menu are Creole specialities of the region with the emphasis on fish, crab, lobster and other seafood delicacies. Grilled, curried, served with ginger – all are to a high standard and delicious. The more adventurous might even try turtle soup or grilled bat.

In the evening the Blue Marlin Bar, with its sweeping ocean views, is a popular retreat serving cocktails and pre-dinner drinks to the tones of light classical music and jazz.

225

 US$500–665 (48)

 US$780 (2)

US$40

US$25

Honeymoon specials
Champagne, fruit and gifts for newly-weds on arrival.

Leisure facilities
Swimming, Scuba diving, snorkelling, tennis, golf, volleyball, billiards, boules, ping-pong, deep-sea fishing, sailing, plus other watersports. Bicycle hire.

Sightseeing
Visits to nature reserves, bird sanctuaries, coral reefs. Trips by chartered boat to neighbouring islands, particularly La Digue and Praslin. World Music Day in May, jazz and international food festival in July. Discovering the capital of Mahé with its restaurants, art galleries and markets.

Hotel L'Archipel

Route des Cocotiers
Anse Gouvernement
Praslin
Seychelles

✈ Mahé 7km

tel +248 232 242
fax +248 232 072

archipel@specialhotels.com
www.specialhotels.com

Tour operators:
UK Elegant Resorts

226

Praslin is the second largest island in the picturesque group that makes up the Seychelles. Some believe it is the most beautiful and that's an opinion you may well believe yourself as you drive up the lush wooded drive to L'Archipel and arrive at your villa overlooking the perfect curved bay of soft sand and sparkling blue sea beyond.

Beamed ceilings and muslin drapes characterise the traditional fittings of the 24 airy rooms here. All contain lovely sea-facing verandahs and suites also have their own private Jacuzzi bath.

Dining is available in the main building, beachside or on the privacy of your own verandah – but wherever you choose the food is always superb. Dishes are overseen by the creative influence of the hotel's French trained chef. On less formal nights, the Creole buffet definitely should not be missed.

During the day you can explore Praslin's two tiny villages or simply set out on your own. Every part of the island can be reached within one hour's drive. Closer to home, the hotel's enticing calm bay offers many water activities including windsurfing and snorkelling. For ultimate romance, take a cruise to one of the many secluded islets that dot the sea and enjoy your own desert island for a day.

 from US$402* (21)

 US$516-664* (3)

 included

 included

Honeymoon specials
Basket of fruit, bottle of sparkling wine in room on arrival. Room upgrade subject to availability.

* Prices are on a half-board basis.

Sightseeing and leisure
All watersports, from windsurfing to snorkelling, and private cruises to secluded islets. Deep-sea fishing, diving and bottom fishing can be arranged but cost extra. You can also hire bicycles.

Sri Lanka

**climate/
when to go**
Tropical monsoon,
north-east monsoon
(Dec-Mar).
South-west monsoon
(June-Oct). Dec-Mar
is best for the south
and west coasts,
May-Sept on the
north and east.

currency
Sri Lankan Rupees.

language
Tamil, Sinhala and
English.

getting around
Plenty of buses and
trains. Hiring a car is
a popular option.

health
Immunisation against
cholera and hepatitis,
plus anti-malaria.

Once upon a time Sri Lanka was known as 'Serendib'. From this we have devised the word 'serendipity' – a happy and unexpected accidental discovery.

True to form, the pear-shaped island nation set in the Indian Ocean is both happy and unexpected. Only 240 miles long and 140 miles across at its widest point, it is nevertheless a wonderful mix of extremes.

Dry desert plains are set against jungles, home to leopards and elephants. The fresh mountain tea estates, serene and isolated, soar above the bustling capital of Colombo. A single day can see the sun rise and set over the ruins of majestic civilisations and modern luxury beach resorts to be found along the long stretches of glorious sandy beaches and deep crystal clear waters.

A land of tea and coconuts, monasteries and temples, quiet villages and frenetic festivals, Sri Lanka will provide one unexpected delight after another. Discover it all for yourself.

227

Mahaweli Reach

35 PBA Weerakoon
Mawatha
PO Box 78
Kandy
Sri Lanka

✈ Colombo 125km

tel +94 74 472727
fax +94 8 232068

mahaweli@specialhotels.com
www.specialhotels.com

228

Kandy was the ancient capital of Sri Lanka and as such offers many sights to enthral the visitor. Positioned directly on the banks of the river, which is Sri Lanka's longest, Mahaweli which loops the town, this luxurious resort offers a superb base for exploration.

The 116 air-conditioned rooms are comfortably furnished and all have balconies overlooking either the river or the hotel's huge freeform swimming pool. They also contain television and mini bar.

The on site restaurant specialises in Sri Lankan cuisine, which is renowned for its rich flavours and original use of spices. Delicious local and international dishes are also served at regular theme nights and barbecues. The hotel also offers nightly entertainment such as dance troupes, live music and romantic river cruises.

On site facilities at the Mahaweli Reach are superb with billiards, tennis and river fishing just an example of the activities available. Off site, you can choose from excursions to many of Sri Lanka's phenomenal sights. Essential visits during any stay are to the Temple of the Sacred Tooth Relic, the Sigiriya rock fortress, the Esala Perahera with authentic folk dancers, and the endearing Elephant Orphanage. Don't miss bathtime at 3pm.

 US$120-150 (112)

 US$200-450 (2)

US$15

US$7-11

Honeymoon specials
Champagne, cake, chocolates and flowers in room on arrival. Also, souvenirs from the hotel and upgrade to a suite depending on availability. Note: Minimum stay of three nights to qualify for above special.

Sightseeing and leisure
The hotel offers billiards, swimming, tennis and boating on site. Golf course and beauty salon nearby. Excursions include Temple of the Sacred Tooth relic, Royal Botanical Gardens, Kandyan Arts & Crafts, the Elephant Orphanage at Pinnawela and colourful bazaars.

Taj Exotica

Dharmawijayarama
Mawatha
Bentota
Sri Lanka

✈ Katunayak 90km

tel +94 34 75650-8
fax +94 34 75160

exotica@specialhotels.com
www.specialhotels.com
exotica.bentota@tajhotels.com

Taj toll free reservations:
UK 0800 282 699
US/Canada 800 458 8825

Member of:
The Taj Group of Hotels

Palm trees, golden sands and deep blue sea cradle Sri Lanka's south-west coast and nestled within this 150 kilometres of total paradise lies one of the finest hotels in the region, the Taj Exotica.

There are 169 rooms or suites to choose from and each overlooks the sweeping bay. Lie in your king-sized bed to watch the sun rise over the water or settle in to one of the comfortable rattan chairs on your balcony and enjoy an exotic fruit breakfast courtesy of the hotel's 24-hour room service.

Out of room dining also offers a luxurious culinary experience. Three speciality restaurants offer intricate menus based around both local and international cuisine. After your meal it is easy to unwind with a tropical cocktail at one of the hotel's two bars.

By day, step just yards from your door to wander the miles of shoreline and beachcomb some of the beautiful shells left behind by the flowing tide of the Indian Ocean. To cool off take a dip in its calm clear waters, visit the hotel's large swimming pool or try one of the many watersports on offer. If you'd prefer to travel further afield, car hire is easily arranged at the hotel and allows easy access to the many unique sights Sri Lanka has to offer.

229

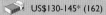 US$130-145* (162)

 US$250-350* (7)

 from US$35

 US$8

Honeymoon specials

Package includes charges for registrar, hairdressing and dressing up of bride, bridal bouquet and button hole for groom, wedding cake, bottle of sparkling wine, one photo, fruits and flowers in room, special candlelit dinner on wedding night. Price: US$225.

* Prices subject to change.

Other Taj hotels

The Taj Group of Hotels has an extensive selection of fine hotels across south Asia. You can choose to stay in one of their 'gateway' hotels: The Taj Palace Hotel or Taj Mahal Hotel, New Delhi; Taj Mahal Hotel, Bombay; or Taj Coromandel, Madras; all members of Leading Hotels of the World, en route to your chosen Taj honeymoon spot.

Saman Villas

Aturuwella
Bentota
Sri Lanka

✈ Colombo 92km

tel +94 34 75 435
fax +94 34 75 433

saman@specialhotels.com
www.specialhotels.com

Tour operators:
UK Elegant Resorts
Premier Holidays

Member of:
Small Luxury Hotels

230

Described as Sri Lanka's most luxurious resort, Saman Villas perches on a rocky headland on the island's west coast by a quiet fishing village. Behind you lie lush avenues of green coconut palms, to each side stretches miles and miles of pure white sand, and in the distance all you see is the beautiful blue waters of the Indian Ocean.

Twenty-seven suites make up the resort and all are angled to ensure each verandah or balcony offers superb coastal vistas. Inside, wooden floors, traditional matting and rattan furnishings create an air of simple elegance. They are all spacious, consisting of a living room, sleeping deck, dressing room and sumptuous bathroom with courtyard.

 US$110-290* (27)

 US$6-20*

 US$7-11*

Prices subject to additional charges, enquire with hotel.

Honeymoon specials

Champagne, heart-shaped cake and flowers on arrival. Mangala Pavilion for private use for one full day, a private five-course al fresco dinner. Hand-made stationery and gift of hotel souvenir. Free upgrade to deluxe suite, subject to availablity. The special launch rate for this package is US$240 plus room rate, based on a stay of at least three nights. Price includes service charge and government tax.

The two restaurants are also perfectly positioned with either sea or garden views. Choose from a wide selection of Western, Eastern and spicy Sri Lankan dishes. And service is immaculate.

Facilities at the hotel are perfect for the active. There is an on site fitness room for those who want to stay in shape, plus a sauna; while a variety of watersports and archery can be found close by.

Waterbabies will also love the infinity-type swimming pool that, from ground level, appears to merge with the Indian Ocean. The pool connects with a large terraced garden which extends along the rest of the seafront from north to south.

Traditional Sri Lankan weddings can be arranged by the hotel and tailored to the couple's religious specifications. Held in traditional costume with singing and music native to the area it's a colourful way to celebrate your vows.

Sightseeing

Turtle hatchery, fish market, Buddhist temple, Coral Sancuary, river cruises and tours.

Leisure facilities

Fitness centre, boutique, sauna, massage, aromatherapy. Swimming, table tennis, badminton, snooker, and other indoor games. Library facilities and evening entertainment programmes.

India

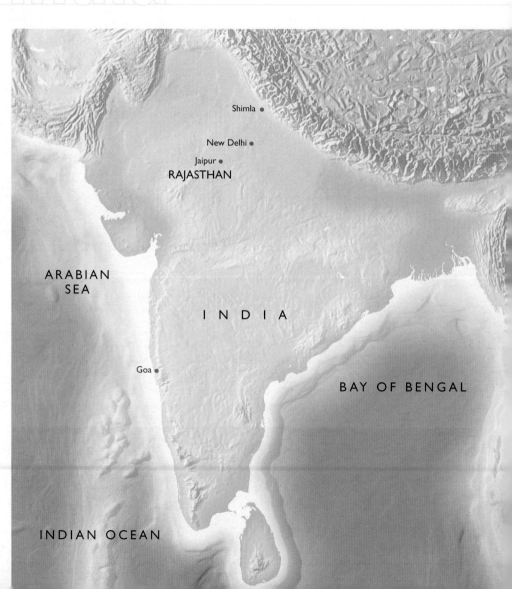

232

flying time
To: Delhi, Bombay,
Calcutta, Madras
London: 10-12 hrs
NY: 17-19 hrs

**climate/
when to go**
Four seasons: spring,
autumn and two
monsoons. It varies
according to location
and altitude. The
mountain resorts of
the north stay cool
at 10-20°C. Further
south things hot up;
in May Delhi sizzles
at up to 40°C. Tourist
season is Oct-Mar.

currency
Indian rupee.

language
There are over 1,000
languages and
dialects. Hindi is the
most popular, but
many speak English.

health
Innoculations against
typhoid, tetanus,
polio, hepatitis and
meningitis. Take
malaria pills.

getting around
Unless you are flying,
travel in India is slow.
Buses, taxis, cycle and
rickshaws are good
for short hops.

Shimla

New Delhi

Jaipur

RAJASTHAN

ARABIAN
SEA

I N D I A

Goa

BAY OF BENGAL

INDIAN OCEAN

W andering through ruined temple cities, bargaining in bazaars, inhaling the scents of spices and incense, staying in a maharajah's palace... whatever you want from a honeymoon, it is here in India.

The north is by far the most visited area of this vast country, by virtue of its cooler climate, imposing Mughal architecture and wide range of attractions – the fairytale desert forts of Rajasthan; the hill stations of Himachal Pradesh; the pilgrimage sites of Bihar and Uttar Pradesh and Varanasi on the sacred river Ganges; and, most famously, the strikingly unforgettable Taj Mahal.

Old Delhi is still a medieval place of forts, mosques and bazaars; colonial New Delhi meanwhile is an elegant metropolis of broad avenues, stately homes and landscaped gardens with some of the best hotels, restaurants and facilities. Close to Delhi are three places that together provide many of the images with which

India is associated – Agra, Khajuraho and Varanasi.

Further west, the desert territory of Rajasthan, 'Land of Princes', is as famous for its gardens and lakes, festivals and handicrafts as for its fortress theatres of war. It encompasses the Pink City of Jaipur, the towering fort of Jodhpur, medieval Jaisalmer and elegant Udaipur, a famous lake city of charming gardens and palaces.

Southern India has become increasingly popular with travellers – especially the beaches of Gokarn and Kovalam, and historic Cochin. In the old Portuguese colony of Goa, with its unique subtropical blend of Asia and the Mediterranean, fishermen leave their long hardwood boats to worship at the white-fronted Baroque churches and grand colonial houses share space in the villages with palm-thatched huts.

HRH Group of Hotels

Fateh Prakash Palace Hotel
City Palace
Udaipur 313001
Rajasthan
India

✈ Udaipur Dabok 20km
tel +91 294 528016
fax +91 294 528006

UK marketing office:
25 Chepstow Place
London W2 4TT
tel +44 171 792 8562
fax +44 171 727 7875

234

historic@specialhotels.com
www.specialhotels.com
hrhindia.com

Tour operators:
UK Pettits India,
Abercrombie & Kent
US Int. Ventures & Travel

City Palace, Udaipur

Fateh Prakash

The Fateh Prakash Palace Hotel, Udaipur, Rajasthan

For a truly memorable holiday, honeymooners might consider a tour of Rajasthan, one of India's most beautiful and colourful regions, stopping off on the way in a number of hotels which are part of HRH Group of Hotels.

A good itinerary might be to begin at the Fateh Prakash Palace, Udaipur – the city of lakes. Situated on the banks of Lake Pichola, it is part of the city Palace complex and has been restored to its pristine glory with original furnishings, tapestries and carvings decorating the seven suites to create an air of sumptuous, regal comfort.

Two hours north of Udaipur is the 15th century Kumbhalgarh Fort. Twenty miles of high walls snake over the ridges beneath the fort and the Aodhi Hotel is set in the hills just walking distance from the ramparts. A joy for nature lovers, it adjoins a wildlife sanctuary. Then move on to Jodphur where

 from US$100* (9)

 US$200-250 (7)

 US$50-125

 US$8

*Prices for Fateh Prakash only.

Honeymoon specials
Fruit and flowers in room on arrival.

The Fateh Prakash
Palace Hotel

Gajner Palace

City Palace, Udaipur

Kumbhalgarh Fort

Shiv Niwas, Udaipur

the Durjan Niwas Hotel is in the heart of this fascinating city.

After city comes desert and the Gorbandh Palace Hotel away from the noise of the city enjoy the calm and clear starry sky. The dances and folk music for which Rajasthan and specially Jaisalmer is famous can be enjoyed by campfire in open air at night. In the northern part of the desert the Gajner Palace is an incomparable jewel built on the shores of a lake. The surrounding woods are now an animal sanctuary, rich in wild boar, antelopes and other endangered species.

The magical tour ends with a visit to the recently renovated and stunning Karni Bhawan Palace in Bikaner, built by a Maharaja in the art deco style which was very popular in the '40s.

Suggested itinerary:

3 nights Fateh Prakash Palace, Udaipur
2 nights Aodhi, Kumbhalgarh
1 night Durjan Niwas, Jodhpur
3 nights Gorbandh Palace, Jaisalmer
(optional 1-night camel safari)
2 nights Gajner Palace
1 night Karni Bhawan, Bikaner

Leisure facilities

Visit the city Palace Museum which contains beautiful Indian miniatures, and on the uppermost terrace a hanging garden. Walk in the old city of Udaipur which is a maze of narrow winding lanes. Enjoy a boat ride at sunset on Lake Pichola.

Lake Palace

PO Box 5
Udaipur
Rajasthan
India

✈ Udaipur 26km

tel +91 294 527 961
fax +91 294 527 974

Taj toll free reservations:
UK 0800 282 699
US/Canada 800 458 8825

236

lake@specialhotels.com
www.specialhotels.com
lakepalace.udaipur@tajhotels.com

Member of:
The Taj Group of Hotels

Built two and a half centuries ago by Maharana Jagat Singh II, the Maharana of Udaipur, the Lake Palace sits on a rocky island which rises from the broad waters of Lake Pichola. The slender columns of white marble, fountains, filigreed screens, domed chattris and intricate mosaic were once the sole preserve of princes. Today it is a luxury hotel whose guests have included the likes of Queen Elizabeth II, actress Vivien Leigh and Jackie Onassis.

The suites echo with historic memories. Walls are frescoed with ancient water colours, inlaid with miniature paintings. Light dances on the walls, reflected from the waters of the lake through stained glass of every hue. Chandeliers, marbled and wooden flooring, Indian rugs and balconies looking out onto the lily pond below make this a hotel as beautiful as it is unique.

In the two restaurants and bar, secret recipes, passed down through the years are still on the menu for the best of Rajasthan's creamy yoghurt sauces and delicately spiced fish dishes. Meals may also be taken on one of the barges on the lake.

In the evening, you can wander around the lily pond or watch the lights reflected in the lake's glassy waters as the night settles to the liquid strains of a soulful sitar playing in the distance.

🛏 US$210-245* (84)

🛏 US$325-550*

🍴 US$33

☕ US$6

Honeymoon specials
Flowers and complimentary wine on arrival. Honeymoon package available on request (US$675).

Sightseeing and leisure
Local markets, City Palace Museum, Jagmandir. Also, folk dances in the hotel. Beauty parlour at hotel.
* Prices are subject to change.

Other Taj hotels
The Taj Group of Hotels has an extensive selection of fine hotels across south Asia. You can choose to stay in one of their 'gateway' hotels: The Taj Palace Hotel or Taj Mahal Hotel, New Delhi; Taj Mahal Hotel, Bombay; or Taj Coromandel, Madras; all members of Leading Hotels of the World, en route to your chosen Taj honeymoon spot.

The Leela Palace

Information & Reservations
UK 0870 606 1296
INT. +44 870 606 1296

Mobor
Goa, 403731
India

✈ Dabolim 50 mins

tel +91 834 746 363
fax +91 834 746 352

leela@specialhotels.com
www.specialhotels.com
leela.goa@leela.sprintrpg.ems.
vsnl.net.in

Member of:
Leading Hotels of the World

A short drive through rambling coconut groves brings you to the secluded luxury of The Leela Palace hotel where 137 opulent guestrooms and suites rest within 75 acres of lush gardens and stunning, sparkling lagoons.

All the rooms are decorated with the plushest furnishings with rattan and woodcarvings used to give a traditionally Indian feel. Private terraces ensure seclusion and offer the perfect spot for dinner *à deux*. Those in the Presidential Villa or the Royal Villas can take a private moonlit dip as these offer you the luxury of individual plunge pools.

Jamavar is the hotel's hot new restaurant which features traditional Indian fare cooked with the finest local ingredients. Alternatively, the Riverside Restaurant set alongside the bank of the River Sal offers the opportunity to dine under the stars.

No trip to Goa would be complete without an excursion to explore some of its magical temples and captivating markets; or take in the exuberant performances by folk troupes, musicians and dancers. Closer to home, tee off at the hotel golf course, work out at the gym or tennis courts, or simply choose to while away the time on the bleached white sands of the nearby Mobor beach, leaving only as the sun sets over the turquoise sea.

237

US$195-295 (54)

US$295-759 (83)

from US$25

from US$14

Honeymoon specials
Wine and flowers on arrival. Packages available upon request.

Sightseeing and leisure
Visit to churches and temples, historic monuments of Vijayanagara Empire architecture, flea markets, bird watching, sunset cruises.

The Cecil, an Oberoi Hotel

Chaura Maidan
Shimla
India

✈ Delhi 385km

tel +91 177 20 4848
fax +91 177 21 1024

cecil@specialhotels.com
www.specialhotels.com

Member of:
Leading Hotels of the World

From many of the 79 suites and rooms of this classic Shimla hotel, the Himalayan forests and hills can be seen stretching, mist-capped, into infinity. Shimla, the summer capital of India during the days of the British viceroys, has cool mountain air, exotic valleys, gushing streams and glorious green hill slopes.

Inside The Cecil, infinite pains have been taken to restore this historic hotel to its original splendour. Warm wood, rich details, parquet flooring and luxurious fabrics make staying here a sensuous and memorable experience.

In the restaurant, too, the senses come alive with the rich mix of Asian and European cuisine on offer.

The library, billiard room and extensive health club, including massage, steambaths and a large heated indoor pool, only add to the charm and tradition of the gracious hospitality on offer here. There are also several interesting heritage site walks within Shimla itself and, for sports lovers, there is a 9-hole golf course nearby.

Around Shimla, activities include day trips and picnics to Mashobra and Kufri, affording great views of the mountain scenery. Longer treks can also be organised, deep into the foothills, where in summer the fragrance of fresh flowers pervades these beautiful, enchanting peaks.

 US$175-250* (71)

 US$250-330* (8)

🍽 from US$12

☕ included

Honeymoon specials

Fruit, flowers and sparkling wine in the room on arrival. Room upgrade subject to availability.

Prices include breakfast and one major meal per day.

Sightseeing and leisure

Tennis, waterskiing, windsurfing, sailing and snorkelling are complimentary. Scuba diving, deep-sea fishing, island excursions, cocktail cruises, private yacht hire and golf on a championship course can be arranged for a fee. Beauty centre nearby.

Information & Reservations
UK 0870 606 1296
INT. +44 870 606 1296

Rajvilas – an Oberoi Hotel

Goner Road, Jaipur
303012 Rajasthan
India

✈ Jaipur 16km

tel +91 141 64 01 01
fax +91 141 64 02 02

rajvilas@specialhotels.com
www.specialhotels.com
www.oberoihotels.com

This individually styled hotel is located over 30 acres of beautiful orchards and herb gardens, pools and fountains in the peaceful Rajasthani countryside and offers high standards of facilities, flawless service and superb attention to detail. None of this was left to chance, with over 10,000 candidates being interviewed for the hotel's opening and only 140 available vacancies.

The deluxe rooms have four-poster beds and sunken marble bathrooms; while the exotic Rajasthani-style tents come with lavish bathrooms, teak floors and outdoor decks; and romantic villas give guests the opportunity to revel in the luxury of private swimming pools and dining pavilions.

The hotel's restaurant, Surya Mahal, offers an exotic mixture of Asian and European cuisine and that East-meets-West feel continues in the beautifully designed lobby and library bar.

Guests can be pampered at The Spa, housed in a *haveli*, a classic Rajasthan mansion, with a whirlpool, hot and cold plunge pools and terraces for meditation and yoga. Ayurveda-inspired treatments provide a holisitic approach to well-being.

A special wedding blessing can be organised with traditional Indian ceremony at the ancient Shiv Temple with traditional costumes and music.

239

 US$280* (54)

 US$300-1,000* (17)

 US$30

 US$15

Honeymoon specials

Three night's stay in a deluxe room with breakfast in bed every day. A romantic private dinner with chocolate fondue, near the Shiv temple on a small island floating at the centre of a large pool. Basket of exotic flowers and incense in room each day. Complimentary spa therapy (one per person). Jaipur block printed designer sarongs. Airport transfers by luxury car, in-room check-in and welcome drink.
Cost: from US$850 till 30/9/99, $950 till 31/3/2000.

Sightseeing and leisure

Private excursions to Jaipur, many attractions like forts, festivals, bazaars and palaces. A wide range of treatments available at the hotel's spa.

* Prices exclusive of taxes and vaild till end Sept 1999.

Rambagh Palace

Bhawani Singh Road
Jaipur 302 005
Rajasthan
India

✈ Jaipur 11km

tel +91 141 381 919
fax +91 141 381 098

Taj toll free reservations:
UK 0800 282 699
US/Canada 800 458 8825

rambagh@specialhotels.com
www.specialhotels.com
rambagh.jaipur@tajhotels.com

240

Member of:
The Taj Group of Hotels

The legendary palace of Rambagh, once home to none other than the Maharaja of Jaipur, stands majestically in gardens renowned for their elegance and exotic foliage. Today it's still grand and one of the 20 most popular hotels in the Pacific Rim, as voted by the readers of Condé Nast *Traveller* magazine in 1998.

The interior of the palace is breathtaking. Guests can stay in the former personal chambers of the Royal family such as the Prince's suite with marble floors, golden sculptures and an indoor fountain. Antiques, wood panelling and high ceilings give the Potikhana, once the Maharaja's study and now a lavish bed-sitting room, an elegant warmth. Each of the 20 luxury rooms are individually decorated. Intricate painted ceilings, chandeliers and original furniture hark back to a glorious age.

Indian, Continental, Chinese and local Rajasthani specialities are served in regal splendour from the Suvarna Mahal dining hall to the more intimate Neel Mahal, decorated in every shade of blue and open round the clock. The Polo Bar offers a nice variety of spirits and liqueurs.

In the evenings the Palace's original amphitheatre comes to life with song and dance, performed by folk artistes under a canopy of trees.

 US$135-370* (102)

 US$350-675* (4)

 from RS800

 from RS300

Honeymoon specials
Basket of fruit, Indian sweets, flowers in room. Buggy and elephant ride on request.

Sightseeing and leisure
Area known for fine emeralds, antiques, Jantar Mantar, Hawa Mahal, Amber Fort, City Palace. Pool, fitness and beauty centre, tennis, squash. Golf, horseriding on request.

Other Taj hotels
The Taj Group of Hotels has an extensive selection of fine hotels across south Asia. You can choose to stay in one of their 'gateway' hotels: The Taj Palace Hotel or Taj Mahal Hotel, New Delhi; Taj Mahal Hotel, Bombay; or Taj Coromandel, Madras; all members of Leading Hotels of the World, en route to your chosen Taj honeymoon spot.
* Prices are subject to change.

The Taj Goa

Sinquerim
Bardez 403 519
Goa

✈ Dabolim 50km

tel +832 276 201/10
fax +832 276 044

goa@specialhotels.com
www.specialhotels.com
village.goa@tajhotels.com
fortaguada.goa@tajhotels.com
hermitage.goa@tajhotels.com

Taj toll free reservations:
UK 0800 282 699
US/Canada 800 458 8825

Member of:
The Taj Group of Hotels

Goa, on India's western coast, has been attracting visitors to its palm-fringed shores for many years. Now, there's even more reason to go as the Taj has not one but three resorts spread over an 88-acre complex. Paradise awaits, so close your eyes and count to three.

One...the Aguada Hermitage has exquisite villas amidst a profusion of flowers and trees. Stroll from your villa through the colourful gardens and onto the beach and ocean. Two...the Fort Aguada Beach Resort is built into the ramparts of a 16th-century fortress. Not far from your terrace suite is a vast and golden beach. Three...the Taj

Holiday Village has pretty pink honeymoon cottages, surrounded by palms. With the Arabian Sea lapping at the coastline, seafood is a speciality.

Each resort has its own distinctive charm. The Taj Holiday Village is Moorish in design and quietly quaint; the Aguada Hermitage, originally designed for Commonwealth Heads of State, is stately and stylish; modernist chic characterises Fort Aguada.

The beauty of the Taj Goa is that it doesn't matter which one you choose. The whole resort complex is at your disposal. This means more restaurants and bars, more swimming pools, more opportunities for recreation and romance.

241

 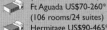
Holiday Village US$60-250*
(137 rooms/7 suites)
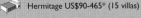
Ft Aguada US$70-260*
(106 rooms/24 suites)

Hermitage US$90-465* (15 villas)

🍽 from RS450

☕ from RS250

Honeymoon specials
Basket of fruit, Indian sweets, flowers in room on arrival.

Sightseeing and leisure
Church of St Francis of Assisi, Bascilica of Bom Jesus. Beach tour, river and sunset cruises, trips to markets, birdwatching. . Pool, sports complex, watersports, mini golf course.
* Prices subject to change.

Other Taj hotels
The Taj Group of Hotels has an extensive selection of fine hotels across south Asia. You can choose to stay in one of their 'gateway' hotels: The Taj Palace Hotel or Taj Mahal Hotel, New Delhi; Taj Mahal Hotel, Bombay; or Taj Coromandel, Madras; all members of Leading Hotels of the World, en route to your chosen Taj honeymoon spot.

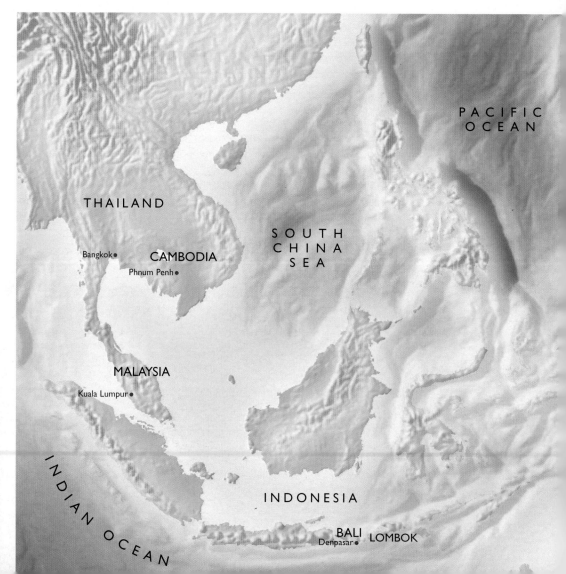

PACIFIC
OCEAN

THAILAND

Bangkok●

CAMBODIA

Phnum Penh●

SOUTH
CHINA
SEA

MALAYSIA

Kuala Lumpur●

INDONESIA

INDIAN OCEAN

BALI LOMBOK
Denpasar●

Bali & Lombok

This mountainous island of startling beauty is the jewel in Indonesia's crown. Emerald-green rice terraces hug the contours of the hills, reflecting the clouds scudding over the frittering palm fronds.

Everywhere there are tiny shrines, adorned with mossy statues and offerings – incense sticks laid on tiny rice packets, and gifts of magnolia, hibiscus and richly scented frangipani flowers. Bali is a prayer to the gods, where heaven and earth are held in balance by daily obeisance. The Balinese know their luck: this is one of the world's most charmed places.

Tourism has come to Bali, but it has been skilfully marshalled. The biggest hotels are clustered on the palm-fringed peninsula of Nusa Dua in the south, away from the more raucous backpacker streets of Kuta, or its quieter twin Sanur. Ubud, set among wooded valleys inland, is the old artistic capital where you can slake off the day's dust with a coconut-shell scoops of water under open skies. Bali is perfect for honeymooners, poetic and spiritual, yet comfortable and accessible. The Balinese regard marriage as a sacred union of the physical and the spiritual, blessed by the gods. 'Where is Wayan?' they ask all young couples. 'Where is the first born?' Families are at the centre of their lives and you will have a special place among them.

flying time
London: 18 hrs
LA: 18 hrs
NY: 24 hrs

climate/ when to go
May-Sep, in the dry season, is ideal. But any time of year is good, although you might need to shelter under a big banana-leaf umbrella during a wet-season downpour in Dec-Feb. The high season for religious ceremonies is Oct-Nov, but there are lots of smaller ceremonies that take place all year.

getting around
By taxi, bus, *bemo* (covered pick-up truck) or *dokar* (horse-drawn trap). It is also easy to hire your own car, jeep, motorbike or bicycle.

Begawan Giri

PO Box 54 Ubud
Bali 80571
Bali

✈ 45km

tel +62 361 978 888
fax +62 361 978 889

begawan@specialhotels.com
www.specialhotels.com
begawan@indo.net.id

244

For those who like the idea of relaxing in their own private estate set in lush, tropical gardens, Begawan Giri ('Wise Man's Mountain') may just be the answer. Here, in the serenity of a hilltop garden fed by Holy springs, five peaceful residences are set amidst lovingly tended gardens, overlooking the Ayung River.

Each of the villas (which can be hired in part or whole) has been individually designed, with an eye to *feng shui*, to ensure the maximum of comfort and peace. Each one is designed to be in harmony with an aspect of nature or the spirit, and all are furnished with antiques, handmade furniture and exquisite fabrics as well as boasting a personal butler, private pool, king-size beds and verandahs.

The emphasis at Begawan is on freedom. If guests want a romantic supper in their suite, or a picnic by the springwater plunge pool, then it's up to them.

 US$475-2,575* (21)

 from US$15

 from US$8

Honeymoon specials

Sparkling wine, flowers, fruit platter in suite on arrival. Complimentary airport transfer, plus outdoor 'his & her' massage and cleansing dip in spring pool.

* Prices quoted are based on two people per suite per night and subject to 21% tax & service charge.

If they want a candlelit meal at the Kudus House Restaurant, they can have that too.

For real pampering, the resort has its own holistic traditional spa. Enjoy a Balinese massage with aromatic oils, or exotic body treatments such as Javanese Lulur and Balinese Spice. The nearby village of Ubud with its artists' studios, antique shops, tucked away temples and village markets, is a fun place to visit.

Local attractions

Bali's cultural centre, the village of Ubud, is close by. Artists' studios, antique shops, temples and village markets are all worth taking time to visit. The hotel can organise excursions, white-water rafting, sightseeing and various shopping trips.

Leisure facilities

Holistic massage and beauty treatments at The Source, library, water gardens and natural spring pools.

Damai Lovina Villas

Jalan Damai
Lovina
Bali

✈ Ngurah Rai 80km

tel +62 362 41008
fax +62 362 41009

damai@specialhotels.com
www.specialhotels.com
www.damai.com

246

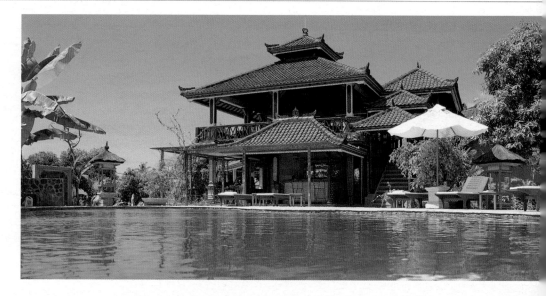

Nestled in the gentle hills overlooking the bay of Lovina, among rice paddies, spice plantations and stunning jungle-clad ravines, are the Damai Lovina Villas, Bali's gourmet retreat. Quiet, secluded and very romantic, they make a perfect hideaway. Located only a couple of hours' drive from the airport and the crowds of the south, they are a secret gem offering two of the greatest luxuries of all – beauty and tranquillity.

The eight bungalows are built in traditional Balinese style and have a cool, open-plan opulence. Stylish four-poster beds, antiques, beautifully and meticulously crafted teak furniture, textiles which recreate ancient Indonesian patterns and striking

 US$168-206 (8)

 US$40

 US$10

Honeymoon specials

Champagne, a basket of tropical fruit, and a beautiful arrangement of flowers each day. An extensive range of packages available on request.

open-air bathrooms with spas create a warm
atmosphere of tropical style and elegance.

A mouth-watering blend of French and tropical
cuisine – as colourful as it is varied – is presented
simply and beautifully by the resident French chef,
who creates a new set menu each night.

Enjoy the excitement of a full Balinese wedding
ceremony with a reception for up to 40 guests
which can be easily arranged on request.

The Damai is light years away from the crowds
of the south and to those who have visited, it's a
slice of heaven here on earth. Being off the beaten
track, it may take a bit of effort to find but, once
discovered, it is almost impossible to leave.

Leisure facilities

Diving at Mendangan, swimming in the bay in
Lovina and golf in the volcanic crater
at Bali Handara Golf Course. Beautician by
appointment. Traditional Indonesian massage,

Local attractions

Watching dolphins playing at sunrise. Walks in the unspoilt
countryside, watching the sun set behind Java's volcanoes.
The waterfalls of Git-Git, the hot springs of Banjar and spice
plantations.

Nusa Dua Beach
Hotel & Spa

PO Box 1028
Denpasar
Bali

✈ Ngurah Rai 12km

tel +62 361 771 210
fax +62 361 772 617

nusadua@specialhotels.com
www. specialhotels.com
www.hotelnusadua.com

Member of:
Leading Hotels of the World
The Audley Group

248

Set on Bali's southern shores, the Nusa Dua Beach Hotel & Spa is immersed in the pageantry of one of the world's most vibrant cultures. An aquamarine ocean, azure skies stretching into the distance, silver sands, a golden sun and the deep greens of the beach-side palms are the palette with which the Balinese gods painted this fabled isle.

The guestrooms are regal and celebrate the richness of Balinese culture in a sumptuous tapestry of classical decor and unmatched comfort. Personalised rooms offer a rich panoply of the island's arts and crafts, including Balinese ikat and batik textiles and ornately painted wall panels.

Guests can dine in high style in any number of fabulous venues ranging from gourmet Asian cuisine enjoyed *al fresco* to a colourful Italian bistro or a sizzling beachside barbecue.

Recalling the royal water palaces of Bali's last kings, a particularly beautiful feature of the hotel is the lagoon pool. Here you will find a perfectly tranquil oasis of soothing fountains, tropical scented gardens and sparkling water where romance and relaxation go hand in hand – a true taste of paradise to enjoy.

 US$200-350* (335)

 US$500-2,000* (45)

 from US$35

 US$15

Honeymoon specials

Flowers, fruit and chocolates on arrival.
* Prices subject to 11% tax plus 10% service charge.

Leisure facilities

Massage treatments, body scrubs, spa with sauna, lap pool, steam rooms, Jacuzzi, hair and beauty salon and gym. There is an 18-hole golf course five minutes away from the hotel.

Sightseeing

Traditional open-air theatre for classic cultural performances at hotel. Club Iabuh, the hotel disco, presents a variety of evening programmes throughout the week. *Ulu Watu*, temple to the sea spirits, is nearby.

The Oberoi, Bali

Legian Beach
Jalan Kayu Aya
PO Box 3351
80033 Denpasar
Bali

✈ Denpasar 9km

tel +62 361 730 361
fax +62 361 730 791

oberoibali@specialhotels.com
www.specialhotels.com

Tour operators:
UK Elegant Resorts

Member of:
Leading Hotels of the World

Situated beside Legian Beach on the enchanting island of Bali is the secluded and decidedly deluxe Oberoi. It is a resort that manages to combine a high degree of luxury and service with a sense of carefree independence.

Beautiful individual bungalows and villas, set in 15 acres of tropical gardens, are designed in traditional Balinese style with intricately carved teakwood beds, Balinese artworks, elegant furnishings and marble floors. Nestling behind coral stone walls, some of the villas have their own private pools set in a palatial courtyard. Sea breezes waft through the landscaped garden, mingling with the sweet scent of hibiscus and densely growing bougainvillaea.

Traditional Balinese cuisine may be enjoyed either in a private villa pavilion or in the Kura Kura restaurant. Beside the beach, the Frangipani Cafe provides lighter snacks. There are many other places to eat, whether it is a light snack from a hawker's cart or something more fancy at one of the many quality restaurants nearby.

The Legian Beach is breathtakingly beautiful and one of Bali's best. Here, for many visitors, basking in the golden glows of the setting sun can become something of an evening ritual.

249

US$225-275 (60)

US$300-475 (15)

US$35-45

US$17

Honeymoon specials
Honeymooner guests are welcomed with a congratulation gateau with the compliments of the general manager and personalised stationery.

Sightseeing and leisure
The health spa features open-air massage pavilions overlooking tranquil ponds filled with tropical water plants and golden carp. Library of books, films, music and games. Gym, tennis court, chess pavilion, golf arranged.

The Oberoi, Lombok

Medana Beach, Tanjung
PO Box 1096
Mataram 83001
NTB
Lombok

✈ Mataran 28km

tel +62 370 638 444
fax +62 370 632 496

lombok@specialhotels.com
www.specialhotels.com

250

Tour operators:
UK Elegant Resorts

Member of:
Leading Hotels of the World
Small Luxury Hotels

The Oberoi, Lombok is a secluded cluster of just 50 luxurious villas and terrace pavilions set in tropical gardens along the sparkling golden sands of Medana Beach. Lombok, only 80 kilometres from east to west, is an unspoilt island paradise with excellent beaches and soaring mountain scenery.

The villas and terrace pavilions are single-storey thatched cottages with pleasantly shaded terraces, which overlook the gardens or the beach. All are comfortably appointed and decorated in the warm colours and textures of local fabrics and adorned with traditional artefacts. The spacious bedrooms with teak wood flooring and sumptuous marble

bathrooms provide a sense of luxury.

Beyond these delights, the resort boasts a variety of other attractions including exclusive access to a secluded beachfront, a magnificent swimming pool, a Holistic Spa and health club and a huge variety of watersports from Scuba diving to snorkelling, and boat cruises for you to indulge in.

Dining is also a treat, with Asian and international cuisine served in the elegant restaurant, or dine in the open-air around the hotel's ampitheatre. The cocktail bar provides the ideal setting for sipping cool drinks as the last glimmers of the golden sun fade away into the night.

 US$200-250 (30)

 US$300-650 (20)

 US$34-35

 US$17

Honeymoon specials

Honeymooner guests are welcomed with a congratulation gateau with the general manager's compliments and personalised stationery.

Sightseeing and leisure

Health spa treatments, gym, Jacuzzi, herbal bath, massage pavilion. Library of films, music, books and games. Mountain bikes. Snorkelling, Scuba diving, sunset cruises.

Sheraton Laguna
Nusa Dua

Information & Reservations
UK 0870 606 1296
INT. +44 870 606 1296

PO Box 77
Nusa Dua Beach 80363
Bali

✈ Phuket Int. 12km

tel +62 361 771 327
fax +62 361 771 326

sheraton@specialhotels.com
www.specialhotels.com
www.sheraton.com

251

The scenic island of Bali with its rice terraces, jungle gorges and deep blue seas, is home to the Sheraton Laguna. Clustered in a horseshoe round cool swimming lagoons and tropical gardens and sandwiched between rich palms and the beautiful sands of Nusa Dua Beach, the Sheraton Laguna promises an ocean of pleasure and relaxed intimacy.

Many of the spacious rooms and suites, with their timbered floors and rich Balinese artworks, directly adjoin the refreshing lagoons. Whether it be an early morning plunge or a late-night dip, the cool, azure waters are only a wish away.

The resort boasts an 18-hole golf course, tennis and watersports facilities, elegant restaurants, intimate bars and a poolside terrace. Situated right on Nusa Dua Beach – miles of silver sands and calm, clear water. For that extra pampering touch, there is also a luxurious, fully-equipped Laguna spa. Why not try a bath of milk and honey or the ultimate relaxation of a Shiatsu massage?

If guests can tear themselves away from the luxury, comfort, and myriad ways to breeze through the days, then the island of Bali, with its shadow puppet plays, gamelan orchestras and rich art traditions, is waiting to be explored in all its wonder and fabled beauty.

US$235-380

US$480-1,800

US$85

included

Honeymoon specials
Honeymooners receive special room assignment, daily flower arrangement in room, chocolates, plus honeymoon liquor on arrival.

Sightseeing and leisure
The hotel has its own leisure and beauty facility called Laguna Spa for extensive body treatments. Meanwhile, the Spa Villa provides a more private experience ideal for romantic couples. Also, the hotel has its own 18-hole golf course on site at Bali Golf & CC.

Information & Reservations
UK 0870 606 1296
INT. +44 870 606 1296

Jalan Karang Mas Sejahtera
Jimbaran 80364
Bali

✈ Ngurah Rai 10km

tel +62 361 702 222
fax +62 361 701 555

rcbali@specialhotels.com
www.specialhotels.com

Member of:
Leading Hotels of the World

252

Perched high on a bluff, with panoramic views across the Indian Ocean and vibrant tropical sunsets, this deluxe hotel provides its guests with a true taste of paradise.

Exotic flowers abound, including cascades of sweet-scented bougainvillea, and trees such as the almost-mythical banyan are set amid tiered lawns featuring lily ponds, sculpted fountains and waterfalls. Stone steps, cut into a cliff, lead to a lush ravine that forms the entrance to the secluded beaches that stretch for miles.

Thirty-six thatched-roof villas are part of the hotel's distinctive Balinese design. Each features a carved door opening onto tropical gardens, private

 US$220-360 (323)

 US$450-2,200 (30)

 US$35-65

 US$17-23

Honeymoon specials

Each couple may select two of these activities: complimentary massage, two hour tour by boat including picnic and visit to secluded surfers beach, rose petal drawn bath, champagne, intimate feasts, full-day chauffeur driven shopping excursion. On the final night, a marriage certificate written in Balinese Sanskrit presented. "Love by Design" package: US$168-398 per night based on a stay of five nights.

plunge pools and *bale bengongs* (open-air lounges), with an interior of Balinese furnishings and art, and a two-person bathtub. Intricately woven coconut leaf baskets filled with flowers and incense are placed in the room daily as an offering to the gods for a harmonious sojourn.

The hotel beautifully combines the romance of this enchanting island with highly attentive service and excellent, wide-ranging cuisine.

There is a choice of six restaurants and lounges ranging in atmosphere from informal to intimate, serving dishes ranging from Balinese *rijstaffel* to Japanese *sushi*. Most dramatically, skewers of meat, chicken and seafood are famed next to the tables

in a sand-floored restaurant which has been carved out of the cliff, with dramatic effect.

After dinner, cigars, brandy and robust Indonesian coffee or spiced teas are served on the characterful Damar Terrace, which is romantically illuminated by dozens of candles.

Marriage blessings in Balinese costume can be arranged in the hotel's temple. Receptions for up to 540 guests are catered for in the Canang Sari, a traditional Balinese wedding gazebo constructed of coconut-palm wood and limestone flooring. Young Balinese girls welcome the bride and groom, dressed in traditional costume, while a musician plays the *gender* – a local instrument.

Sightseeing

Trips to Denpasar's Bali museum, Sangeh's sacred monkey forest, Mount Batur volcano, art centre, sacred springs and temples and giant sea turtles on the island of Serangan.

Leisure facilities

Tennis, golf, swimming, boating, rafting, diving, deep-sea fishing, hiking, surfing, windsurfing and snorkelling. Fully-equipped spa with sauna, Turkish bath and private massage rooms.

Cambodia

flying time
To: Siem Reap
London: 14 hrs via
Bangkok
LA: 9 hrs

**climate/
when to go**
Three major seasons:
cold from Nov-Jan,
hot from Feb-Apr,
rainy from May-Oct.
Temperatures are
fairly uniform (avg
23°C), although
humidity is often in
excess of 90%.

currency
Cambodian Riels, but
US dollars generally
accepted.

language
Cambodian, but
English and French
are spoken in hotels.

getting around
Taxis and local
transport. Hotel
shuttles dependable
and the safest.

visas
One-month tourist
visa can be obtained
(US$20) upon
arrival. You should
bring four photos
with you.

254

The Khmer Royal City of Angkor and its most renowned temple, Angkor Wat, rightly ranks alongside the Pyramids of Egypt as one of the most awe-inspiring and important monuments in the world.

It has extraordinary serenity and beauty, which is made all the more compelling by its remote location in north-eastern Cambodia.

Angkor is huge, with more than 60 temples. Angkor Wat itself dates back to the 12th century when it was dedicated to the Hindu God, Vishnu. Its famous five towers represent the five peaks of Mount Meru, the home of the gods and the very centre of the Hindu universe. It features the longest continuous bas-relief in the world, which runs along the outer gallery walls, narrating stories from Hindu Mythology. With the decline of the ancient Khmer Empire, Angkor became a Buddist Temple and has been continuously maintained.

Now, for the first time, access to the greater temples is available from nearby Siem Riep international airport with services from Bangkok and Phnom Penh.

And as Cambodian weddings are renowned for romance and rich tradition, Lolei Travel, a local tour operator, is now offering a special 'journey' for honeymooners along the same lines. Incorporating a shortened version of the traditional three-day Cambodian wedding, the honeymoon couple will enjoy a one-day romantic ceremony with traditional dress, breakfast, transport by elephants to a temple for lunch before enjoying another elephant ride through Angkor Tom and to the Grand Hotel D'Angkor. Following the day's extravaganza, a laid-back, private sunset cocktail tour on the lake of Tonle Sap on board a traditional wooden boat rounds off the unforgettable Cambodian experience.

Grand Hotel d'Angkor

1 Vithei Charles de Gaulle
Khum Svay Dang Kum
Siem Reap
Cambodia

✈ Siem Reap 10 mins

tel +855 63 963888
fax +855 63 963168

dangkor@specialhotels.com
www.specialhotels.com

Member of:
Small Luxury Hotels

Just eight kilometres away from the magnificent Angkor temple, Grand Hotel d'Angkor has been catering to discerning travellers for the past 70 years and was recently restored by Raffles International to its original splendour. The 131 guestrooms and suites are all equipped with art deco country style furnishing and Cambodian *objet d'art*. Several room categories are available including individually appointed Personality Suites and two luxurious villas.

Wining and dining takes place in eight restaurants and bars offering buffets, set menus and *à la carte* meals featuring both international and Asian cuisine.

The 60,000-square-metres of tropical gardens fronting the hotel offers much to explore. Beautifully landscaped, it can be traversed by foot or bicycle. Or, spend an adventurous day exploring the many temple ruins in Angkor, and on your return, visit the hotel's excellent spa to relax both body and mind.

The hotel can also organise a traditional Khmer wedding with the bride and groom in full regalia accompanied with classical Khmer music played by a live orchestra. The wedding vows may take place at the hotel's grounds and officiated by a monk. After much celebration, end the day with a glorious sunset on top of Angkor Wat.

255

 US$360-390

 US$410-1,900

 US$18-80

 US$14

Honeymoon specials
Flowers and wine on arrival. Free beauty treatment for ladies and a free massage for gentlemen.

Sightseeing and leisure
Cambodia and especially Siem Reap offers centuries of history and some of the world's most resplendent temples. Just one of the most notable temples to visit is the awe-inspiring Angkor Temple.

Malaysia

flying time
To: Kuala Lumpur
London: 12¹/₂ hrs
NY: 20 hrs
LA: 18-19 hrs

**climate/
when to go**
Tropically hot and
humid all year. Try to
avoid wet seasons,
which affect beaches
and watersports. The
west coast gets most
rain Apr-May and
Oct-Nov; the east,
Nov-Feb. There are
many Chinese, Indian
and Christian festivals,
such as Chinese New
Year (Jan-Feb) and
Deepavali (Oct-Nov).

currency
The Malaysian ringgit,
or 'dollar'.

language
Bahasa Malaysia.
Chinese, Tamil and
English are widely
spoken.

health
Immunisation against
typhoid, tetanus,
polio, hepatitis and,
for some areas,
anti-malaria tablets.

The world's tallest structure, the Petronas Twin Towers complex, soars above Malaysia's capital Kuala Lumpur – a new and powerful symbol of the country's headlong race into the 21st century. Malaysia has embraced the manufacturing industry and the latest technology, but it is still a destination where you can discover untamed nature at its most tropical. Also, compared with a few years ago, Malaysia is a real travel bargain, as the local currency has weakened considerably against the dollar and the pound.

Driving through peninsular Malaysia, the land link between Singapore and Thailand, you soon escape the cities and find yourself amid plantations of rubber and palm oil trees. A day's drive from Kuala Lumpur brings you to the Taman Negara National Park where you can go jungle trekking, on the look out for giant monitor lizards and brilliant butterflies. On the jungle-clad island of Borneo, which contains the Malaysian states of Sarawak and Sabah, you can climb south-east Asia's highest mountain, Mount Kinabalu, see orangutans, take

a river trip through tropical rainforest and stay in traditional bamboo longhouses with families of the Dayak tribe, sharing communal meals and finding out about their still quite primitive way of life.

Malaysia has fine, empty beaches for those who like solitude, and newly developing beach resorts like Kuantan and Cherating on the east coast of the peninsula, where watching leatherback turtles lay their eggs in the sand, is one of the night-time attractions.

Off the peninsula's more built-up and industrial west coast are the islands of Langkawi and Penang, where you find busier resorts, though by the standards of, say, Thailand's Pattaya, even these are sleepy.

As a contrast to the sun-baked beaches and steamy jungles, there are the cooler highlands, places like Fraser's Hill, Genting Highlands and the Cameron Highlands, all within easy reach of Kuala Lumpur. For

British civil servants in Malaya in the 19th century, the hill station in the Cameron Highlands, with its fruit orchards and tea plantations, was like a chunk of home. It has something of the old colonial atmosphere and today's recreation includes tennis, golf and hill walking.

To get a feel for the earlier colonial history, go to Melaka and see the legacy of 16th-century Portuguese churches and rusty pink-brick mansions put up by Dutch traders in the 1600s. Like the rest of Malaysia, Melaka has a mixed population of Malays, Indians and Chinese. It is in the old Chinese quarter that you feel most sharply the clock being turned back as you walk between the old-style shop houses and dragon-roofed temples. Medicine shops sell dried snakes and strange potions, tinsmiths beat metal into shape on the street, and darkened doorways reveal coffin-makers at work. Like so much of Malaysia, it's a spectacle to behold.

The Datai Langkawi

Jalan Teluk Datai
07000 Pulau Langkawi
Kedah Darul Aman
Malaysia

✈ Kuala Lumpur

tel +604 959 2500
fax +604 959 2600

datai@specialhotels.com
www.specialhotels.com

Tour operators:
UK Elegant Resorts

258

Tucked in the middle of an ancient and tropical rainforest and perched on the fringe of a jungle cove on the north-western tip of Langkawi, The Datai has a secluded white beach caressed by the gentle waves of the Andaman Sea.

The Datai's villas are scattered throughout the forest and linked to the main hotel and other facilities by a series of pathways. Each has its own terrace and an elevated dining verandah. Inside, calm tones, soft lighting and warm, red balau flooring carry through the atmosphere of lush foliage and jungle to be found outside.

Open air dining among the tree tops is a rare treat that be enjoyed every day at the Datai in the Pavilion, an authentic Thai restaurant. *Al fresco* dining is available at the Beach Club while an enticing blend of Malaysian and international cuisine is on offer in the hotel's main dining room.

To soothe body and soul, the Datai has its own spa, situated next to a secluded stream, which offers massage, aromatherapy, and traditional Malaysian body treatments.

If that doesn't appeal, there is an 18-hole golf course right next to the resort which promises not only a fine game but the most incredible views of the nearby mountains while you play.

 RM1,760-6,700

 RM1,045-1,700

 US$25-50

 US$15

Honeymoon specials
Fruit, flowers and bottle of champagne on arrival. The hotel can assist in arranging ceremonies, at no charge, however, there are charges on application for licences.

Leisure facilities
Health club with gym. Snorkelling, windsurfing and sailing. Scuba diving and deep-sea fishing can be arranged off site.

Sightseeing
Langkawi is a mystical island of jungle-covered mountains, lakes, caves and waterfalls to explore. Take a boat ride to Pulau Dayang Bunting, otherwise known as Lake of the Pregnant Maiden. Other attractions include the hot spring Telega Air Hangat, the Gua Cerita, and the black sandy beach of Pantai Pasir Hitam.

Penang Mutiara
Beach Resort

1 Jalan Teluk Bahang
11050 Penang
Malaysia

✈ Penang 40km

tel +604 885 2828
fax +604 885 2829

penang@specialhotels.com
www.specialhotels.com

Tour operators:
UK Kuoni

Member of:
Leading Hotels of the World

Penang Mutiara is located on the prime beachfront of Teluk Behang, translated as 'glowing bay'. A long, landscaped driveway leads gradually up to the granite rendered *'porte cochere'*. Here, royal blue flooring introduces the pearl-white resort perfectly, with the emerald green gardens, turquoise sea and blue sky beyond.

The hotel is a fine example of contemporary Malaysian elegance. Spacious guestrooms, each with a balcony overlooking the crystal-clear sea, are furnished in pastel shades with rattan furniture and a combination of carpet and parquet flooring. Warm wooden shutters and exotic fabrics lend an air of timelessness and tropical romance while the bathrooms are of a sumptuous marble with extra-deep baths.

Gracious living is the key to the cuisine as well. Delicate Cantonese, Italian and Japanese recipes are served in a number of intimate and individual restaurants. Or perhaps you'd prefer a starlit dinner for two in one of the several open-air gazebos.

For centuries, travellers and traders were drawn to these sun-drenched shores. Their influence can still be seen in the island's rich cultural heritage. In

259

the architecture, savoured in the intoxicating aromas spilling from the markets, tasted in the spicy flavours of the magnificent food and certainly experienced in the warm welcome extended to guests at the Penang Mutiara.

 US$145-200 (406)

 US$395-1,975 (32)

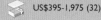 US$21

 US$13

Honeymoon specials
Honeymooners are given fruits, flowers, kingsize bed decorated with flower petals. Room upgrade subject to availability. One bottle of house wine for a five-night stay.

Leisure facilities
Fitness centre on site: gym, whirlpool, sauna and steam bath. Also, salon with beauty facilities.

Sightseeing
Visits to butterfly farm, botanical garden, Penang Hill Railway, Kek Lok Si Temple, Fort Cornwallis, Snake Temple, international sports arena. Five shopping centres. Many traditional and religious festivals throughout the year.

Thailand

flying time
To: Bangkok
London: 14 hrs
NY: 22-23 hrs
LA: 19 hrs via Seoul

**climate/
when to go**
The best months are
Oct-Feb. A particular
attraction is the
festival of Loy
Krathong, held in Nov,
when thousands of
little candle-lit boats
are floated on the
country's waterways.

currency
Baht, but US dollars
widely accepted.

language
Thai. English is also
widely spoken.

getting around
There is an efficient
rail system; hire cars
are cheap and readily
available. Bangkok is
best negotiated from
the boats and ferries
that ply their trade on
the canals or in a *tuk-
tuk*, a three-wheeled
motor scooter.

Formerly known as Siam, and still referred to proudly by Thais as Muang Thai or 'Land of the Free', Thailand is a small, friendly kingdom where 20th-century modernity exists alongside a charming and unique 700-year-old culture.

Amazingly, Thailand has managed to preserve its cultural heritage to a unique degree. So for visitors, Thailand has much to offer. Take some time to sample the exotic pleasures of Bangkok, the Venice of the East, on a cruise through its countless waterways passing glorious illuminated temples and the world famous floating market on the way. While there, visit The Grand Palace and Temple of the Emerald Buddha, two of the oldest and largest temples in Bangkok built by King Rama I nearly 200 years ago, one of which houses the gigantic gold-plated 'Reclining Buddha'.

Go beyond the cities where there are some enthralling natural environments. Dense bamboo forests, fields of delicate orchids, waterfalls and velvet green mangroves, as well as areas of sumptious cultivated land of coconut and rubber plantations and acres upon acres of rice fields.

For a different scene, North Thailand affords plenty of scope for both cultural sightseeing and refreshing escapes into the vast countryside. Chiang Mai is the best base for exploring the region, offering its own sights and numerous hiking and trekking options. Finally, move to the coast and discover glorious beaches, Thailand style, watched over by 40-feet-high Buddha statues.

Whatever the location, the spiritual calm of Buddhism – over half the male population has passed through monkhood – enthuses all aspects of Thai life.

ℒAID BACK IN PARADISE

Chase moon shadows,
roll over the edge *of* a warm
gentle turquoise sea,
feast *on* beach-side banquets.
Indulge *in* your whims here...
Samui, Pha-ngan, Krabi *and* Phuket.

a m a z i n g **THAILAND**
EXPERIENCE The SPLENDOURS Of A KINGDOM

Contact: Tourism Authority of Thailand, Le Concorde Building, 202 Ratchadaphisek Rd., Huai Khwang, Bangkok 10310, Thailand
Tel. (66 2) 694-1222 (80 lines) Fax. (66 2) 694-1220, 694-1221 E-mail: center@tat.or.th Internet: www.tourismthailand.org or www.amazingthailand.th

Le Royal Meridien
Baan Taling Ngam

295 Moo 3
Taling Ngam Beach
Koh Samui
Suratthani 84140
Thailand

✈ Samui Int. 45km

tel +66 77 423 019
fax +66 77 423 220

taling@specialhotels.com
www.specialhotels.com
sawadee.com/samui/meridien/

Tour operators:
UK Elegant Resorts

Set among the green trees of a coconut plantation, overlooking one of Koh Samui's most beautiful beaches, Baan Taling Ngam lives up to its translation of 'your home on a beautiful cliff'.

The secluded grounds of the resort hide 42 deluxe rooms and suites, 28 luxury villas and our premier accommodation – the Royal Villa (Baan Napa), all with traditional teak interiors and private balconies or patios. If you'd prefer to be closer to the soft sands take one of the nine beach suites.

Dining takes place in the clifftop Lom Talay restaurant, which serves exceptional Mediterranean and Thai cuisine, or try the delicious fresh seafood in the seafront Promenade restaurant.

You'll certainly have worked up an appetite with all the facilities the hotel offers. Snorkel, dive, windsurf, or waterski in the tranquil waters of the Ang Thong Marine National Park that surrounds the resort. Or you can take a sunset island cruise. Back on dry land, mountain biking or four-wheel drive safaris are easily arranged.

Whatever you choose, the massage, sauna or dip in one of the seven hilltop pools will help you wind down ready for the next perfect day in paradise.

263

 US$300-330 (40)

 US$400-3,000 (28 villas/9 suites)

 US$18-30

 US$20

Honeymoon specials
Card from general manager, rose petal in heart shape at turn down on first day, brass bell, a bottle of white wine.

Sightseeing and leisure
Ang Thong Marine National Park, Chawaeng beach, butterfly park, Hin Ta Hin Yai. The hotel also boasts seven outdoor pools, licensed PADI dive school, tennis courts, mountain biking, snorkelling, kayaking, plus most other watersports. Full range of hair styling and beauty treatment, therapeutic massage, sauna, work-out facilities.

Dusit Laguna

390 Srisoontorn Rd
Cherngtalay District
Amphur, Thalang
Phuket 83110
Thailand

✈ Phuket 22km

tel +66 76 324 320
fax +66 76 324 174

dusit@specialhotels.com
www.specialhotels.com
www.dusit.com

264

Member of:
Leading Hotels of the World

White silvery sands. Beautiful lagoons. The salty tang of sea breezes. Abundant coconut groves. Shimmering, emerald Andaman waters. In the distance a solitary boat sways gently to the rhythm of the waves. Overhead a clear sky of unbelievable blue stretching away to infinity is lit by the everlasting tropical sun. All this and more is to be found at the romantic Dusit Laguna on the exotic island paradise of Phuket.

Classic simplicity and elegance are the hallmarks of the resort's rooms and suites. A king-size bed is crowned with a white, damask canopy. Golden brown interiors are suffused with discreet occasional lamps while outside sunlit balconies overlook magnificently landscaped gardens.

Exquisite regional and international cuisine can be enjoyed at the hotel's four restaurants and two bars. Immaculately prepared Thai dishes, freshly barbecued seafood, cool refreshing drinks and delicious snacks are all available, accompanied by Thai musicians and the famous Phuket sunset.

The wedding package including a Thai Buddhist ceremony, complete with three Buddhist monks, photographer, room upgrade, flowers and garlands, plus champagne breakfast and a candlelit Thai dinner, costs from US$2,600.

US$270 (213)
US$430-750 (13)
US$35-65
US$14

Honeymoon specials

Honeymooners are guaranteed a king-size bed, complimentary fruit and flowers, a honeymoon cake and a bottle of wine on arrival. A splendid Thai wedding ceremony is available (see details above).

Sightseeing and leisure

Jungle treks on elephants, Jeep safaris, canoe trips to nearby islands and visits to Wat Chalong, Phuket's largest temple. Mountain biking, sailing, Scuba diving, windsurfing, fishing, canoeing, swimming, beach volleyball, tennis, table tennis and golf nearby. Beauty salon and massage by appointment.

The Maiton Resort

PO Box 376
Phuket 83000
Thailand

✈ Phuket 44km

tel +66 76 214 954
fax +66 76 214 959

maiton@specialhotels.com
www.specialhotels.com
maiton@samart.co.th
www.phuket.com/maiton/
index.htm

The Maiton Resort is the sole occupant of a private island in the emerald Andaman Sea, nine kilometres southeast of Phuket. Absolute beachfront and ocean view villas, surrounded by the arches of coconut palms, are a mere step from the sugary beach – the longest continuous stretch of private beach in Thailand offering guests an unparalled tropical sanctuary. All villas are crafted in the Thai tradition and have marble bathroom, spacious living room, mini bar and verandah.

Guests are spoilt for choice when it comes to dining. Make your selection from the classic French restaurant, Japanese or Asian cuisines and superb tastes of Thailand on the terrace of the Sala Thai Restaurant or grilled seafood at the Hillside Grill.

Staff aim to provide exceptional personal service for all guests and can arrange daily excursions. Take a dolphin cruise as the island is home to several pods of dolphins and sightings are usual. For watersport fanatics, there is everything that could be desired, such as diving, snorkelling, waterskiing, game fishing, windsurfing, sailing or kayaking.

On dry land there are pools as well as a Jacuzzi, sauna, fitness centre and tennis court. For the lazy at heart, relax with a Thai massage, learn about Thai cooking, try the Thai fruit carving class or indulge yourself in the beauty salon with a wide selection of facial and body treatments.

265

 65 villas

 included

 included

Honeymoon specials
Champagne and hand made chocolates in villa on arrival, rose petals decorating the bed. For stays over 10 nights, a clothing trouseau of choice prepared by the personal resort tailor. Honeymoon package from 21,480Tb per couple per night, which includes beachfront villa, all meals and drinks, limo transfers, room service and service charges.

Sightseeing and leisure
On Phuket Island there are markets, temples, golf and shopping. Dolphin cruises and all watersports. Jungle treks, beach volleyball, massage, gym and sauna, plus Thai cooking and carving classes.

Paradise Beach Resort

18/8 Maenam Beach
Koh Samui 84330
Thailand

✈ Samui 10 min

tel +66 77 247 227/32
fax +66 77 425 290

paradise@specialhotels.com
www.specialhotels.com

Tour Operators:
UK Kuoni

266

Nestled on the shores of the central part of the tranquil Maenam Beach in a luscious tropical garden, this small, personal resort offers you the chance to truly relax and get away from it all in an island eden. Endless white beaches welcome sun and sea lovers and watersport enthusiasts. Or guests can relax around the resort's fresh water swimming pool or take a dip in the Jacuzzi.

All rooms have private balcony or verandah and are creatively furnished and provided with modern comforts including air-conditioning, mini bar, refrigerator and satellite TV and video.

The Paradise Terrace beachfront restaurant provides the opportunity to sample Thai and continental cuisine and a wide range of freshly caught fish and local specialities. From the comfort of your resort you can decide which excursions to take – ranging from a variety of sightseeing tours, diving, deep sea fishing, island hopping or even a romantic moonlight cruise.

 US$140-167 (86)

 US$162-189 (19 villas)

US$11-15

US$10

Honeymoon specials
Complimentary flowers, fruits and champagne. Candlelight dinner and room upgrade when available.

Leisure facilities
Fresh water swimming pool, Jacuzzi, water sports, diving, deep sea fishing, island hopping and moonlit cruises.

Sightseeing
Big Buddha, water falls, monkey theatre, Zen Thai cultural village and zoo.

Information & Reservations
UK 0870 606 1296
INT. +44 870 606 1296

84 Moo 5
Bophut
Ko Samui
Surat Thani 84320
Thailand

✈ Samui 3km

tel +66 2 254 0056/62
fax +66 2 254 0054/55

tongsai@specialhotels.com
www.specialhotels.com
tongsai@loxinfo.co.th
tongsaibay.co.th

Peace. Quiet. Private bay and beach. Twenty-five acres of beautiful tropical gardens. Romantic. Secluded. Picturesque. The Tongsai Bay.

When the resort was built in 1986, the owner did not cut down one single tree. The land on the hill was so naturally beautiful that the cottages were built around the trees and coconut palms. It could be said that Mother Nature is the real architect.

The new Grand Tongsai Villas which opened in December 1998 are specially created for romance. Muslin curtains frame the bed and every room has an open-air terrace from which to sneak panoramic views of this idyllic tropical hideaway. In these, the air-conditioned bedroom alone is 54 square metres with polished teak floor, rattan furniture, celadon lamps and lovely Thai silk curtains.

The huge open-air Maka-wood terrace provides the *piece de resistance:* open-air bathtubs where you can lie back and soak up the incredible views. There is even a gazebo where you can sleep, gazing at the moon and stars above (mosquito net included).

Style runs right through Tongsai where there are three top restaurants – some of the best Thai on the island – and four bars for the discerning palette.

US$277-555

US$42

US$14

Honeymoon specials
Complimentary bottle of sparkling wine, fruit basket and flowers in room on arrival. Traditional Thai wedding packages are also available from Baht 35,000, which include various services which are rituals in the Thai community. Contact the resort for details.

Sightseeing and leisure
Hin Lat and Na Muang waterfalls, Samui Hin, one of the highest points on Ko Samui, the unique stone formations of Hin Yai. Temples and the Samui Monkey Theatre are worth seeing. The resort also boasts an exercise room, snooker room, tennis and offers most watersports. Diving and deep-sea fishing available through a third party.

South Pacific

flying time
To: Fiji, Cook's via
Rarotonga, Bora Bora
via Tahiti
London: 22-25 hrs
LA: 12-14 hrs
NY: 18-20 hrs

**climate/
when to go**
Tropical and pleasant
all year. Average
annual temperature
is 25°C.

currency
The Fijian dollar;
New Zealand dollar
in the Cook's;
Central Pacific Franc
(CFP) in Bora Bora.
US dollars welcome
almost everywhere.

language
English is generally
spoken along with
the indigenous South
Pacific languages.

getting around
Frequent inter-island
air services. Often
islands can be
reached by ship or
launch. On the
ground, local taxis
are available in main
centres.

268

Few places in the world can match the romance, magic and allure of the South Pacific islands. Fiji, the Cook Islands, Bora Bora, Vanuatu and Tongo...magical names and magical places to visit, too. It is hard to find anywhere more remote than these lonely outposts, but what they lack in ease of access they more than make up for in the sheer beauty and romance of their setting and atmosphere.

The Cook's 15 islands occupy just 93 square miles amidst 850,000 square miles of ocean. Rarotonga, the main island, is spectacular, with mist-capped mountains and dense jungle. Protected by a coral reef, it has palm-fringed beaches and clear waters, teeming with fish. Here, and on Aitutaki (said to have the finest lagoon in the Pacific), there are picture-postcard beaches and entertainment aplenty. In the past, explorers, pirates and mutineers washed up on the islands. Those who could tear themselves away returned home and raved of the enchanted land they had found. Unlike their accounts of sea monsters and mermaids, these stories were true.

Like the Cook Islands, the island of Bora Bora is a copywriter's delight. Words flow as easily as the peaceful and unhurried days in this warm and sunny climate to conjure up everyone's idea of the South Pacific. On your doorstep a colourful lagoon, perfect breakers thundering on the distant reef, coral gardens alive with fish, soft breezes in the palms, warm sand drifting through warm toes, the heady smell of hibiscus, singing, dancing, eating and drinking under the happy-go-lucky tropical sun and the magic of shore-side walks under the lustrous Pacific moon.

Another gem in this part of the world is Fiji, a sophisticated tropical idyll with marvellous beaches, colourful coral reefs and rose-tinted sunsets straight from a picture-perfect book. And for the more authentic Fiji try the Yasawa islands, first sighted by Captain Bligh on his epic journey and also the setting for the film *Blue Lagoon*. For honeymooners, these islands are unadulterated paradise.

NORTH PACIFIC
OCEAN

FIJI   COOK   BORA BORA
        ISLANDS

SOUTH PACIFIC
OCEAN

Bora Bora Lagoon Resort

Information & Reservations
UK 0870 606 1296
INT. +44 870 606 1296

Motu Tooppau
B.P. 175
Vaitape, Bora Bora
French Polynesia

✈ 20 mins by boat from
Bora Bora airport (10km)

tel +689 60 40 00
fax +689 60 40 01

bora@specialhotels.com
www.specialhotels.com
bblr@mail.pf

Member of:
Leading Hotels of the World

Tour operators:
UK Elegant Resorts
US Islands in the Sun

Discovered by Captain Cook in 1769, Bora Bora, has been described as the most beautiful island in the world. And set on an atoll in the midst of this paradise's crystal clear lagoon, is Bora Bora Lagoon Resort, the ultimate in romantic getaways.

You sleep in a 528 square foot bungalow modelled on a traditional Tahitian home. Thatched roofs and gleaming wood interiors house king-sized beds, separate seating area and individual sundeck. The magnificent over-water bungalows offer private swimming areas and, spectacularly, an illuminated glass coffee table to view (and even feed) the lagoon's colourful marine life without getting your feet wet.

Dining is always special here. Whether you sample the five-star cuisine of the over-water Otemanu restaurant, informal menus at the Café Fare, buffet or á la carte, or dine *al fresco* at one of the weekly Tahitian feasts, you won't be disappointed.

During the day you can canoe across the still surface of the lagoon or swim with turtles at the nearby Lagoonarium. Feed sharks on the nearby reef, take a 4x4 excursion into the main island's lush interior, or simply relax on the talcum fine sand and enjoy the silence that characterises this magical resort.

269

 US$520-710 (78)

 US$820 (2)

 US$55-80

 included

Honeymoon specials

Unforgettable Honeymoon/Romance Package includes three nights in over-water bungalow, floral greeting on arrival as well as fresh flowers and champagne, one canoe breakfast for two, American breakfast daily, romantic dinner with a bottle of wine, shark feeding excursion, disposable underwater camera, resort logo gift items. Package price: US$2,580 per couple, available until 20 December 1999.

Sightseeing and leisure

The hotel is located on a private island where the main attraction is the lagoon and most of the activities are focussed here. Also, guests may take advantage of having a massage either privately in their bungalow or in the massage room in the hotel. Plus complimentary use of outdoor pool, two flood-lit tennis courts and gym.

Information & Reservations
UK 0870 606 1296
INT. +44 870 606 1296

Aitutaki Lagoon Resort

PO Box 99
Aitutaki
Cook Islands

✈ Aitutaki 7 mins

tel +682 31 201
fax +682 31 202

aitutaki@specialhotels.com
www.specialhotels.com

270

This beautiful, romantic tropical island hideaway gives you the chance to truly get away from it all. The island is located 140 miles north of Rarotonga, the capital of the Cook Islands (approximately 45 minutes by air) and is one of 15 in the Cook Islands' group. The resort is located on a secluded inlet linked by a causeway to the main island.

You can choose from deluxe beach, lagoon view or garden accommodation, all with secluded private terrace, fridge, direct dial IDD phones, mini-bar and private bathroom. For the ultimate in relaxation,

enjoy drinks at the beach bar or swimming pool, dance to the Island String Band, immerse yourself in the culture of the islands with twice weekly Cultural Shows, or try the famous Seafood Buffet every Wednesday evening.

A range of watersports are also available. Choose from snorkelling, diving, windsurfing, game fishing and kayaking. For exploring this luscious island there is the lagoon cruise, or organised island tours. If you would rather explore on your own, hire a car, or perhaps rent a bike and cycle your way round.

 NZ$305-665 (25)

NZ$665 (5)

NZ$12-45

NZ$16.50-25

Honeymoon specials
Fruit bowl, flowers and champagne on arrival.

Leisure facilities
Complimentary snorkelling, kayaks, canoes and windsurfing. Golf course 10 minutes from resort. The locals are often willing to lend guests their golf clubs, balls etc.

Sightseeing
A bustling market is nearby. Boat trips to feed the fish in the lagoon and island tours can be arranged.

Turtle Island Resort

c/o Turtle Island Holidays
Level 1, Rialto North Tower
525 Collins St
Melbourne
Vic 3000 Australia
Fiji

✈ Viti Levu 45 miles

tel +61 3 9 618 1100
fax +61 3 9 618 1199

USA contact:
+800 255 4347

www.turtlefiji.com
usa@turtlefiji.com
turtlemelb@micronica.com.au

Turtle Island, Fiji, has been voted one of the 'Top 10 Most Romantic Resorts Worldwide'. A five-star award-winning resort on a 500-acre privately owned Fijian Island, it is an unspoiled tropical treasure and a journey into Fijian culture. Situated on the famous Blue Lagoon, it is home to just 14 couples. Fourteen separate powder sand beaches, acres of rainforest, fields of yellow grass and 100 friendly Fijian staff make this an island jewel.

The charming Fijian-style two room cottages (bures) situated alongside the Blue Lagoon have a four-poster bed, verandah for napping in the sun-flecked shade of the palms and an indoor Jacuzzi which set the scene for romance.

Guests enjoy world-class cuisine with a gourmet picnic on a private beach, dinner for two on a mountain top under the stars or a festive lovo (Fijian-style banquet) with other guests. Island grown fruit and vegetables, abundant freshly caught seafood, chilled champagne and wines are all on the menu at Turtle Island.

Turtle Island is more than a honeymoon. It is a life experience. It is where you bathe in the delights which have been lost to modern society...the warm loving Fijian staff, the beauty of an island untouched by industry, where the ecology is a primary concern and where people understand that your honeymoon is a special time which can never be recreated.

271

 £741* (14)

 included

 included

 (incl)

Honeymoon specials

Wedding packages include marriage license, transport on the lagoon to chapel by billi billi (wedding raft), wedding set-up and bouquet, Fijian apparel, flower leis, choir, minister, video, Fijian band, Kava ceremony, wedding feast and cake, beverages, film and Tapa Bound wedding album. Package price on application. * Price fully inclusive per couple per night. Seaplane transfers £539 per couple per return.

Sightseeing and leisure

Turtle Island is one of the most secluded and romantic islands in the South Pacific. All activities – deep-sea fishing, diving, horseriding, mountain biking, snorkelling, jungle and mountain walks, windsurfing, private beach picnics, sailing, fly fishing, tours, sunrise champagne breakfasts, Kava ceremonies and more are included in the price. Also, visit the local village church or school or take a sunset champagne cruise.

Celebrity Cruises

Worldwide

Contact:
Celebrity Cruises
Royal Caribbean House
Addlestone Road
Weybridge
Surrey KT15 2UE
England

tel +44 1932 834200
fax +44 1932 820286

UK Reservations:
Freephone 0800 018 2525
+44 1932 834310

celebrity@specialhotels.com
www.specialhotels.com
www.celebrity-cruises.com

What could be more romantic than getting married or honeymooning on a five-star cruise ship as it glides effortlessly through the high seas? Travelling to some of the world's most exotic and fascinating destinations from tranquil Bermuda to the sun-splashed Caribbean, through the mighty Panama Canal or the awe-inspiring glaciers of Alaska, Celebrity Cruises offer diverse and original excursions in every port of call. Marriages can be arranged either on board in port or ashore in various destinations, please contact Reservations for further details.

On board any one of the five state-of-the-art liners, luxury and elegance are premium. The state rooms and suites are modern and spacious with warm wood-finish furniture, artworks on the walls and soft, atmospheric lighting. Some come complete with verandahs

 from £1,039*

 from £1,969*

 included

 included

Honeymoon specials

Breakfast in bed including champagne, boxed set of engraved glasses, floral arrangement, single rose on pillow, Celebrity bathrobes, personalised certificate (cost £80). All honeymoon couples will receive a one-category upgrade (subject to restrictions). Weddings can be arranged through Weddings Abroad: +44 171 941 1122.

* Based on Century 9-night Caribbean 19-11-99.

while others enjoy a full butler service.

The tables in the expansive dining rooms are set with fine linen, sparkling crystal and polished silverware and graced with fresh flowers. A new menu is on offer every evening. Appetizers such as North Atlantic Shrimp might be followed by a chilled Gin and Tomato Consommé, a Roquefort salad, Yakutat Bay Halibut steak and Pear Flan Soufflé to finish. After dinner there are convivial piano bars, intimate night clubs, casinos and pulsating discos to enjoy.

During the day, trips ashore are equally varied. Whether it be renting a moped to visit Bermudian villages, visiting the Alaska Chilkat to see one of the world's largest colonies of bald eagles, enjoying the excitement of the Big Apple or just soaking up the sun on a Caribbean beach, Celebrity Cruises provide some of the best the world can offer.

Sightseeing

Depending on the cruise: Panning for gold or whale watching in Alaska, train rides through the Rocky Mountains, travelling the length of the Panama Canal, sightseeing in Niagara Falls, visiting the Elmorro Fortress in San Juan, shopping for souvenirs in Nassau's straw market or sampling Grand Cayman's famous rum cake.

Leisure facilities

On board: numerous bars and lounges, health clubs, aqua spas (including massage, fitness programs, aromatherapy, etc), shops, pools, wine tasting, auctions, cookery classes, West End-style shows and productions and casino.
On shore: golf, tennis, watersports, fishing, diving, sailing, canoeing, walking, hiking.

Royal Caribbean International

Worldwide

Contact:
Royal Caribbean International
Royal Caribbean House
Addlestone Road
Weybridge
Surrey KT15 2UE
England

tel +44 1932 834200
fax +44 1932 820286

UK Reservations:
Freephone 0800 0182020
+44 1932 834300

274

royalcruise@specialhotels.com
www.specialhotels.com
www.royalcaribbean.com
londonoffice@miamail01.rccl.com

Member of:
Passenger Shipping Association

Tour operator:
UK Royal Caribbean International

Inspired by a bygone age when travel was a romantic adventure rather than just a means to an end, a Royal Caribbean cruise removes the problem of picking just one honeymoon destination.

The warm sandy beaches and gentle trade winds of the Caribbean, the bright coral reefs of the Bahamas, the bustling seaports and quaint villages of Bermuda, the ice-blue glaciers and pristine wilderness of Alaska, and the ancient medieval cities of Europe – all can be visited by passengers on a majestic cruise ship, sailing sedately through the world's great oceans and seas.

Most of the luxury cabins offer magnificent ocean views, some have private balconies and sitting areas. All are bright, well proportioned and decorated to a high standard, with discreet lighting, pretty fabrics and solid, well-built furniture.

 UK£1,789* (9 nights)

 UK£959* (9 nights)

 included**

 included**

Honeymoon specials
Complimentary bottle of Moët et Chandon.

* Based on Grandeur Of The Seas, sailing 27/11/99.
** Beverages are not included.

Guests wake every day to a new culinary adventure: pastries on deck at sunrise, pancakes and maple syrup in the lavish dining room, afternoon tea by the pool, a barbecue on a private island, or a romantic dinner for two served in the luxurious privacy of the cabin.

Royal Caribbean International also offers a special Royal Romance wedding package on selected cruises. From US$600, couples can be married on board and expect VIP priority check-in, onboard co-ordination, wedding cake for two, flowers, marriage certificate, photos and, of course, the ceremony. Should couples really want to splash out, US$1,200 will buy numerous extras including a chauffeured limousine. A whole host of extras are available such as island weddings, receptions, music, video, ice sculptures, and beauty appointments.

Sightseeing

Depending on the cruise, the many shore excursions on offer include guided tours through the Canadian Rockies, shopping in New York, whale-watching in Alaska, visits to the volcanoes of Honolulu, the Bridge of Sighs in Venice, or the Peter and Paul Cathedral in St Petersburg. These cost extra.

Leisure facilities

On board: beauty salon, boutiques, casino, indoor/outdoor pools*, library, miniature 18-hole golf course*, fitness centre and spa, solarium*, video games room, nightclub. On shore: depending on the cruise, guests might go snorkelling in the Caribbean, paddle-boating in Haiti, gambling in Monaco, horseriding in Mexico, salmon fishing in Alaska, mountain biking in Curaçao, sailing in Marseille or submarining in Aruba.

* On selected ships.

Information & Reservations
UK 0870 606 1296
INT. +44 870 606 1296

The Nile
Luxor
Aswân
Egypt

tel +20 23 83 32 22/3444
fax +20 23 83 77 77

philae@specialhotels.com
www.specialhotels.com
obmhosm@oberoi.com.eg
www.oberoihotels.com

Why pick just one holiday destination when every day a new, vivid and wonderful vista can roll into view? Aboard The Oberoi Philae Nile Cruiser 5,000 years of history are waiting to be discovered and enjoyed. Discover the glories of ancient Egypt in the same magnificent manner the Pharaohs themselves travelled.

Luxury is the key word aboard the five-decked cruiser from the elegant wood floored reception with its large picture windows and oriental carpets to the cabins and suites with their balconies, king-size beds and air-conditioning.

The itinerary includes a visit to the temples at Luxor, the Valley of the Kings and the Temples of Horus and Edfu and many other attractions. Every moment while sedately cruising down the Nile, is a sightseeing opportunity. On board there are a variety of activities for you to enjoy from the Captain's welcoming cocktail party to fancy dress and nightly entertainment. Elegant restaurants abound and there is also a fully equipped gym and sundeck plunge pool.

When the sun sets over the Nile, guests can dine under a canopy of stars while the cruiser makes its regal way into the still night.

 US$2,070 (4 nights)

 US$3,105 (6 nights)

 included

 included

Honeymoon specials
Package includes full board accommodation for four to six nights, daytime excursions to the most popular tourist spots in Upper Egypt. Wedding cake, wine, flowers on arrival, plus special pharaonic souvenir and photo.
Cost: US$1,600 (4 nights); US$2,400 (6 nights).

Leisure facilities
Large sundeck plunge pool and bar, fully equipped indoor gym, hairdresser, beauty salon.

Information & Reservations
UK   0870 606 1296
INT. +44 870 606 1296

c/o 39 Orchid Magu
Malé 20-02
Maldives

tel +960 32 3080
fax +960 32 2678

island@specialhotels.com
www.specialhotels.com
www.unisurf.com

Island Explorer

The glassy calm seas of the Maldives were made for exploration by sea and what better way to truly discover the beauty and wonder of this archipelago of tranquil islands than by taking a cruise around its highlights.

On board ship, comfort and luxury are guaranteed. Each stateroom, although compact, offers comfortable sleeping facilities, seating areas and air-conditioning. Most cabins also contain large picture windows so you can watch the incredible scenery float past – they're also prime viewing territory for the dolphins and porpoise that often play alongside the ship's bow.

Of course, dining is excellent. Most meals are buffet style with the exception of the Captain's gala dinner that offers a chance to dress up and enjoy a gourmet sit down meal.

Your itinerary sees you visiting five of the Maldives most beautiful and uninhabited islands. Snorkels are available for hire on the boat and you won't want to miss this chance to swim undisturbed through this remarkable marine area. Excursions to local fishing villages, shopping areas or cultural events are also arranged. Life on board ship can be as lazy or active as you make it – all you need do is enjoy yourself.

US$68-180* 60 cabins

included

included

Honeymoon specials

Fruit and flowers in the cabin on arrival. Room upgrade subject to availability.

* Prices quoted are per person per night and include all meals, excursions and return transfers from airport.

Sightseeing and leisure

As you are cruising the Maldives, there are plenty of watersports to appreciate. There are also excursions to Kuda Bandos, RAA Atoillfuru, Ungoofaaru and Kudakurathu, among other inhabited and uninhabited islands.

WEDDINGS ABROAD DIRECTORY

	Licensed for weddings	Wedding co-ordinator available	Prior registration with local authorities for wedding couples	Music for ceremony arranged	Photographs for ceremony arranged	Honeymoon packages	Wedding packages	Wine/champagne on arrival	All-inclusive	Reception facilities	24-hour room service	Limousine/car service for honeymooners	Special Honeymoon Suite	Beach wedding
Aitutaki Lagoon Resort, Cook Islands	●	●	★	●	●	●	●	●		●				●
Ajman Kempinski Hotel & Resort, UAE						●		●		●	●	●		
Al Bustan Palace Hotel, Oman						●		●		●	●	●	●	
Albergo Pietrasanta, Italy	●		★	●	●	●		●		●	●	●	●	
American Colony Hotel, The, Israel	★		★	●	●	●	●	●		●	●	●	●	
Arlberg Hospiz Hotel, Austria	●		★	●	●		●			●	●	●		
Baan Taling Ngam, Thailand	●	●	★	●	●	●	●	●		●	●		●	●
Badrutt's Palace Hotel, Switzerland						●			●	●	●		●	
Baros Holiday Resort, Maldives						●				●	●		●	
Bay, The, South Africa	●	●	●	●	●					●	●		●	●
Begawan Giri, Bali	●	●	★			●		●		●	●		●	
Belvidere Manor, South Africa	●	●	●					●		●				
Benguerra Lodge, Benguerra Island	★					★	★							
Bora Bora Lagoon Resort, Bora Bora	●		★	●	●	●	●	●					●	●
Borana Lodge, Kenya	★			●	●	●		●	●	★			●	
Cairo Nile Hilton, Egypt	★	★		★	★	●	●	●		●	●	●	●	
Cambridge Beaches, Bermuda	●	●	★	●	●	●	●			●	●		●	●
Camino Real Acapulco Diamante, Mex.	●	★		●	●	●	●	★		●	●		●	
Camino Real Cancun, Mexico	●	●	●	●	●	●	●			●	●		●	
Camino Real Las Hadas, Mexico	●		●	●	●	●	●			●	●		●	●
Camino Real Puerto Vallarta, Mexico	●	●		●	●	●	●			●	●		●	
Castello Del Sole Ascona, Switzerland	★					●		●		●	★	●	●	
Celebrity Cruises	●	★	★	●	●	●	★	●	★	●	●	★	●	★
Chateau de la Chevre d'Or, France	●	●		●	●					●	●		●	
Chateau Eza, France	●	●	★	●	●					●	●		●	
Chewton Glen, England	●	●	★	●	★	●	●		●	●	●		●	
Ciragan Palace Kempinski Istanbul, Tky	●		★	●	●	●	●			●	●		●	
Colony Beach & Tennis Resort, Florida	●	●	★	●	●		●	★		●			●	●
Colony Club Hotel, Barbados	●	●		●	●	●	●			●	●		●	●
Conrad Int. Sharm el Sheikh, Egypt	●	●		●	●	●				●	●	●	●	
Damai Lovina Villas, Bali	●	●	●	●	●	●	●			●	●		●	
Dan Eilat, Israel	●		★							●	●		●	
Datai Langkawi, The, Malaysia		●	★	●	●	●				●	●			
Desert Rose, Kenya								●	●					

Information supplied by hotels and correct at the time of going to press.
● Denotes the hotel provides the indicated service. ★ Please contact the hotel direct regarding this facility.

Hotel	Licensed for weddings	Wedding co-ordinator available	Prior registration with local authorities for wedding couples	Music for ceremony arranged	Photographs for ceremony arranged	Honeymoon packages	Wedding packages	Wine/champagne on arrival	All-inclusive	Reception facilities	24-hour room service	Limousine/car service for honeymooners	Special Honeymoon Suite	Beach wedding
Domaine du Royal Club Evian, France						●	●	●		●	●	●	●	
Dusit Laguna, Thailand	●		★			●	●	●		●	●	●	●	
Eilat Princess Hotel, Israel	●	●	★	●	●	●	●	●		●	●	●	●	
Elounda Mare, Greece	★			●	●	●		●		●	●	●		
Fateh Prakash Palace Hotel, India	●	●		●	●	●	●	●		●		●		
Fawsley Hall, England	●			●	●	●		●		●		●		
Fiesta Americana Cancun, Mexico	●	●	★	●	●	●	●	●		●	★	★	●	●
Fisherman's Cove, Seychelles	★					●	★	●		●	★	★	●	
Forte Village Resort, Sardinia	●	★	★	●	●	●	●	●		●		●	●	★
Four Seasons Hotel, Cyprus	●	●	★	●	●	●	●	●		●		●	●	
Full Moon Resort, Maldives						●							●	
Galdessa Camp, Kenya						●			●	●			●	
Grand Hotel Cocumella, Italy		●	★	●	●	●	●	●				●	●	
Grand Hotel d'Angkor, Cambodia	●	●	★	●	●	●	●	●		●		●	●	
Grand Hotel Excelsior Vittoria, Italy		●	★	★	★	●	●	●		●		●	●	
Grand Hotel Zermatterhof, Switzerland	★			●	●	●		●		●		●	●	
Grand Lido Negril, Jamaica	●	●	★	●	●	●	●	●	●	●		●	●	●
Halcyon Hotel, England		●		●	●	●	★	●		●		●	●	
Hide Safari Camp, The, Zimbabwe	●		★	●	●	●		●		●			●	
Hilton Beach Club Dubai, The, UAE	●					●	●	●		●	●	●	●	●
Hilton Dahab/Red Sea Cruise, Egypt						●	●	●	●	●			●	
Horizons & Cottages, Bermuda	●	●	★	●	●	●	●	●		●			●	
Hotel da Lapa (Lapa Palace), Portugal	●			●	●	●	●	●		●	●	●	●	
Hotel Du Palais, France	●	●	★	●	●	●	●	●		●	●	●	●	
Hotel Europa & Regina, Italy	★			●	●	●		●		●	●	●	●	
Hotel Hacienda Na Xamena, Ibiza										●	●	●	●	
Hotel Hoffmeister, Czech Republic	★		★	●	●	●		●		●	●	●	●	
Hotel La Reserve, Portugal				●	●			●		●		●	●	
Hotel L'Archipel, Seychelles	●	●	★	●	●	●	●	●		●				★
Hotel Le Maquis, Corsica				●	●									
Hotel Martinez, France	★	●	★	●	●	●	★	●		●	●	●	●	
Hotel Mocking Bird Hill, Jamaica	●	●	★	●	●	●	●	●		●		●	●	●
Hôtel Plaza Athénée, New York	●	●	●	●	●	●	●	●		●	●	●	●	
Hotel Puente Romano, Spain	●			●	●			●		●	●	●	●	

	Licensed for weddings	Wedding co-ordinator available	Prior registration with local authorities for wedding couples	Music for ceremony arranged	Photographs for ceremony arranged	Honeymoon packages	Wedding packages	Wine/champagne on arrival	All-inclusive	Reception facilities	24-hour room service	Limousine/car service for honeymooners	Special Honeymoon Suite	Beach wedding
Hotel Quinta do Lago, Portugal				●	●	●	●	★		●	●		●	
Hotel Royal Monceau, France				●	●	●	●			●	●		●	
Hotel Santa Caterina, Italy						●	●			●	●	★	●	
Hotel Schloss Fuschl, Austria			★	●	●	●	●	●		●	●	●	●	
Hotel Schloss Mönchstein, Austria	●	●	●	●	●	●	●	●		●	●	●	●	
Hotel Vistamar de Valldemossa, Mallorca	★	●		●	●	●	★	●		●		●	●	
Hyatt Regency La Manga, Spain	●	●		●	●	●	●	●		●	●	●	●	
Hyatt Regency Marinasmir, Morocco	●			●	●	●	★	●		●	●	●	●	
Il Melograno, Italy		●		●	●	●	●	●		●	●	●	●	
Inn at Manitou, The, Canada	●	●	●	●	●	●	●	●	★	●	●	●	●	
Island Explorer						●			★	●	●		●	
Jerusalem Hotel, Israel	★			●	●	●	●	●	★	●	●		●	
Katete Safari, Zimbabwe						★			●	●			●	
Kedar Country Hotel, South Africa	●	●	●	●	●	●	●	●		●			●	
Kempinski Hotel Atlantic, Germany	●	★	●	●	●	●	●	●		●	●	●	●	
Kempinski Resort Hotel Estepona, Spain	★			★	★	●	●	●		●	●	●	●	★
Kinasi, Mafia Island, Tanzania	●	★	★	●	★	●	●	●	●	●	★		●	★
Kirurumu Tented Lodge, Tanzania	●		★	●	●	●	★	●		●			●	
Kivotos Clubhotel, Greece	●	★	●	●	●	●	●	●		●	●		●	
La Cocoteraie, Guadaloupe	★			●		●		●		●	●		●	
La Gazelle d'Or, Morocco	★					●	★	★	●	●	●	●	●	
La Mamounia, Morocco				●	●	●	●	●		●	●	●	●	
La Pinsonnière, Canada						●	★	●		●	★	●	●	
La Posta Vecchia, Italy						●	●	●		●	●	●	●	
La Residencia, Mallorca			★	●	●	●	★	●		●	●	●	●	
Laguna Beach, Maldives						●					●		●	
Lake Palace, India	●	●		●	●	●	●	●		●	●	●	●	
Lapa Rios, Costa Rica	★		★	★	★	●	★	●	●	●			●	
Las Dunas Beach Hotel & Spa, Spain				●	●	●	●			●	●	●	●	
Las Mananitas, Mexico	●	●	★	●	●	●	●	●		●	●	●	●	
Le Meridien Limassol, Cyprus		●	★	●	●	●	●	★		●	●	●	●	
Le Montreux Palace, Switzerland	●	●	●	●	●	●	●	●		●	●	●	●	
Le Silve Di Armenzano, Italy						●	●	●		●	●		●	
LeSPORT, St Lucia	●	●		●	●	●	●	●		●	●		●	★

Information supplied by hotels and correct at the time of going to press.
● Denotes the hotel provides the indicated service. ★ Please contact the hotel direct regarding this facility.

Hotel	Licensed for weddings	Wedding co-ordinator available	Prior registration with local authorities for wedding couples	Music for ceremony arranged	Photographs for ceremony arranged	Honeymoon packages	Wedding packages	Wine/champagne on arrival	All-inclusive	Reception facilities	24-hour room service	Limousine/car service for honeymooners	Special Honeymoon Suite	Beach wedding
Le Toiny, St Barts	★			●	●	●	★	●	★	●	★		●	★
Leela Palace, India	●	★	★	●	●	●	●	●	●	●	●	●	●	★
Litchfield Plantation, South Carolina	●	●	★	●	●	●	●	●		●	●	●	●	
Lodge & Spa at Inchydoney Isl., Ireland	★	★		●	●	★	●	●	●	●	★	★	●	
Mahaweli Reach, Sri Lanka	●	●	★	●	●	●	●	●	●	●	●	●	●	
Maiton Resort, The, Thailand	●	●	★	●	●	●	●	●	●	●	●	●	●	●
Marbella Club, Spain							★			●	●		●	
Mauna Lani Bay Hotel & Bungalows, HI	●	●	★	●	●	●	●	●	●	●	●	●	●	★
Mena House Oberoi & Casino, Egypt				●	●	●	●	●	●	●	●	●	●	
Misty Hills Country Hotel, South Africa	●	●		●	●	●	●	●	●	●	●		●	
Mombasa Serena Beach Hotel, Kenya	●	●	★	●	●	●	●	●	●	●	●		●	★
Musango Safari Camp, Zimbabwe				●	●	★		●	●	●	●		●	
Nakatchafushi Tourist Resort, Maldives						●				●	★		●	
Nusa Dua Beach Hotel, Bali	●	★	★	●	●	●	●	●		●	★	★	●	★
Oberoi, Bali, The, Bali	●	★		●	●	●	●	★		●	●	●	★	
Oberoi Cecil, Shimla, India	●	●	★	●	●	●	●	★		●	●	●	●	
Oberoi, Lombok, The, Indonesia	●		★	●	●	●	●	★		●	●		●	
Oberoi Philae Nile Cruiser						●		●	●	★			●	
Ol Donya Wuas, Kenya	●					●		●	●	●	●		★	
Ottley's Plantation Inn, St Kitts	●	●	●	●	●	●	●	●	★	●	★		●	
Palace Hotel Gstaad, Switzerland				●	●	●	★	●		●	●		●	
Paradis, Mauritius	●	★	★	●	●	●	●	●	●	●	★	★	●	●
Paradise Beach Resort, Thailand	●	●		●	●	●	●	●	●	●	●		●	
Park Hotel Sonnenhof, Liechtenstein				●	●	●	●	●		●		●	★	
Penang Mutiara Beach Resort, Malaysia	●	★	★	●	●	●	●	●	●	●	●	●	●	
Pink Beach Club, Bermuda	●	●	●	●	●	●	●	●		●	●			●
Rajvilas – an Oberoi Hotel, India	●	●	★	●	●	●	●	●		●	●		●	
Rambagh Palace, India	★	●	★	●	●	★	★	●	★	●	●		●	
Ras Kutani, Tanzania	★	★				●	★	●	●	●			●	
Reid's Palace, Madeira				★	★	★		●		●	●		●	
Residence, The, Mauritius	●	●	★	●	●	●	●	●		●	●		●	★
Ritz-Carlton, The, Bali	★			●	●	●	★	●		●	●		●	
Romantik Hotel Poseidon, Italy		●		●	●			●		●			●	
Royal Beach Hotel, Israel	★	★		★	★	●	★	●		●	●		●	

Information supplied by hotels and correct at the time of going to press.
● Denotes the hotel provides the indicated service. ★ Please contact the hotel direct regarding this facility.

281

	Licensed for weddings	Wedding co-ordinator available	Prior registration with local authorities for wedding couples	Music for ceremony arranged	Photographs for ceremony arranged	Honeymoon packages	Wedding packages	Wine/champagne on arrival	All-inclusive	Reception facilities	24-hour room service	Limousine/car service for honeymooners	Special Honeymoon Suite	Beach wedding
Royal Caribbean Int.	●	●	★	●	●	●	●	●	●	●	●	●	●	●
Royal Palm, Mauritius	●	★	★	●	●	●	●	●		●	★	★	●	★
Saman Villas, Sri Lanka	●	●	★	●	●	●	●	●		●	●	●	●	
Santa Marina Hotel, Greece	●			●	●	●	★	●		●			●	
Sanyati Lodge, Zimbabwe	●	★		●	●	●	★	●		●	★		●	
Secret Harbour Resort, Grenada	●	●	★	●	●	●	●	●		●			●	
Shandrani, Mauritius	●	●	★	●	●	●	●	●	●	●	★	★	●	★
Sheraton Laguna Nusa Dua, Bali	●	●	★	●	●	●	●	●		●	●	●	●	★
Shutters on the Beach, California	★			●	●	●	★	●		●	★	★	●	
Siboney Beach Club, Antigua	●			●	●	●	●	●		●			●	★
Sofitel Alexandria Cecil, Egypt				●	●	●	●	●		●	●	●	●	
Sofitel Old Cataract, Egypt				●	●	●	●	●		●	●	●	●	
Sofitel Winter Palace, Egypt	★	★	★	★	★	●	●	★		●	●	●	●	
Soneva Fushi, Maldives						●	●	●	★	●			●	
Sopa Lodges, Tanzania	●	●	★	●	●	●	●	●	●	●			●	
St Nicolas Bay, Greece	●	●	★	●	●	●	●	●		●			●	
Stonepine Resort, California	●	●	★	●	●	●	●	●		●			●	
Suvretta House, Switzerland		●		●	●	★	●	●		●	●	●	●	
Ta' Cenc, Malta	●	●	●	●	●	●	●	●		●	●	●	●	
Taba Hilton Resort, Egypt	★	★				●	●	●		●	●	●	●	
Taj Maldives						●		●		●				
Taj Exotica, Sri Lanka	●	●	★	●	●	●	●	●		●	●	●	●	●
Taj Goa, The, India						●	★	●		●	●	★	●	
Thumhers Alpenhof, Austria				●	●	●		●		●	★	●		
Tongsai Bay Cottages & Hotel, Thailand	●	●	★	●	●	●	●	●		●			●	●
Treasure Beach, Barbados	●	●	●	●	●	●	●	●		●			●	★
Trou Aux Biches, Mauritius	●	●	★	●	●	●	●	●	●	●	★	★	●	★
Turtle Island Resort, Fiji	●	●	★	●	●	●	●	●	●	●	★		●	★
Victoria Falls Hotel, The, Zimbabwe	●	●	●	●	●	●	●	●		●	●		●	
Vila Vita Parc, Portugal						●	●	●		●	●	●	●	
Villa Cipriani, Italy		●		●	●	★	●	●		●		●		
Waterloo House, Bermuda	●	●	★	●	●	●	●	●	★	●		●	●	

Information supplied by hotels and correct at the time of going to press.
● Denotes the hotel provides the indicated service. ★ Please contact the hotel direct regarding this facility.

Elegant Resorts

CONTACT:

Call for a copy of one of our brochures and let Elegant Resorts make your dream a reality.

- Caribbean
- Worldwide
- Europe
- Skiing
- Villas

Tel +44 (0) 1244 350408
Fax +44 (0) 1244 897750
enquiries@elegantresorts.
co.uk
www.elegantresorts.co.uk

Your honeymoon is a once-in-a-lifetime experience. We at Elegant Resorts know this only too well and go to the ends of the earth to create and offer you blissful, individually tailor-made honeymoons to some of the most exotic destinations around the world.

Our philosophy is to provide the finest quality holidays backed by a personal service that is second to none.

We pride ourselves on offering a unique collection of some of the most splendid destinations – some wild, some remote and simple, others sophisticated and opulent, and with every conceivable amenity.

Whether your dreams take you off on a yacht around the Caribbean, a romantic tour of Tuscany, a sleek city break to Prague, a skiing trip to the picture-postcard Rockies, or an exotic island adventure in south-east Asia, we will take care of every detail, leaving you free to concentrate on the details of the big day, and more importantly, on each other.

Our team of experts, with their highly creative approach, extensive knowledge of world-wide venues and unrivalled attention to detail, can provide a programme tailor-made to meet all your needs.

All our brochures reflect the exclusivity of our holidays and each one is full of imaginative ideas for discerning travellers.

283

INDEX

284

285

286

Kempinski Hotels & Resorts are located in some of the world's most exciting resorts and historical cities, all perfect for an unforgettable honeymoon.

Luxurious accommodation, fine cuisine, discreet service – Kempinski Hotels & Resorts offer everything a newly-wed couple could wish for. All year-round, our properties worldwide offer memorable 'Honeymoon Packages' at special all-inclusive prices.

'Heavenly Honeymoons' include all the benefits of Leisure Concierge (e.g. late check-out, destination welcome pack, use of health centre) plus:

- Luxurious accommodation in the room category of your choice with an automatic upgrade to the next available room type upon arrival.
- Full breakfast for two served in your room or in the hotel's restaurant.
- A complimentary bottle of wine with any one meal taken in the hotel's restaurant.
- Fruit, flowers, chocolates and champagne in your room.
- A wedding gift of two embroidered bathrobes to take home as a souvenir.
- A complimentary voucher for a one-night stay in the Kempinski Hotel of your choice on your first wedding anniversary.*

(This package is subject to availability and may change without prior notification.)

For further information on 'Heavenly Honeymoons' and the full Leisure Concierge programme, please call one of our toll-free numbers or the hotel of your choice directly.

* Restrictions may apply.

TOLL-FREE NUMBERS

Argentina	0800 671 30	Canada	1 800 426 3135	Hong Kong	800 96 8381	Norway	800 11 626
Australia	1 800 623 578	Denmark	1 800 185 76	Japan	0120 326 733	Singapore	1 800 735 46 22
Austria	0660 86 46	France	0800 852 852	Netherlands	0800 022 43 06	Spain	900 122 351
Belgium	0800 716 36	Germany	0130 33 39	New Zealand	0800 446 368	Sweden	020 450 520
Brazil	0800 550 378	Gt Britain	0800 868 588	North America	1 800 426 3135	Switzerland	0800 55 0626

Travel Agents and Tour Operators
United Kingdom & Ireland

Abercrombie & Kent
tel +44 171 730 9600
fax +44 171 730 9376

Africa Archipelago
tel +44 181 780 5838
fax +44 181 780 9482

The African Connection
tel +44 1244 355 330
fax +44 1244 310 255

Amathus Holidays
tel +44 171 831 2383
fax +44 171 831 9697

Art of Travel
tel +44 171 738 2038
fax +44 171 738 1893

Barwell Leisure
tel +44 181 397 4411
fax +44 181 974 1442

Best of Greece
tel +44 1784 492 492
fax +44 1784 492 493

British Airways Holidays
tel +44 1293 723 161
fax +44 1293 722 624

Cadogan Holidays Ltd
tel +44 1703 828 313
fax +44 1703 228 601

Caribbean Connection
tel +44 1244 341 131
fax +44 1244 310 255

Caribtours
tel +44 171 581 3517
fax +44 171 225 2491

Carrier
tel +44 1625 582 006
fax +44 1625 586 818

Castaways
tel +44 1737 812 800
fax +44 1737 812 207

Cazenove & Lloyds Safaris
tel +44 181 875 9666
fax +44 181 875 9444

Celebrity Cruises
tel +44 1932 834 200
fax +44 1932 820 286

Citalia
tel +44 181 686 5533
fax +44 181 681 0712

Classic Collection
tel +44 181 876 5769
fax +44 181 876 9916

CV Travel
tel +44 171 591 2800
fax +44 171 591 2802

Elegant Resorts
tel +44 1244 350 408
fax +44 1244 897750

Erna Low
tel +44 171 584 2841
fax +44 171 589 9531

First Choice Holidays
tel +44 161 745 7000
fax +44 161 588 680

Gozo Holidays
tel +44 1923 260 919
fax +44 1923 263 482

Grenadier Safari
tel +44 1206 549 585
fax +44 1206 561 337

Gullivers Travel Agency
tel +44 171 696 5700
fax +44 171 696 5690

Hayes & Jarvis
tel +44 181 222 7833
fax +44 181 741 0299

Hoopoe Adv. Tours
tel +44 181 428 8221
fax +44 181 421 1396

Indian Ocean Conn.
tel +44 1244 355 320
fax +44 1244 355 309

Italian Expressions
tel +44 171 435 2525
fax +44 171 431 4221

Jules Vernes
tel +44 171 616 1000
fax +44 171 723 8629

Kuoni Travel
tel +44 1306 740 500
fax +44 1306 744 222

Pan Pacific Worldwide
tel +44 171 323 2133
fax +44 171 323 1791

Pettits India
tel +44 1892 515 966
fax +44 1892 521 500

Premier Holidays
tel +44 1223 516 516
fax +44 1223 516 615

Prestige Holidays
tel +44 1425 480 400
fax +44 1425 470 139

Prima Sales Office
tel +44 171 936 2332
fax +44 171 493 7773

Principal Promotions
tel +44 171 485 5500
fax +44 171 485 6600

Royal Caribbean Int.
tel +44 1932 834 200
fax +44 1932 820 286

Silkcut Travel
tel +44 1730 265 211
fax +44 1730 230 399

Simply Spain
tel +44 181 987 6112
fax +44 181 742 2330

SuperClubs
tel +44 1749 677 200
fax +44 1749 677 577

Thermalia Travel
tel +44 171 586 7725
fax +44 171 722 7218

Thomas Cook Holidays
tel +44 1733 417 000
fax +44 1733 417 784

TTI Ltd
tel +44 1367 253 810
fax +44 1367 253 812

Unique Hotels
tel +44 1453 835 801
fax +44 1453 835 525

Utell Int.
tel +44 181 661 2263
fax +44 181 661 1234

Western & Oriental
tel +44 171 313 6600
fax +44 171 313 6601

Whole World Golf Travel
tel +44 181 741 9987
fax +44 181 741 1171

USA & rest of the world

Abercrombie & Kent
tel +630 954 2944
fax +630 954 3324

Africa Travel Inc.
tel +818 5077 893
fax +504 596 4407

Apple Vacations
tel +847 631 2383

Classic Safari Camps of Africa
tel +27 11 465 6427
fax +27 11 465 9309

Explorers World Travel
tel +847 295 7770
fax +847 295 8314

Frontiers Int. Travel
tel +724 935 1577
fax +724 935 5388

Fun Safaris
tel +800 323 8020
fax +630 529 9769

GoGo Tours
tel +201 934 3812
fax +201 934 3793

Hideaways
tel +800 843 4433
fax +603 430 4444

Hilton Sales Worldwide
tel +800 HILTONS
fax +570 450 1596

Homeric Tours
tel +212 753 1100
fax +212 753 0319

Int. Lifestyles
tel +954 925 0925
fax +954 925 0334

Int. Ventures & Travel
tel +91 11 469 8532
fax +91 11 462 2579

Islands in the Sun
tel +310 536 0051
fax +310 643 9609

Liberty GoGo
tel +212 689 5600
fax +212 545 8050

The Meridian Group
tel +757 340 7425
fax +757 340 8379

Pan Pacific Worldwide
tel +212 757 4938
fax +212 757 4637

Preferred Hotels
tel +800 323 7500
fax +407 679 3361

Quest of the Classics
tel +353 754 8891
fax +353 754 8891

Richard Bonham Safaris
tel +254 288 2521
fax +254 288 2728

Spa Finders
tel +212 924 6800
fax +212 924 7240

Travel Impressions
tel +516 845 8000
fax +516 845 8095

Utell Int.
tel +402 398 3200
fax +402 398 5484

Zeus Tours & Yatch Cruises
tel +212 221 0006
fax +212 764 7912

Hotel Groups

Best Loved Hotels
tel +44 1454 414 786
fax +44 1454 415 796

Charming Hotels
tel +39 08711 940
fax +39 08711 955

Classic Safari Camps of Africa
tel +27 11 465 6427
fax +27 11 465 9309

Concorde Hotels
tel +33 140 712 121
fax +33 140 712 131

Hospitality in Historic Houses
tel +39 0577 632 256
fax +39 0577 632 160

Hyatt Resorts USA & Caribbean
tel +44 181 742 8888
fax +44 181 742 2222

Johansens Recommended Hotels
tel +44 171 490 3090
fax +44 171 490 2538

Kempinski Hotels & Resorts
tel +44 181 307 7693
fax +44 181 544 9893

Leading Hotels of the World (UK)
tel +800 181 123
fax +44 171 493 7773

Leading Hotels of the World (US)
tel +800 223 6800
fax +212 758 7367

Passenger Shipping Association
tel +44 171 436 2449
fax +44 171 636 9206

Preferred Hotels
tel +44 181 348 0199
fax +44 181 347 8998
toll free +1 800 893 391

Relais & Chateaux
tel +800 960 239
fax +33 145 729 669

Small Luxury Hotels of the World
tel +44 1372 361 873
fax +44 1372 361 874

The Meridian Group
tel +757 340 7425
fax +757 340 8379

The Taj Group of Hotels
tel +800 282 699(UK)
tel +800 1 LUV TAJ (US)

Universal Resorts
tel +960 323 080
fax +960 322 678

Warwick Int. Hotels
1 500 556 555 (UK)
+800 203 3232 (USA)

Zimbabwe Sun (HMI)
tel +44 181 908 3348
fax +44 181 904 0094